T0340120

Teaching Mikadoism

Teaching Mikadoism

The Attack on Japanese Language Schools
in Hawaii, California, and Washington,
1919–1927

Noriko Asato

University of Hawai'i Press
Honolulu

Publication of this book has been assisted by grants from the Kajiyama Publications Fund for Japanese History, Culture, and Literature at the University of Hawai'i and the School of Hawaiian, Asian, and Pacific Studies, University of Hawai'i.

Paperback edition 2020
Printed in the United States of America
25 24 23 22 21 20   6 5 4 3 2 1

LIBRARY OF CONGRESS CATALOGING-IN-PUBLICATION DATA
Asato, Noriko.
Teaching mikadoism : the attack on Japanese language schools in Hawaii, California, and Washington, 1919–1927 / Noriko Asato.
p. cm.
Includes bibliographical references and index.
ISBN-13: 978-0-8248-2898-1 (hardcover : alk. paper)
ISBN-10: 0-8248-2898-4 (hardcover : alk. paper)
1. Japanese language—Study and teaching—United States.
2. Education and state—United States—History—
20th century. 3. Japanese—United States—
History—20th century. I. Title.
PL520.U5A83 2006
495.6'071073—dc22
2005022330

ISBN-13: 978-0-8248-8847-3 (pbk.)

Designed by University of Hawai'i Press Production Department

Contents

Notes on Terminology

This book deals with the experience of ethnic Japanese or *Nikkei* in America in the early twentieth century. Japanese Americans use Japanese terms to identify generations. The immigrant generation is called *Issei*, while their American-born children are *Nisei* (second generation).

The other half of this story is the interplay between Nikkei and anti-Japanese activists. The final years of World War I marked the peak of a nationalistic and anti-immigrant mood that fostered a movement to "Americanize" the country. During this Americanization period, educators and the public at large advocated a policy of "100 percent English," reflecting rising xenophobia stemming from America's World War I experiences. This movement aimed at eradicating all foreign language schools and newspapers. As Roger Daniels demonstrated in *The Politics of Prejudice*, these anti-Asian activists adopted the "yellow peril" myth—that Asians would take over the West through the number of immigrants and their offspring (68).

Japanese exclusionists recycled this racist scenario into the term "Mikadoism." They tried to instill paranoia about Nikkei as subjects of the Japanese emperor, the Mikado. Japanese language schools became a core aspect of the exclusionists' attack. These schools, they argued, transformed American citizens into Imperial subjects.

Preface

Every Saturday morning during the school year in 1930, Minoru "Min" Yasui and his brothers and sisters walked two miles from their home to the Nihon Gakkō (Japanese school) in Hood River, Oregon's community of Nikkei, or ethnic Japanese.[1] The official name of the school was the Hood River Japanese Language School, and it met weekly in the Hood River Japanese Community Hall. Min and his fellow Nisei, second-generation Japanese Americans, were taught by Rev. Isaac Inouye, a Harvard-educated Methodist minister.[2] Although Rev. Inouye had a powerful reputation, the Nisei kids thought that he had an irascible and testy nature.[3] Still, it was he who taught them how to read the native tongue of Issei.

Twelve years later, in November 1942, Min Yasui was in Portland's federal district court, charged with deliberately violating the curfew imposed on "all persons of Japanese ancestry" by the United States military.[4] Yasui, who studied law at the University of Oregon, was challenging the government's racial discrimination policy—why only Japanese Americans had to obey a restrictive curfew under the army's guise of "military necessity," which Yasui rejected. Judge James Alger Fee, however, refused to appreciate Yasui's constitutional defense and implied that Yasui gave up his rights because he attended a Japanese language school for three years, became proficient in the language, and then secured a job at the Japanese consulate in Chicago.[5] His case was later appealed in the United States Supreme Court, which ruled in 1943 that he and another register, Gordon Hirayabashi, were indeed guilty of violating military orders. The government argued that the forced mass relocation of Japanese Americans was necessary since the military had stated that some Japanese Americans were fifth columnists—suppressing evidence from the FBI and other agencies that there had not been one case of espionage or sabotage by a Japanese American. The court relied on the final report of Lieutenant General John DeWitt, which suggested that Nisei, despite being American citizens, were a threat because the majority had attended Japanese language schools. DeWitt argued that these institutions were designed for "cultivating allegiance to Japan."[6] Thus, the knowledge to speak, read, and write Japanese, and the existence of Japanese language schools, were used to "prove" that the entire community of Japanese Americans might be disloyal to the United States. Their conviction "left a suspicion about loyalty that 'hangs as a cloud over 120,000 Japanese Americans' who were shipped to the internment camps."[7]

This book explores the origin of the Japanese language school issue, focusing on a history of the Japanese language school controversy from 1919 to 1927. The school debate became a battleground among various factions for control over Japanese Americans' lives and their future. Under the influence of the "Americanization" movement, invigorated during World War I, nativists demanded that the question of Japanese language schools was a challenge to Japanese assimilability into white society. Activists in the Japanese exclusion movement raised the "Japanese language school problem" to question Japanese Americans' loyalty to the United States and endeavored to use this issue to halt the economic "invasion" and, further, Japanese immigration to the United States. American officials, anti-Japanese newspapers, and Japanese exclusionists manufactured an image of Japanese language schools as evil institutions, and this disinformation was so widespread that many believed it rather than the truth. Even white supporters of Nikkei and some Japanese Americans themselves saw the Japanese language schools as an abdication of parents' responsibility to give their children an education that would best raise them as American citizens. The history of the Japanese language school issue is parallel to the Japanese immigrants' struggle to secure fundamental civil rights in the United States. In this book, I explore the origins of the Japanese language school "problem," from the early 1900s through its development in Hawaii, California, and Washington, focusing on how the Japanese language school controversy was created in these three locations and was used to pursue different objectives for various parties.

Many studies of Japanese American history briefly mention Japanese language schools. However, few offer a detailed examination of those schools in relation to the Japanese exclusion movement. Three exceptions include unpublished dissertations and a master's thesis. Yoshihide Matsubayashi (1984) treated the development of Japanese language schools in Hawaii and California from 1892 to 1941. He made extensive use of Japanese American newspapers and documents from Japanese education associations. The weakness of his study is that he provides a developmental rather than a critical analysis of Japanese language schools and how their policies changed with the concurrent "Japanese language school problem." Matsubayashi did not compare or analyze the different motivations behind the Japanese language school debate in places that differed politically, socially, and economically.[8] Ann Halsted's 1989 dissertation displays rigorous use of archival documents to show how the Hawaiian territorial government imposed "Americanization" policies on Nisei children and controlled their language schools. Her study does an excellent job of depicting conflict between Hawaii's authorities and the Nikkei community.[9] Mariko Takagi studied prewar Japanese language schools in Hawaii by comparing textbooks produced by Hawaii's Japanese language teachers and the Japanese ministry of education. Her sociology thesis (1987) examines the changes in Hawaii's textbooks, especially their moral elements, in accordance with Hawaii's social environment surrounding Japanese language schools.[10] Although both Halsted and Takagi depicted Hawaiian Nikkei's struggle to maintain Japanese language schools, neither of them explored the impact of Hawaii's language school debate on the West Coast.

There are several published studies on Japanese language schools, which mostly approach them as educational policy studies. Some highlight identity conflicts between a cultural and racial background rooted in Japan and pressures for Americanization and assimilation into a new generation of Japanese Americans. Eileen Tamura's *Americanization, Acculturation and Ethnic Identity* (1994) explores the effects of Americanization on Hawaii's Nisei education and their assimilation procedures during Hawaii's territorial period.[11] Yukuji Okita examines the changing perspectives on Japanese education in Hawaii and the movement toward the question of raising future generations of Japanese Americans. Okita utilized pioneer-era Japanese newspapers and Japanese diplomatic records, which cast new light on the early Hawaii Issei's problem of education for their offspring.[12] Toyotomi Morimoto (1997) uses archival materials from UCLA's Japanese American Research Project to highlight the meandering textbook compilation process taken by the Japanese Language School Association, and the controversy surrounding this process in the ethnic community.[13] Teruko Kumei (2000) investigates the Japanese government's policy on Nisei education between 1906 and World War II.[14] In another article (2002), Kumei demonstrates how Issei parents faced the challenge of preserving Japanese spirit, heritage, and language through Japanese education.[15] From a related angle, Yoon Pak (2002) explores early Nisei education in Seattle by examining letters and compositions written by Japanese American seventh and eighth graders, just before they were sent to the Puyallup Assembly Center in 1942, and later to concentration camps.[16]

This book builds on these works, but reframes the question as to how the anti-Japanese language school campaign evolved and how the Nikkei community reacted to the situation. By looking in detail at the situations between 1919 and 1927, grounded in the history of three communities, it is possible to highlight the power dynamics concerning Japanese language schools in the Territory of Hawaii and the states of California and Washington. Comparison of the attack on Japanese language schools and community responses in three different locations helps us to see the "distinctive histories" and also the connections of "shared experiences," which, as Yuji Ichioka has pointed out, have been neglected in studies of Issei history.[17] By using a variety of primary sources, I also hope to show some of the complexity of Issei opinion and Japanese diplomatic action. This study is not a final conclusion but is written in the hope of broadening the history of Japanese language schools. Although the focus is on the period following World War I, emphasis is on the impact of the long-lasting scar that the anti-Japanese movement created by suggesting the disloyalty of Japanese Americans and their language schools. It also suggests a need for further research on the question of religion in Nikkei history.

Chapter 1 briefly introduces Japanese immigration to Hawaii and the contiguous United States. The chapter also introduces the origin of Japanese language schools and religious conflicts over the schools in Nikkei communities. The policies of the Japanese foreign and education ministries concerning the education of Japanese Americans are also explored in this chapter.

In chapter 2, the very origin of the Japanese language school controversy is examined, based on archival materials from the 1919 Federal Survey of Education in Hawaii. Japanese language schools were originally subsidized and encouraged by sugar planters. However, as Japanese Americans gained power as the largest group of plantation laborers, their language schools were abruptly targeted as the primary focus of the Territorial Department of Public Instruction (DPI). This chapter attempts to explore the different players, and questions the rationale that promoted the Japanese language school controversy in Hawaii.

Chapter 3 shows how the "Japanese language school problem" quickly spread to California. On the surface, it seems to have been based on Hawaii's model; however, its development was closely tied with California's 1919 alien land law and the Japanese exclusion movement. The chapter probes how and why California's Japanese exclusionists attacked Japanese language schools as one of their targets. This chapter also explores the efforts of California's Japanese consul general to resolve the "Japanese language school problem."

Although Washington state had the third largest Japanese population, few scholars have explored its Japanese language schools or the wider anti-Japanese movement in the state. The Japanese language school debate there was definitely less intense than in Hawaii or California. However, an examination of Washington's case (chapter 4) highlights the importance of a local historical context for our understanding of the Japanese language school issue as well as its importance for both Nikkei and anti-Japanese activists.

In the final chapter, I explore the meaning of the "Japanese language school problem" in each location, highlighting differences and similarities. The chapter also briefly discusses the situation of other foreign language schools in American history for comparison, and suggests further research on the functions of language schools for a nation of immigrants. It includes comparison of the Supreme Court decisions on Japanese language school laws and other foreign language school cases in terms of the catalysts behind these controversies. It is the author's contention that more detailed studies of other language school issues will challenge our historical consensus on the Americanization period following World War I and will lead to a more nuanced understanding of this important period of American history.

Acknowledgments

Writing this book has felt like wading into the Pacific Ocean. I left the beach as a language teacher, then got wet from my toes to my knees until I felt completely immersed in Japanese American history. I was not sure what the swim would be like, but the people I met in the course of my explorations were nothing but warm; they inspired me with their courage and intelligence. I sincerely want to thank that very special group of people whose stories definitely changed my perspectives about life. Meeting the Nisei who attended the University of Nebraska during World War II after they were interned in concentration camps profoundly impacted me in many ways. Above all, they showed me that history is made up not only of the stories of policymakers and their decisions but also of how these policies impact people, and how people can make history with their own thoughts and actions.

Writing this history would not have been possible without the help of several historians, librarians, and archivists. I want to thank historian Roger Daniels (University of Cincinnati) for kindly commenting on early drafts of this monograph, literally chapter by chapter. He offered countless suggestions, which helped me improve the foundations of my monograph. Roger taught me what it takes to do a "good history."

Meeting University of Hawai'i education historian Eileen Tamura at the History of Education Society Annual Meeting in 2001 changed my perspectives. Her patience and knowledge nourished my work and her high expectations for research challenged me when I contributed an article for her special issue of the *History of Education Quarterly*.

I am also truly indebted to Arthur Hansen (California State University, Fullerton, and Japanese American National Museum). Art went through several drafts of my manuscript. His warm advice and support truly encouraged me to persevere, and his help was always there when I needed it most.

I also want to thank Duncan Ryūken Williams (University of California–Irvine) and Moriya Tomoe (Hannan University) for suggestions on Buddhism that expanded my research framework. Professors Louis Fiset and Gail Nomura of the University of Washington also kindly offered comments and early encouragement on this study, as did Sandra C. Taylor (University of Utah) and the late Rosalee McReynolds. I especially want to thank S. Frank Miyamoto (University of Washington) for his warm advice and sharing stories and analysis of his Issei parents and his childhood experiences. It really helped me feel the early years of one Japanese American's life. I also appreciate Homer and Miyuki Yasui's sharing memories of Min Yasui.

My work builds on my predecessors' pioneering research on Japanese language schools, such as Professors Teruko Kumei (Shirayuri University), Yukuji Okita (Dōshisha University), and Toyotomi Morimoto (Waseda University). I especially would like to thank Dr. Kumei for her encouragement and wealth of knowledgeable advice. She further impressed me by sending a copy of an article from *Hankyō*, a magazine that many librarians told me could no longer be found.

Historians all owe a great debt to librarians and archivists. I would specifically like to acknowledge the assistance of Betty Falsey, Reader Services Librarian, Houghton Library, Harvard University; Karri Samson, Auburn-Placer County [California] Library; Catherine Hanson-Tracy, Reference Librarian, California State Library; Heidi Dodson, Reference Archivist, Rashida Ferdinand, and Lori Carr, Amistad Research Center, Tulane University, New Orleans; and Jolyn Tamura, former State Archivist of Hawaii.

I also want to thank Toshiko McCallum, Japanese American National Museum; DeSoto Brown, Bishop Museum; Dana Brenner, Record Center, California Teachers Association; Frank Tapp, Archives Special Collection Department, Auraria Library, Colorado University; Teresa L. Conaway, and Sandra B. Placzek, Schmid Law Library, University of Nebraska; Junko I. Nowaki, Librarian, Edwin H. Mookini Library, University of Hawai'i at Hilo; Kathleen A. DeLaney, University at Buffalo Archives; Stephen Janeck, Drexel University Archives; Gail Kleer, Western Washington University; Judi Olson, Yankton College Records Manager; Bob Schuler, Tacoma Public Library; Steve Barrett, Idaho State Historical Society; Dave Hastings, Washington State Archives; Ann Kailani-Jones and Ann Bregent at the Washington State Library; and Asako Yoshida, University of Manitoba Library. I am also grateful to Jannette O'Brien, Washington Education Association, and Etsuko Ichinose, Japanese Consulate of Los Angeles, for further assistance.

Several colleagues, librarians, and archivists in Japan helped me to locate and acquire materials there. I want to thank Yuriko Nakamura, University of Tokyo; Harumi Yakushiin and Kayoko Murakami, Kyoto University; Kazuhiko Tomizuka of the Diplomatic Record Office; as well as Kazuyuki Arai and Hisako Iwami of Seijō University.

I am grateful to Reiko Ogawa Harpending, Director of the Kawasaki Reading Room for Japanese Studies, and the Inter-Library Loan staff of the University of Nebraska–Lincoln Libraries, for assistance to obtain books, articles, and many, many microfilms.

Different stages of this research were supported by grants from the University of Nebraska–Lincoln Human Rights Human Diversity Grant, Humanities Center Grant, and an Arts and Humanities Research Enhancement Seed Grant. I am also grateful to Modern Languages and Literatures Chair Russell Ganim for his support, encouragement, and for several readings of my grant proposals.

I was fortunate to have Masako Ikeda as my editor at the University of Hawai'i Press. She provided several helpful suggestions on the conclusion, and offered guidance and patience on producing my first monograph. I would also like to thank indexer Ellen Chapman.

My family in Japan has been a great support and always reminded me who I am. I want to especially thank my father, Kiyoshi; my brother, Toshio; and his wife, Sumie, for letting me know I always have a home to come back to.

This monograph would not be realized without Andrew Wertheimer's support. His expertise on Japanese American history helped me develop many aspects of my work. I also thank my son, Joey, for giving me so many reasons for migrating to America. He also helped me by copying piles of books and microfilms and feeding the cats while I was away doing research.

CHAPTER 1

Immigration, Education, and Diplomacy

Japan, the United States, and the Origins of the Language School Controversy

She replied in a peculiar mixture of different languages, "Me mama hanahana yo konai." "Me mama" was a pidgin English phrase for "my mother"; "hanahana" was the Hawaiian word for "work"; and that "yokonai" was a Japanese expression equivalent to "can not come." . . . I felt keenly the need of establishing a school.

—Reverend Takie Okumura, *Seventy Years of Divine Blessings*

apanese American history began in 1868, when 148 Japanese emigrants, called the *gannenmono* (people of the first year), left Japan in the first year of its modern Meiji era (1868–1912). They were recruited to be contract laborers, meaning that the immigrants had a fixed-term contract to work in exchange for wages and passage.[1] This initial migration was not a success, and Japan did not allow further emigration until 1885. In this second stage of emigration, 945 *kanyaku imin*, or government-sponsored contract laborers, initially went to Hawaii.[2] Most of them originally came from small-scale farming families, primarily from southeast Japan's rural prefectures. These Issei were escaping depressed conditions, the result of a series of natural disasters and inflation from Japan's rapid modernization, which was financed on the back of agricultural taxpayers. The Japanese government administered twenty-six separate shiploads, totaling 30,000 emigrants to Hawaii, until 1894 in this *kanyaku imin* period.[3] These emigrants considered themselves *dekasegi*, or sojourners, who intended to return after fulfilling a three-year contract. Hawaii's planters recruited the immigrants to satisfy the growing sugar industry's appetite for efficient and inexpensive laborers.[4] Planters earlier recruited Chinese laborers, but were unhappy that few chose to remain after fulfilling their contracts. Chinese immigration was halted in 1900, when the newly annexed territory enforced America's Chinese Exclusion

Act of 1882. Japanese laborers were perceived as an ideal solution to Hawaii's labor shortage.[5] By 1890, Japanese laborers, accounting for 42.2 percent of Hawaii's entire plantation workforce, outnumbered Chinese laborers; by 1902, Nikkei made up 73.5 percent.[6]

Japanese workers were also desired in the contiguous United States by industrialists in the expanding railroad, agriculture, mining, lumber, and fishing businesses. Their offers of higher wages enticed Issei from Hawaii and Japan. Labor contractors played a major role in this third period. Although contract labor was banned in the United States in 1885, Japanese labor contractors secretly made deals between employers and laborers in exchange for a percentage of their wages. Labor contractors recruited some 27,400 Japanese as *jiyū imin*, or free immigrants, to work in the West Coast states and Alaska between 1891 and 1900 and another 42,500 between 1901 and 1907. In addition to these new immigrants from Japan, 38,000 Nikkei workers from Hawaii remigrated to the Pacific Coast states in search of higher wages and a better life.[7] Observing that anti-Japanese sentiment was on the rise, and that agitation seemed to be following the path of the earlier Chinese exclusion movement, the Japanese government halted issuing passports to the United States in 1900 for two years, although more Nikkei continued to arrive on the West Coast fleeing the miserable conditions in Hawaii.[8]

Hawaii's Japanese Language Schools, 1893–1920

Since most Issei were bachelor sojourners with little intention to settle, children's education was not a concern for them. During the *kanyaku imin* period (1885–1894), the Japanese consulate in Honolulu reported that 1,305 Nisei (632 boys and 673 girls) were born in Hawaii. In addition to these Hawaii-born Nisei, some children came to Hawaii along with their parents, bringing the school-aged Nikkei population to 2,000 during this period. In 1888, however, only 54 Nikkei children attended Hawaii's public schools (out of a total school population of 8,770). This number slowly rose to 60 (out of 10,712) and 113 (out of 11,307) Nisei pupils in 1892 and 1894, respectively.[9] Unlike white children who attended private schools, until the mid-nineteenth century, most school-aged Nisei did not attend any school.

Plantation owners encouraged Japanese laborers to remain beyond their contracts and to bring their wives. Planters also improved conditions to persuade immigrants to extend their stay, such as underwriting Japanese language schools on plantations for workers' children. Issei parents believed these schools were needed to help their children learn Japanese so they could make a smooth transition to public schools in Japan. Issei also needed language schools as daycare for their children, who otherwise were placed under a tent in the cane fields, while husbands and wives both toiled.[10]

Reverend Shigefusa Kanda established the first Japanese language school in 1893 in Kohala on the island of Hawaii. It was followed by Methodist missionary Reverend Tamaki Gomi's school in Maui (see Fig. 1). These early Christian missionaries tried to recruit Nikkei children to their schools, but few Issei enrolled their children at the schools because they were suspicious of Christianity.[11]

Honolulu's first Japanese school, the Honolulu Nihonjin Shōgakkō (Japanese Elementary School) was begun by Reverend Takie Okumura, a graduate of Dōshisha University of Theology, with thirty students in 1896.[12] It was similar to a *terakoya*, a private temple school, where reading and writing were taught during the Tokugawa era.[13] The goal of Okumura's school was to provide Japanese education to Nikkei six years of age or older. Classes were held after public school for one or two hours. Oku-

Fig. 1. Kula Japanese Language School, Maui (ca. 1899). The first Japanese language school in Maui. Merchant Seiji Fukuda (right) opened the school in 1895, with Methodist Church Rev. Tamaki Gomi (left) as the teacher. Students from other ethnic groups also attended the school, as it was the only one in the area. (Courtesy of the Bernice Pauahi Bishop Museum)

mura's school offered reading, calligraphy, and composition, along with *shūshin* (moral education) and physical education, using textbooks compiled by the Japanese ministry of education (the Monbushō). The school employed teachers certified by the Monbushō.[14] Okumura requested that the Monbushō support the school, and so it sent a copy of the Japanese Imperial Rescript on Education (Kyōiku Chokugo Tōhon), national textbooks, and physical education equipment.[15] Teachers tried to operate the schools on the basis of Japan's public education system. In this sojourner stage, it is understandable that language schools celebrated national holidays, such as the emperor's birthday, following elementary schools in Japan.[16]

In 1898, the Hongwanji or Jōdoshinshū (the True Pure Land Buddhist sect) Honpa Hongwanji opened three Japanese schools on the island of Hawaii, followed by one on Kaua'i in 1900.[17] In Honolulu, the Hongwanji Fuzoku Shōgakkō (elementary school attached to Hongwanji) was started in 1902 with 162 students under Reverend Hiseki Miyazaki. Plantation manager Saiji Kimura donated $350 for the school's desks and chairs. Three years later, the school built a new elementary school building with support from the Hongwanji headquarters and Prince Fushimi. Like Christian schools, the curricula were based on the presumption that children would "return" to Japan with their families.[18]

In the early days of Buddhist missionary work in Hawaii (especially in the smaller sects), priests visited plantations scattered across districts to teach children because Nikkei lived on plantations throughout the Islands. One solution to the itinerant life was building dormitories or boarding schools. This was the case for Reverend Senri Soma's school attached to the Jōdoshū (the Pure Land) temple, both of which were established in 1904. When his wife Mine joined him, they established a dormitory to house sixty to seventy Nisei children, which spared Reverend Soma from having to visit several branch schools.[19]

Like other Americans, Nikkei attended public schools during the day. Later in the afternoons, most also went to a Japanese language school for one to two hours every day. There, they studied Japanese language, culture, and other subjects taken from Japan's national curriculum. The schools were primarily supported by tuition. In the early 1900s, monthly tuition at these schools cost around 35 cents.[20] Language schools were also subsidized by sugar planters and ethnic communities. The Japanese consulate sometimes subsidized fees for students in need. Although some schools were secular, most were affiliated with Buddhist temples or Christian churches. In smaller communities, priests often earned extra

Fig. 2. Okumura's Honolulu Japanese Boarding School engaged in military exercises (1901). The man in a suit (left) is Rev. Takie Okumura. (Courtesy of the Bernice Pauahi Bishop Museum)

money by teaching.[21] While some teachers were hired locally, many were recruited from Japan; schools would submit a request to the Japanese consulate. The foreign ministry forwarded the requests to the Monbushō. The Monbushō then contacted a prefectural governor who asked the education department to send a particular teacher.[22] Those selected were usually certified and experienced teachers. In many cases, a husband and wife were recruited together to operate a language school.

Christian and Buddhist schools competed to recruit students. This caused friction among religious leaders, and this "problem" spread within the Nikkei community. In 1899, when Okumura's school built a new building and was preparing to expand, Okumura was advised to transfer school administration to the Nikkei community because his school, run by a Christian clergyman, might become an excuse for Buddhists to establish their own schools. Okumura accepted this advice and transferred power to an educational committee of thirty-three community leaders, chaired by Consul General Miki Saitō. Despite the transfer, three years

Fig. 3. The Hongwanji Temple in the Aiea Sugar Plantation, Oahu (ca. 1902). The temple was established in 1902 on permanently free-leased land from the plantation. Japanese language teaching began inside the temple in 1903. The temple was located in the center of the plantation, surrounded by the mill and Japanese camp houses. (Courtesy of the Bernice Pauahi Bishop Museum)

later the Hongwanji temple opened its own school in Honolulu. According to Okumura, this damaged his "secular" school since it lost many of its students to the Hongwanji Fuzoku Shōgakkō. According to Okumura, the Hongwanji promoted that its schools practiced purely the spirit of Japanese education or *chūkun aikoku* (loyalty to the emperor and love of country), and aggressively built schools on each island and plantation, even in communities that already had a Japanese school. This, Okumura claimed, was the origin of the Japanese school problem in Hawaii.[23]

For both Christian and Buddhist priests, Japanese language schools were tools to attract Nikkei followers and expand their influence. Christians had difficulties attracting converts since their faith was illegal in Japan until 1873.[24] Japanese schools appealed directly to Issei parents' primary concern—their children's education. The Buddhist clergy had their own difficulties in disseminating their religion. Christianity was the dominant religion in Hawaii, and whites saw Buddhism as a "barbarous worship of idols." However, most Issei were originally Buddhist. Hongwanji had the largest number of adherents in Hawaii since most Japanese immigrants originally came from Hiroshima, Yamaguchi, Kumamoto, and Fukuoka prefectures, where people were predominantly members of Jōdoshinshū.[25] Unlike many other Buddhist sects, Jōdoshinshū was developed for commoners. Hongwanji Bishop Yemyō Imamura, head of the Hawaii Hongwanji, taught Issei that they were the "true guests of the Amitabha Buddha." His teaching appealed to Issei, who were often looked down upon as coolies. Imamura studied at the Hongwanji Bungakuryō (later Ryūkoku University). Before he came to Hawaii as a missionary in 1899, he studied under Yukichi Fukuzawa at Keiō Gijuku (later Keiō University).[26] Imamura adapted Buddhism to American society and constructed the foundations for Hongwanji to prosper during his service as the second Hongwanji bishop in Hawaii. Imamura declared that constructing Japanese language schools and Hawaii's main temple were his priorities.[27]

By 1903 there were twenty-two Japanese language schools scattered across the Territory. In November, with Hawaii's Consul General Saitō as the president, the Central Japanese Association was established in Hawaii. This landmark move indicated Japanese immigrants' self-identity shift from temporary "sojourners" to "permanent settlers." By that time, the Nikkei population reached over 65,000, almost half of the Territory's population.[28] One of the association's primary goals was to improve Nisei education. When Hawaii was annexed by the United States in 1898, Japanese children born in Hawaii became entitled to American citizenship, unlike their Issei parents or other Asian immigrants, who were aliens ineligible for citizenship—federal naturalization laws gave the right of naturalization only to free white men and Africans.[29] Nisei also held Japanese citizenship, since the Japanese government adopted the *jus sanguinis* system—whereby one's nationality was based on paternal citizenship. This dual nationality put Nisei in an awkward situation. Nativists called this the evidence of divided loyalty. Issei leaders needed to redirect the policy for Nisei education, and sought to raise them as American citizens of Japanese ancestry.[30] The first mission of the Japanese association leadership was to petition Saitō to request the foreign ministry to invite a Monbushō inspector to study Hawaii's Japanese language schools. These leaders understood the difficulties for the schools in following the "Japanese school model" and hoped an inspector could help create appropriate curricula and textbooks. Their petition also was an effort to secure official sanction for the language schools from the Japanese government. Saitō forwarded this petition to Foreign Minister Jutarō Komura, who then passed it on to the Monbushō. One year later the Monbushō responded: it recommended continued use of its national textbooks, which it argued were an inexpensive solution to the problem of unifying textbooks at individual schools.[31] It is not clear if the Monbushō consciously wanted to enforce the national education policy on immigrants overseas or simply did not consider particular conditions in Hawaii. Regardless, Issei hereafter used this connection to recruit certified teachers and principals, and to obtain government recognition of Japanese language schools in the diaspora.[32]

Hawaii's Japanese American history and the fate of the language schools were greatly framed by labor relations on the plantations. In May 1904, Japanese laborers at the Waipahu plantation on Oahu went on strike. They were protesting the actions of a head *luna* (overseer) who was coercing Japanese workers to participate in his lottery scheme.[33] This strike became an opportunity for Bishop Imamura to foster improved relations with plantation owners. Consul General Saitō tried to intervene and failed, but Imamura succeeded in convincing workers to return to work. Again in 1909, Imamura suppressed an Oahu strike for higher wages.[34] These incidents impressed plantation interests, who noted Imamura's influence and may have thought that "Buddhism tended to enhance the docility of their labor force."[35] With the planters' support, Hongwanji schools prospered. By 1910, there were twenty-seven Hongwanji schools with over 6,000 students in Hawaii.[36]

Between 1900 and 1908, seventy-six Japanese language schools grew throughout the Islands.[37] Parallel to this phenomenon, religious rivalry between Christians and Buddhists became intense. In June 1909, the vernacular newspaper *Hawai Shokumin Shinbun* praised the Papaikō Shō-gakkō (established in 1907) as a model school because its secular curriculum closely followed Japanese national education.[38] The newspaper's publisher Kazutami Eguchi, a former Christian missionary, implicitly categorized Buddhist schools as the antithesis of a model school. He condemned the clergy for running schools as a side business.[39] In 1910, the *Shokumin Shinbun* called on Imamura to separate religion from language-school education, for the sake of Buddhism's independence and dignity.[40]

Bishop Imamura did not acquiesce to such criticism, and he responded to the Christians. He wrote directly to Vice Foreign Minister Kikujirō Ishii in 1910, asking the government not to support the Honolulu Nihon-jin Shōgakkō that Okumura originally established and was supported by most Christian Nikkei. In his letter, Imamura explained Hongwanji's achievement in establishing its junior high school, the Hawaii Chūgakkō in 1907, in response to Nikkei demand for a higher education for their off-spring. Imamura claimed that he invited excellent teachers and produced an English prospectus explaining the school's purpose as an invitation for anyone to apply.[41] It received strong support from Nikkei and people outside the ethnic community, attracting an enrollment of ninety-one male and thirty-two female Nikkei students. Then, according to Imamura, the Honolulu Nihonjin Shōgakkō immediately countered by offering its own junior high school class to compete with his school, although it was closed later because of low enrollment. Imamura claimed that Christian parents then sent their children to his school, agreeing that all children, despite religious differences, could learn under the professionally trained teachers in his school. Imamura was upset that the Honolulu Shōgakkō publicly announced opening a junior high school, using its connection with former Consul General Saitō to request a principal and also subsidies from the Monbushō. Imamura explained that, unlike present Consul General Senichi Ueno, Saitō unfairly favored the Honolulu Shōgakkō over his school, thus provoking Buddhists and creating more competition. Imamura argued that the Christians' attempt not only damaged his efforts toward communal harmony but also disturbed the peace, which should not be tolerated.[42]

Some Christians also tried to impede Buddhist schools by appealing to local authorities. In 1911, Consul General Ueno reported that a group of Christian missionaries sent Hawaii's Department of Public Instruction a petition regarding the use of a public school building in Waialua. The petition accused Buddhists of using their Japanese schools to build temples and expand control over Japanese in Hawaii. The petitioners claimed that these Buddhist schools opposed the Americanism that Hawaii's public schools promoted. They claimed that offering Japanese language instruction at public school would help sever the tie between Buddhists and the language school business, and also prevent anti-Americanism from spreading among Japanese. Ueno claimed that this was very misleading, and the Department of Public Instruction simply denied the request. Ueno explained that in earlier times, Japanese were not organized and had to rely on the clergy to take care of children's education. However, he continued, Japanese had slowly become independent and no longer needed the clergy's support. Ueno added that even some of the language schools originally affiliated with Hongwanji were no longer related to the denomination. He further argued that Japanese schools had been established in order to help children maintain their language ability, and even these sectarian schools were not teaching Japanese nationalistic ideas that hampered Americanism, as the petitioners claimed. Ueno explained that the petitioners' official motive was to make all Japanese schools secular and to remove anti-American factions. However, he explained this was rooted in the feud between Christian and Buddhist missionaries. Ueno argued that the petition was supposedly submitted by American missionaries, but that it was actually part of the Japanese Christians' plan to eradicate their opponents' schools.[43]

Some Nikkei leaders were unhappy about making their children pawns in this religious war. They claimed that "the Hongwanji attached school naturally teaches Buddhist ideas" and said they wanted to build a *Nihonjin shōgakkō* that would be secular and adhere to the teachings of public elementary schools in Japan. They petitioned the Monbushō to authorize their private Japanese language school.[44]

Saburō Kurusu, who was deputy consul general in 1912, recalled that regardless of time or place, there "always were problems about Japanese language schools, . . . one plantation had two or three denominations' schools which never conceded to each other." According to Kurusu, the planters thought it was easier to give money to the Japanese consulate, rather than directly to a particular school, and for the consulate to resolve the problems.[45] Planters annually contributed $1,000 to the consulate from 1907 to 1920 to subsidize the schools.[46] In 1914, for example, there were conflicts between schools in more than fifty locations throughout the Islands.[47] This competition was not only between Buddhist and Christian schools, but also among various Buddhist schools.[48] Sometimes different school-support groups, such as people from different Japanese prefectures, fought as to where their schools should be built.[49]

These criticisms of Japanese language schools were mainly directed against Buddhist (especially Hongwanji) schools. By 1909, Hongwanji had the largest school system (see Table 1). Of the eighty-seven language school teachers, thirty-nine taught at Buddhist schools. It is likely that one-third of the Territory's Japanese language school teachers were Buddhist priests. Christians argued that most spoke little or no English and possessed minimal understanding of American civics. Critics also argued that Buddhist-affiliated schools hindered Nikkei assimilation, which became a palpable demand, especially during the World War I Americanization movement. Buddhist teaching was regarded as an antithesis to Christianity, which was frequently used as a measurement of assimilation in America.

In 1915, with mounting attention on Japanese schools, Hawaii's Japanese language teachers formed the Hawaii Education Association (see Fig. 4). That year, 13,552 Japanese American pupils attended public schools in Hawaii, 90 percent of whom also attended language schools.[50] One of the association's first objectives was to unify the schools' curricula. The subjects taught at Japanese schools varied among schools. At the association's first meeting, teachers agreed to teach only Japanese language, while such subjects as moral education, geography, and history would be integrated into language instruction rather than being offered as independent subjects. The purpose of the Japanese language schools, they declared, was to teach standard Japanese to Nikkei children in Hawaii and to cultivate their moral character.[51] At this meeting, the teachers announced an inten-

Table 1: Japanese Language School Affiliations in Hawaii, 1909

Religion	Number of Schools	Number of Teachers
Hongwanji	23	28
Jōdo	11	11
Congregational	6	10
Methodist	2	2
Independent	33	36
TOTAL	75	87

Source: Yukuji Okita, *Hawai Nikkei Imin no Kyōikushi: Nichibei Bunka, Sono Deai to Sōkoku* [History of Japanese immigrant education in Hawaii: Encounter and conflict of Japanese and American culture] (Tokyo: Minerva Shobō, 1997), 114.

tion to write their own textbooks to replace the Monbushō ones to meet Nisei children's environmental and educational needs. They also agreed with Consul General Arita's suggestion to change the schools' names from *"Nihonjin shōgakkō"* (Japanese elementary schools) to *"Nihongo gakkō"* or Japanese language schools.[52] The previous name caused many to believe that they were equivalent to schools in Japan—raising Japanese subjects.

The same year, Hawaii's Hongwanji-affiliated schools, including twenty-nine elementary and three junior high schools (accounting for 25 percent of all Japanese schools in Hawaii), announced a major change of name and educational policies.[53] The Hongwanji education committee explained that "on the surface, Japanese language schools were seen by some as confronting American public schools, imbuing Japanism, and hindering Americanization."[54] The statement declared that the original purpose of the schools was to foster Japanese citizens in order to equip children for public education in Japan. However, as Issei perspectives changed

Fig. 4. Board members of the Hawaii Education Association, established in 1915 (1916). This picture includes Bishop Yemyō Imamura, head of the Hawaii Hongwanji (No. 4), and Christian educator Rev. Takie Okumura (No. 6). (Courtesy of the Bernice Pauahi Bishop Museum)

to settlement, the goal of Japanese education adapted to cultivating children as American citizens. Realizing this change, Hongwanji school officials decided to modify their role to become an "educational home," and offered themselves as a means to connect Nikkei families with public schools. To reflect this, the Hongwanji adopted the name "*gakuen*" (institution) or "educational home" for its schools. The statement was released both in Japanese and English and sent to the Territorial Department of Public Instruction and other school officials.[55] Despite the Hongwanji's new public image, in July 1917, five Japanese teachers, four of whom were Hongwanji teachers, were denied permission to disembark in Hawaii. Immigration officials argued they were contract laborers, which violated a newly established 1917 law.[56] The incident showed growing public hostility. It also made it more difficult to recruit new teachers from Japan.

Another major critic of Japanese language schools came from outside the Islands. Congregationalist missionary Reverend Sidney L. Gulick visited Hawaii for two weeks in 1915 to study the recent "Japanese problem," including Nisei education.[57] Gulick was the leading figure among "pro-Japanese" missionaries. He was a missionary in Japan for twenty-five years, and taught at Kyoto's (Congregationalist) Dōshisha University. Gulick served as secretary of the National Committee for Constructive Immigration Legislation, and he represented the Commission on Relations with Japan of the Federal Council of Churches of Christ in America. Historian Roger Daniels described Gulick as "a mass movement all by himself" because of his tireless publicity work and writings.[58] Gulick promoted the idea of giving fair opportunities to all immigrants in America.[59] To Gulick, Japanese had great potential to become good American citizens, but only if "the Christian religion displaces the superstitious Buddhist sects," and especially "if this rising generation of young Japanese can be won for Christ."[60]

In his 1915 published report, Gulick admonished the public education in Hawaii. He argued that the fifteen years of schooling Nisei received was insufficient to prepare them for citizenship. Outside of public education, he argued, Nisei were conditioned not only in "Oriental homes, but the Japanese at heart have been diligently drilled in language schools by Japanese teachers, many of whom have little acquaintance and no sympathy with American institutions or a Christian civilization."[61] Gulick wrote, "the teachers in the non-religious and Jōdo [the Pure Land] Buddhist schools appeared to be fair-minded, intelligent men," but he criticized others, particularly Hongwanji. They should not "be allowed to stand as teachers of American youth," he asserted.[62] Gulick suggested the Territory should pass a bill that could regulate the "quality" of both private and public school teachers. He argued this would allow the board of education to issue certificates only to teachers possessing "knowledge of English, American history, methods of government, and ideas of democracy." Gulick also warned planters that their "blind subsidizing" of Japanese language schools, where these "teachers and policies tend to obstruct the Americanization of their pupils," might create serious problems ahead "unless Hawaiian-born Japanese are pretty thoroughly Americanized."[63]

To Issei parents, Gulick warned that sending children to Japanese language schools "further retarded" their Americanization, since the "teachers are Japanese who are men less Americanized" than themselves. However, he continued that if parents really needed to send their children to language schools, they should judge if the teachers are "not only well acquainted with American ideas and customs, but are also in sympathy with American ideals." He called for every "American-Japanese school" to display portraits of Presidents Washington and Wilson.[64]

While Gulick lambasted Japanese language schools and their Buddhist teachers, he insinuated that it would be acceptable to send children to Japanese language schools run by Christian missionaries. American protestant missionaries, many of whom devoted their lives to proselytizing Japanese Americans, became their strongest allies in the struggle for equality. However, the question of Japanese language schools challenged the tolerance of missionaries since many schools were outside their control. To Christian missionaries, Buddhist priests took advantage of how Issei parents desperately wanted Nisei children to learn their mother tongue, and through these schools, Buddhists expanded their footing in the United States. Christians, therefore, eagerly offered Japanese classes to compete with those offered by Buddhist temples. This religious competition was not only a phenomenon in Hawaii. Los Angeles Methodist mission leaders, for example, encouraged followers to establish language schools to compete with their rivals.[65] This was perhaps similar to how Christian missionaries in Japan, including Gulick, taught English to disseminate religion, for example, using the Bible as a language textbook.[66]

The Japanese Government and Its Consuls General

In the very early stage of establishing Japanese language schools, Issei teachers and parents wanted to educate their progeny based on Japanese national education, and Japanese language teachers also wanted their schools to be government authorized. How then did the Japanese government perceive immigrant children's education, and what were its educational policies? The Japanese government responded to overseas nationals' individual requests on a case-by-case approach. In 1906, Vice Education Minister Seitarō Sawayanagi sent official instructions on the education of Japanese imperial subjects residing overseas to Vice Foreign Minister Sutemi Chinda. This was a response to Vancouver Consul General Toshirō Morikawa's inquiry to Tokyo for the establishment of the Vancouver Kyōritsu Nihon Kokumin Gakkō (Community Japanese National School). Sawayanagi set two guiding principles: (1) try not to lose the spirit of Japanese subjects and develop Japanese characteristics; and (2) regarding curricula, although there was no absolute, follow the standards of the Shōgakkō Rei (Primary School Order). Other recommendations included: for geography and foreign languages, the curriculum could be slightly modified to adapt to local situations. In the subjects of *shūshin* (moral education) and geography, the relationship between Japan and the host country should be explained, and Japanese dignity and racial solidarity should be emphasized. At ceremonies, national holidays, and other gatherings, Japanese concepts should be fostered.[67] This seems to be the first official Monbushō policy on Japanese immigrants' education, and it was published in the *Ryōjikan Shitsumu Sankōsho* (Consular Guidebook) in 1916 for consulates to follow.[68] It established the core educational philosophy on immigrants' offspring, who were to be raised as Japanese nationals.[69] In the 1906 letter, Sawayanagi also showed enthusiasm for subsidizing overseas schools, "even if they are substandard at present," especially in places where Japanese "might advance in commerce." Sawayanagi asked Chinda to provide information on local school situations for his project.[70]

Two years later, Sawayanagi again requested that the foreign ministry conduct a survey of Japanese schools overseas as a first step to planning subsidies.[71] This time, he received a request to provide the Hōten Shōgakkō in China with a subsidy.[72] In the letter to Chinda, Sawayanagi asserted that he wanted to support "not only the one in Hōten, but other schools located in places with a potential for business."[73] The survey was conducted in Manila, China, and the United States, including Hawaii. However, schools located in the United States and Canada were not included in the list of schools recommended for funding because consuls general in America suggested the funds were unnecessary.[74] Hawaii's Consul General Ueno concurred and explained that sugar planters subsidized Japanese schools. Ueno also argued against official support for these schools, even though they were built by immigrants, because Hawaii was an American territory.[75] American Studies scholar Teruko Kumei suggests that these reports from consulates in the United States manifested concern about the rising Japanese exclusion movement in America. Sawayanagi's enthusiasm for supporting Japanese schools in the United States remains a question, especially considering that he proposed his plan after the 1906 San Francisco school segregation incident and the following Gentlemen's Agreement, which drew international attention to Nisei education. One explanation might be that Sawayanagi was looking at Japanese language schools in China and other Asian countries where Japan had political influence, and he might not have distinguished ones in the United States. This was also after Japan won the Russo-Japanese War and gained territory and national pride.

In any case, at this point, the foreign and education ministries placed Japanese language schools in North America and Hawaii beyond their active control. Sawayanagi's 1906 policy, which was forwarded to consuls general, remained as Tokyo's official policy, but the 1908–1909 decision not to subsidize schools in North America shows that there were exceptions.[76]

In reality, consuls general in Honolulu often deliberately ignored Sawayanagi's 1906 order whenever they encountered real problems. In October 1911, when memories of a 1909 Japanese sugar plantation strike were still vivid, Hawaii Consul General Ueno revealed his view on Japanese children's education to the *Hawai Shokumin Shinbun*. Ueno said that education for Hawaii-born Nisei should focus on raising children loyal to America.[77] Two months later, Ueno said in a public debate that Japanese "children born in the United States are American citizens, so it is natural for the American public to fear providing these children with an education not dealing with the United States." Therefore, he continued, "I hope that these children who are American citizens should have an education consistent with Americanism." He stressed that "it is the duty of farsighted immigrants to raise children who are loyal to America and yet are familiar with Japan's situation."[78] Ueno's statement probably worked both as a gesture reproving Japanese impetuosity in challenging Hawaii's status quo and to soothe whites' animosity toward Japanese.

Speaking at the first Hawaii Japanese Education Association meeting in 1915, Consul General of Hawaii Hachirō Arita recognized the need for Japanese language schools, but he doubted the value of Japanese national education for Nisei. Arita explained that when two countries have unresolvable conflicts, such as over Nisei's dual nationalities, usually the country sending the immigrant yields to the host country in order to avoid conflict. Arita wondered how Americans would react to the fact that Nisei, who were American citizens, received a Japanese education. He called this problematic. If Issei insist on doing this, argued Arita, it might eventually provoke an international incident and perhaps even result in depriving Nisei of their American citizenship. Arita continued, "Imperial Japan has no need to expect much from Japanese residing in Hawaii, so it is hard for me to see why we have to go to such pains to provide national education for our children."[79]

In 1916 Arita's successor, Consul General Rokurō Moroi, expressed a similar stance toward language schools in the Hawaii daily newspaper, *Nippū Jiji*. He admitted the Japanese government had paid little attention to Japanese children's education in Hawaii before achieving victory over Russia in 1905. The United States also began paying attention to Japanese language schools at that time. He said that Americans could no longer ignore the Japanese government's emphasis on emigrant education, because Hawaii was a strategic outpost for American national defense. If, continued Moroi, the American public thought that Japanese language schools purported to instill Japanese ideas, it would be a serious problem, which had to be clarified so that people would not imagine that Japanese were creating Japanese hamlets in Hawaii equipped with Japanese schools.[80] Moroi's statement clearly shows that his mission as consul general was to solve American's "misunderstanding" of Japanese language schools and to avoid conflict between the two nations, rather than to defend the rights of Japanese in Hawaii.[81]

In September 1920, when (as we will see later) Hawaii's territorial legislature tried to pass a bill to control foreign language schools, Hawaii's Consul General Chōnosuke Yada wrote Foreign Minister Yasuya Uchida that "the real issue behind this problem [the Japanese school controversy] is to what extent the Japanese government should maintain control over Hawaiian born Japanese children with dual nationality. . . . For the upcoming legislature, I need to determine my position, and would like to receive the Imperial Government's thoughts and policy on the matter."[82] Uchida replied that the Japanese government "does not intend to interfere with the education of American citizens even if they possess dual nationality." Uchida further instructed Yada that Japanese language schools in Hawaii had developed under special circumstances directly related to immigrant life, which differed from conditions in the mainland United States, and that their treatment required special consideration of the parents' needs. Uchida directed Yada to avoid a situation that would lead to the schools' immediate abolition. Uchida added that more detailed instructions would be difficult to issue without knowing the exact contents of the bill.[83] Yada reported back to Tokyo three weeks later with a strategy to suppress the school control bill based on his evaluation of a recent aggressive public relations campaign. Yada suggested they should explain the contribution of and the need for Japanese language schools and seek support from politically powerful individuals. Yada again asked Uchida for more specific instructions, explaining, "I am having difficulties to act."[84] In November, Uchida finally replied with official instructions on Nisei education and the "Japanese language school problem." He explained, "Since this is related to education for children who have American citizenship, it would not be auspicious for us to outright express disagreement . . . [but] it is in fact a very important matter." Uchida declared, "The situation requires understanding from both sides," and he agreed with Yada's suggestion to approach influential Americans individually "in order to avoid a drastic and abrupt change."[85]

This problem had spread beyond Hawaii. In San Francisco, Consul General Tamekichi Ōta also struggled with a "Japanese language school problem." When California's Japanese language schools began drawing public attention in 1919, Ōta inquired to Foreign Minister Yasuya Uchida about the Japanese government's policy on Nisei education. Ōta explained that he had received various inquiries from Nikkei, including questions on education policy, remodeling school buildings, and plans to build new schools. Each time they sought financial support from the Japanese government.[86] He then summarized how the California legislature discussed reinforcing English education to immigrants in response to the Americanization movement, and also that Hawaii's Japanese language school problem had created volatile disputes. Considering these circumstances, Ōta clarified that he had been trying not to become directly involved in the language school issue, since it might bring about an unfavorable situation if it became public that a Japanese diplomat was involved with institutions seen as hampering Americanization. He asked Uchida to provide him with specific instructions regarding Japanese language schools in the United States.[87] Ōta actually wrote this letter while attending a meeting of the representatives of local Japanese associations on February 10, 1919.[88] When asked to state his opinion on Nisei education at the meeting, Ōta argued that Japanese, as immigrants, needed determination to respect and follow the laws of the host country as long as they lived under its authority. He said that the American government alone had the right to determine educational policy for Nisei children, the majority of whom were born in the United States, possessed American citizenship, and would live as American citizens.[89] After five months of anxiously awaiting Uchida's reply, Ōta sent another inquiry on July 30, 1919, imploring Uchida that "the issue has a critical importance, and a consul general residing in such a place definitely needs instructions from the Ministry";[90] nonetheless, Ōta never received a response from Tokyo.[91]

These exchanges among consuls general in Hawaii, San Francisco, and the foreign minister show how they wanted to diverge from the 1906 Monbushō policy on immigrant education. This policy was created before it was imagined that Japanese language schools could become an international issue and, as Consul General Moroi stated, the foreign ministry "did not give it much consideration" in the early Japanese immigration period. This obsolete government order, however, contradicted the foreign ministry's primary diplomatic directive to alleviate anti-Japanese sentiment and friction. Japanese diplomats attempted to solve Japanese language school controversies using diplomacy, compromising rather than defending immigrants' rights in order to avoid becoming embroiled in controversy. As we will see, for local consuls general who faced countless Japanese exclusion bills and were assigned the role of mediating between Nikkei communities and the American public, following the order literally would have put them in a very difficult position. The foreign ministry, it seems, also did not pressure the consuls general to pursue the education policy. When diplomats asked for official instructions, the foreign ministry could not properly respond because, as education historian Yukuji Okita has pointed out, the foreign minister did not have the authority to determine issues in the purview of the Monbushō. Okita claimed this created a situation whereby the foreign ministry needed to negotiate with the Monbushō, but the large gap between the two ministries' perceptions of the immigrants' situation made it nearly impossible for a policy dictated by the Monbushō to meet the foreign ministry's expectations.[92]

Although the Japanese government withdrew somewhat from Nisei education at this point, it shaped Nikkei life in other ways. Following an American request, it required Nikkei to register their residency and report births, deaths, and marriages through a local Japanese association, just as they would in Japan. The Japanese government also gave citizenship to Nisei if their parents were Japanese. Thus, Nisei possessed dual nationality and might be required to serve in Japan's military if they visited Japan. Based on the 1915 Pacific Coast Japanese Association Deliberative Council's petition for an amendment to the Japanese Nationality Act, in 1916 the government allowed Nisei under age seventeen to apply for expatriation. However, it did not allow those above age seventeen, unless they completed their military obligations.[93] Japanese consulates also positioned themselves above the Japanese associations. These Japanese civic organizations included most Nikkei in America, and they were organized in several hierarchical orders. Through Japanese associations, Japanese consulates coordinated various national events, such as the imperial birthday celebrations and receptions for visits of the Japanese naval fleet or dignitaries. It also used the associations to conduct surveys and maintain the family registration system. Japanese associations had power because the consulates allowed them to perform consular duties, such as processing certificates required of Japanese citizens in the United States. The money raised by consular fees for certificate issuance was the organization's chief form of revenue. Consulates also helped Nikkei to establish Japanese language schools by sending textbooks and recruiting teachers. They mediated between Nikkei communities and the Japanese government, and gave advice on various issues to promote Nikkei welfare. This close contact between Nikkei and the Japanese government (for both control and protection) fostered additional suspicion from Americans, and seemed to support accusations that the Japanese government provided national education to Nisei through Japanese language schools as part of their plan to invade America from inside. Hawaii Governor Charles McCarthy's testimony on the Territory's "Japanese problem," during the 1920 hearings conducted by the House Territories Committee in Washington, D.C., illustrates this fear. He called it a simple "mathematical problem" whereby Japanese American citizens, controlled by Japan, "would control our voting strength."[94]

The fear became dominant in January 1919. Hawaii attorney Albert F. Judd began campaigning to propose a bill to control Japanese language schools. The content of the bill, which he described in the *Pacific Commercial Advertiser*, was identical to Gulick's 1915 call for a bill to regulate Japanese language schools. After subsequent school control bills failed to pass the territorial legislature, the United States Bureau of Education was called in to investigate Hawaii's Japanese language school situation. As the following chapters show, Japanese language schools in Hawaii and elsewhere became pawns in a complex chess game among exclusionists; religious powers; territorial, state, and federal authorities; the Japanese government; and Japanese Americans themselves.

CHAPTER 2

Mandating Americanization

Japanese Language Schools and the
Federal Survey of Education in Hawaii

Under the policies of the United States, it will be very difficult to
prohibit schools of this kind unless it were definitely proven that they
were teaching treasonable things.
　　　—P. P. Claxton, U.S. Commissioner of Education, 1919

Over 20,000 Japanese Americans attended 163 Japanese language
schools in the Territory of Hawaii in 1919. The existence of
the schools had long been a bone of contention between the
Japanese community in Hawaii and the white elite, who dominated the
Territory, and to a lesser extent, within the Japanese community itself.
That year, the Territory's leaders requested the United States Bureau of
Education to conduct an educational survey. Educational surveys were
developed to provide a "first hand study of local conditions" prepared
by national education leaders who could share their expertise with local
authorities so that "children of all the people may be prepared for national
life."[1]

When the federal survey team came to Hawaii, the governor, the
public schools' superintendent, and civic, business, and religious leaders
each had their own research agendas and publicly attempted to shape the
survey team's "scientific study." The legislature primarily requested that
the survey investigate Japanese language schools, which were accused of
instilling "anti-Americanism" in children of Japanese immigrants. During World War I, xenophobia surfaced in America with a vengeance; to the
dominant group, diversity signified disloyalty, creating the impulse for
"100 percent Americanism" throughout the early 1920s.[2] In education,
legislatures in states such as California and Minnesota mandated English
by law as the basic language of instruction in private and public elementary schools, while other states, such as Nebraska, prohibited teaching foreign languages in early grades at any school.[3] In Hawaii, casting Japanese
language schools as an "educational problem" reflected the control aspi-

rations of the Territorial Department of Public Instruction (DPI), sup-posedly representing the people's interests, despite the fact that nearly half of Hawaii's population was of Japanese descent.

Background

As Hilary Conroy, Gary Okihiro, Ronald Takaki, and other historians have demonstrated, the recruitment of Japanese to Hawaii as sugar cane plantation laborers was closely tied with colonialism.[4] Hawaii's sugar industry grew rapidly and became the center of power in the Islands, con-trolled by a group of white elites, primarily descendants of early American and British missionaries.[5] The Reciprocity Treaty of 1875 enabled Hawaii to send sugar tariff-free to the United States and tremendously boosted Hawaii's economy, as can be seen by the growth of plantations from twenty in 1875 to sixty-three only five years later.[6] This increase aggra-vated labor shortages, which were already strained when Chinese work-ers abandoned their abysmal working conditions shortly after completing their contracts. Plantation owners recruited Japanese to meet Hawaii's labor needs.[7] The Nikkei population steadily increased to about 60,000 in 1900, 80,000 in 1910, and 110,000 by 1920, representing 42.7 percent of the Islands' total population.[8] Planters were initially overjoyed when many Japanese workers in the 1900s changed their perspectives from sojourn-ers to settlers. Workers brought wives and "picture brides" from Japan, and by 1920 Nisei made up 44.5 percent of the territory's Nikkei popu-lation.[9] Many whites increasingly worried that Nikkei would dominate Hawaii, a fear exacerbated by their assertiveness in the 1909 and 1920 plantation strikes, as well as by Japan's military victories and colonialism in Asia. This apprehension was compounded by the realization that Nisei, as American citizens (their parents were not allowed to become American citizens until 1952), would become the largest voting block in the terri-tory.

As the school-aged Nisei population grew, the Japanese community became concerned with language education for their progeny. Issei enthu-siastically supported the establishment of language schools on their plan-tations by groups of parents, Christian churches, or Buddhist temples. Hawaii's language schools were unique as many were subsidized by plan-tation owners, who primarily saw the schools as incentives to keep their labor force on the farm.[10] In this stage, planters welcomed Buddhist mis-sions because they used racial/cultural differences to prevent solidarity among laborers and to foster intergroup competition. Buddhist priests and planters saw each other as serving mutual interests. Buddhist priests initially stood on the side of the planters and reconciled troubles between Japanese workers and their plantation managers in exchange for planters' support for their ministries.

With large congregations and the planters' endorsement, Buddhist-denominational schools prospered, especially Hongwanji's, suggesting to some that "the Japanese were determined to stoutly resist assimilation and to reinforce their own religious and cultural heritage."[11] As such, they became a target of the post–World War I Americanization movement, which often blurred the line between "Americanizing" and Christian proselytizing. Christians charged Buddhist schools with raising children as "subjects of the Japanese emperor." As this religious rivalry over language schools escalated, Reverend Okumura, losing so much of the battle to the Buddhist temples, seized any chance to label Buddhist temples and schools as un-American and constantly projected this image to the public.[12] Hawaii's leading English-language dailies, the *Pacific Commercial Advertiser* and the *Honolulu Star-Bulletin*, also alleged involvement of the Japanese government in plotting "a peaceful invasion" of the United States.[13]

Japanese language schools were also perceived as a competitor or threat to public education. Of the 20,651 Nikkei students who accounted for close to 50 percent of Hawaii's public school enrollment in 1920, 20,196 or 97.8 percent also attended Japanese language schools.[14] Language schools celebrated Japanese holidays, including the emperor's birthday. On that day, many Nisei children participated in a ceremony held at their Japanese schools rather than attending public school. During the ceremony, children paid respect to the emperor's picture and listened to a public reading of the Imperial Rescript on Education: this code of morality was created around the idea that loyalty and obedience to the emperor, the head of state, was equivalent to loyalty and obedience to the state. Because so many students were absent, many of Hawaii's public schools simply closed for the day.[15] Public school teachers also complained of Nisei children who spoke "Hawaii Creole English," commonly called "Pidgin English."[16] This was not a "problem" only for Japanese children. In fact, "only 2 or 3 percent of all students entering public school spoke Standard English" as late as 1920.[17] Public school teachers blamed this phenomenon on Japanese language schools. White parents also protested that their children were placed in classes "where Hawaii Creole English was the spoken language, and where, among 'swarms of Orientals,' their children would 'unconsciously pick up and adopt Oriental manners and mannerisms.'"[18] Until 1910, most whites were in the upper class and sent their children to private schools that disallowed or limited admission of non-whites.[19] However, continued migration of middle-class whites, following Hawaii's 1898 annexation by the United States, completely changed the Territory's educational contours. These white children, unable to attend costly and overcrowded private schools, were sent to public schools with Asian American children.[20] Irate white parents complained about the public school system and demanded sweeping changes.[21]

The symbiotic relationship between the Buddhist clergy and plantation interests ended with the 1919 higher wage movement. Bishop Yemyō Imamura of Hongwanji and priests from several other Buddhist sects requested the Hawaiian Sugar Planters' Association (HSPA) to yield to the demands of the Japanese laborers. This eventually worsened into total confrontation as negotiations fell through, leading to the 1920 Oahu sugar plantation strike. Japanese language schools became part of the struggle, serving as places for strike meetings and as shelters for dispossessed workers.[22] Several Buddhist teachers and officials of the Young Men's Buddhist Association also played a prominent role in the six-month strike.[23]

Amid this turmoil, former Territorial Senator Albert F. Judd launched a campaign for a Japanese school control law on January 4, 1919, in the *Pacific Commercial Advertiser*.[24] Judd editorialized on the need for a bill that would require public and private school teachers to pass a certification exam on knowledge of English, American history, and civics.[25] Understandably, Japanese language educators strongly opposed this, because, if enacted, it would mean the death of most schools as few Japanese teachers spoke fluent English. While the ethnic community was conducting a campaign against Judd's proposal, the territorial legislature began its session in March. Contrary to public anticipation, it was Republican Lorrin Andrews, a descendant of an old Hawaii missionary family, who proposed to the House that all private schools be licensed by the DPI, and that an inspector be appointed for foreign language schools.[26] While Andrews' bill was still in the House, the chairman of the House Education Committee, Henry Lyman, revived Judd's original bill on March 20, and on April 11 he introduced another bill to restrict the operating hours of language schools.[27] Facing strong protests from the Japanese community and perhaps with an awareness of the State Department's warning to California legislators to halt the exclusion movement, the territorial legislature passed neither Andrews' nor Lyman's bills.[28] It was after these school control bills failed in 1919 that the legislature passed an act authorizing

Governor Charles McCarthy and Superintendent of Public Instruction Vaughan MacCaughey to request the United States Bureau of Education to conduct a survey of education in Hawaii.[29]

Precursors to the Survey

Momentum for the 1919 Federal Educational Survey developed over several years beforehand. Correspondence between Commissioner of the Bureau of Education Philander P. Claxton and interested parties in Hawaii illustrate how the mission of the federal study evolved, and also how the Japanese language school issue became the focus of the 1919 survey. As early as June 1914, H. B. Penhallow, chairman of the Hawaii Senate Committee on Education, requested the Bureau of Education to investigate the possibility "for the College of Hawaii to take over the Normal School as a preparatory department" and also to study DPI administration.[30] Although Claxton acknowledged Penhallow's request, the commissioner received no response to a follow-up inquiry.[31]

Two years later, Agnes Weaver, chairman of the Service Committee of the College Club, a social reform organization of 200 college-educated women in Hawaii, wrote Claxton.[32] Weaver complained of the poor quality of teachers that the Territorial Normal School supplied for public grammar and primary schools in Hawaii; the majority, she noted, were of Asian ancestry. She claimed that graduates of the Normal School had merely four years of training at the school beyond the eighth grade, and that they had better opportunities for employment than more qualified teachers among "our very own" (presumably whites), who added teacher's training to their high school diploma and college degree on the mainland United States. The club empowered its critique of the status quo by flexing white supremacy. Commenting on a list of Normal School graduates, the College Club stated:

> Notice how largely they are drawn from social groups the least American in blood and bringing up. That these groups should share in all forms of our Island life is best, but that they should dominate our schools, seems doubtful.[33]

Contrary to its claim, however, statistics showing the ethnicity of teachers in Hawaii's public schools in 1916 indicate that whites occupied 52 percent (American 47.8 percent and British 4.2 percent), and Portuguese, Spanish, Chinese, Japanese, and Korean teachers combined accounted for only 15.4 percent of all teaching positions, despite the fact that students of these groups made up over 72 percent of the public school population.[34] We cannot test Weaver's claim as to whether whites who received higher education outside the Islands were treated unequally with graduates of the Hawaii Normal School in either "salary or in other conditions of employment," but the statistics above show that the "social group" Weaver perceived as "the least American in blood and bringing up" certainly did not dominate public education in Hawaii.[35]

Frustrated by months of resistance by Governor Lucius E. Pinkham and Superintendent of Public Instruction Henry W. Kinney against a federal survey, Weaver remonstrated Claxton, "The governor is on the ragged edge of nervous breakdown, senile dementia and insane egotism, [and] the Superintendent . . . has never made good in [*sic*] anything."[36] Weaver characterized the commissioners as big businessmen, who "take their work as Commissioners lightly." She even accused the Inspector General of Schools and the Superintendent of the Normal Schools of being corrupt.[37] Weaver begged the commissioner to come to Hawaii on his own initiative.[38] Governor Pinkham, aware of the College Club's direct plea to Claxton, defended himself, writing Claxton, "there seems to be a rather hazy idea being publicly expressed by these ladies that there should be a Federal Survey made of our schools."[39] After stalling for several months, Pinkham sent an "unofficial" invitation for Claxton to come to the Territory of Hawaii as a "personal visit," but not for an official investigation.[40] He asked Claxton to investigate a way to improve the Islands' institutions of higher education, but insisted that the focus not be on the quality of the Normal School.[41] Later, at a meeting with Weaver and College Club President Kate W. Forbes, Pinkham finally acceded to their demands for a federal survey.[42]

On April 12, 1917, Pinkham signed a bill officially inviting a federal survey; however, the invitation from the governor was not sent for another nine months.[43] Superintendent Kinney also wrote Claxton to welcome his survey committee. In his letter, Kinney described Hawaii's situation as one of getting public school students "to turn toward agricultural and mechanical directions" rather than "clerical and similar occupations." From this perspective, he urged Claxton to send "practical school men, Normal trained and with actual experience as teachers, rather than educational theorists."[44]

The June 22, 1918, appointment of Charles James McCarthy as Pinkham's replacement postponed the survey until the new governor officially reinvited the commissioner's survey team.[45] Claxton wrote McCarthy that he was planning to conduct the survey from January to March 1919.[46] However, the bureau's postwar educational planning work again held back the survey team.

Shortly after the study's postponement, the territorial legislature and media began calling for a Japanese language school control bill. The momentum for a survey to examine Japanese language schools mirrors events of the time. Hawaii was in the midst of a major dispute between plantation workers and the HSPA. Japanese workers reorganized the Association for Higher Wages, dormant since the 1909 strike, and demanded higher wages and changes to the bonus system, which was not meeting skyrocketing postwar inflation. It later went on a major strike at Oahu sugar plantations in January 1920. Hawaii's anti-Japanese sentiment was also influenced by the postwar reanimation of the Japanese exclusion movement in California started by Senator James D. Phelan (Democrat, California) to bring about a more stringent alien land law and federal legislation terminating Japanese immigration and removing Nisei citizenship.[47]

The 1919 Federal Survey

The April 8, 1919, appointment of Vaughan MacCaughey as Hawaii's Superintendent of Public Instruction dramatically changed the scene.[48] MacCaughey wrote Claxton that he was "anxious to hasten the Federal School Survey."[49] A former head of the Department of Natural Sciences and vice-president of the Territorial Normal School, MacCaughey had been professor of botany at the College of Hawaii since 1910 and was also the director of the Hawaii Chapter of the National Education Association (NEA). Unlike his predecessor, MacCaughey seemed obsessed with the idea of bringing the federal survey. He had his own agenda that greatly influenced the investigation. Over the next few months, MacCaughey sent Claxton a flood of anti-Japanese propaganda and editorials against language schools. With false modesty, he wrote Claxton, "I do not wish to 'pester' you with promiscuous clippings, but I do feel that your survey committee should sense our local situation with reference to the Japanese Language Schools." MacCaughey further wrote:

> The bulk of Hawaii's school population attends Japanese language schools six days per week, throughout practically the entire year. The teachers in these schools are all aliens . . . imported from Japan. They have little or no knowledge of American institutions or ideals.[50]

Hawaii's educational problem, to MacCaughey, was the 40,000 alien illiterates, created by an "artificially stimulated immigration" of "low grades of agricultural labor (mostly Asiatic)" to work on the sugar plantations.[51] His sharpest attacks were against the Japanese, the largest ethnic group on the Islands, highlighting that Japanese American pupils constituted 40 percent of the public schools' enrollment, growing from 1,300 in 1910 to 16,000 in 1919, and 20,651 by the following year. The problem, wrote MacCaughey, was not only their dominant and increasing numbers, but also their language schools that were mostly "under the control of reactionary Buddhist priests." He labeled the latter as "medieval, ultra-superstitious and intensely Japanese," teaching "Mikado-worship," and claiming they directly conflicted with "the efforts of the public schools toward genuine Americanization." Emphasizing the importance of religious education in an article published before his appointment, MacCaughey contended that Asian immigration brought an extraordinary number of "Buddhist Oriental households," and that "Hawaii cannot be American until she truly Christianizes her population."[52] MacCaughey's passion to indict Japanese language schools seems rooted in his affiliation with the Congregational Church and the Hawaiian Evangelical Association. A resolution, warning that Hawaiian sugar planters' continuous financial support to non-Christian organizations would hurt Hawaii's welfare as well as hamper the Christianization and Americanization of the foreigners in Hawaii, under the names of MacCaughey and missionaries Takie Okumura, Orramel H. Gulick, and Teiichi Hori, manifested his determination to wipe out Buddhist influence from Hawaii.[53] Louise H. Hunter, who studied Buddhist-Christian conflict in Hawaii, wrote, "With the exception of Takie Okumura, probably no one was more opposed to foreign language schools (the Buddhist in particular) than Vaughan MacCaughey" even before he became superintendent. MacCaughey, in fact, was largely responsible for inflating the Japanese school "issue," as it was not on the federal survey agenda before he succeeded Kinney.[54] Aware of his attitudes toward Buddhist language schools, Hawaii's "Japanese press took careful note of MacCaughey's tirades," and as predicted, the Japanese community found itself amid controversy before the end of MacCaughey's first year in office.[55]

On October 10, 1919, Frank F. Bunker, the bureau's urban education specialist, and the survey's director arrived in Hawaii. The other two members of the commission joined Bunker later that month.[56] They were William W. Kemp, chairman of the education department at the University of California, who studied elementary and normal schools, and

Parke R. Kolbe, president of the Municipal University of Akron, who was charged with investigating higher education.[57] The territorial government allocated $3,000 to finance the survey for three months.[58]

Bunker conferred with Hawaii's civic leaders, including the governor, the superintendent of public instruction, territorial education committee members, the deputy attorney general, immigration officials, principals of Honolulu's schools, former Governor Walter F. Frear, and other leaders. Bunker reported everyone's attitude "toward the survey appears to be all that we could possibly ask." He quickly identified two problems requiring careful study: teacher supply and the Japanese language schools. On the first problem, he explained that most of the rural schools were isolated, remote, and mostly inhabited by "Oriental laborers," offering "no inducement for a refined, educated young woman." He claimed that the teachers from the territorial normal schools were products of "the spell of a desire for numbers." This simply repeated "the vicious circle" in which children of immigrants, whom Bunker believed spoke imperfect English themselves, paralleled "the blind attempt[ing] to lead the blind." Bunker called the Japanese language school issue "beyond all other questions." He asked Claxton to send him the bureau's files on wartime suppression of foreign language teaching including state laws prohibiting foreign language teaching, such as Nebraska's ban on German language instruction.[59]

The survey team visited schools on each of the four major islands by boat, car, and horseback. After visiting public and Japanese language schools on the Island of Hawaii for almost a week, Bunker called the experience illuminating and was confident that he could unravel the complicated problems.[60] Within the first few weeks, Bunker realized they had underestimated the travel expenses for the study, and that he had not understood the importance of private schools.[61] He explained to Claxton that private schools dominated the entire situation, while public schools were considered merely a means to satisfy the "foreigners." After a search for additional funds, the governor approved MacCaughey's suggestion to allocate an additional $2,000 to cover the difference and also the expenses for a fourth survey team member, George R. Twiss, an Ohio State University professor of secondary education and state high-school inspector, to examine the private schools.[62]

In addition to observing schools, survey commission members conferred with "all of the civic clubs of the Islands," including the Social Science Club and the College Club. The commission also sent questionnaires to teachers and principals on the Islands, and solicited opinions of the schools from another 200 unspecified "representative citizens of all races in the Territory."[63] Japanese voices, however, were marginalized or at least not recorded.

News of the federal survey made headlines daily in the Territory's English and Japanese newspapers. Many groups mobilized to influence the commissioners. The Ad Club, a group of elites in advertising and related businesses, met on November 5 to discuss "the Japanese language school problem" in Hawaii. Although not reported by Bunker or any newspaper, MacCaughey was the club's president.[64] Keynote speaker Richard H. Trent, a banker who was president of the Honolulu Stock Exchange, condemned the present territorial legislature for failing to enact laws controlling Japanese language schools. He reprimanded them as "sowing a wind which . . . will be reaped as a whirlwind, and shake the foundation of Americanism." He suggested alternative remedies to what he called the "dual schooling situation." Japanese parents had to choose to send their children to public schools or privately-funded Japanese schools so that no child could attend both; or a special session of the legislature should be called "for the purpose of legislating them out of existence," in which instance he encouraged his audience to note which legislators "betray our Americanism."[65] The Ad Club endorsed Trent's recommendations amid the presence of the invited guests from the federal survey commission. The *Maui News* approved of Trent's proposal and called for immediate action.[66] Four days after Trent's speech, Reverend Albert W. Palmer, pastor of Honolulu's prestigious Central Union Church, spoke on the Japanese language school issue to an audience of American Legionnaires.[67] "These Islands must be 100 percent American," proclaimed Palmer, adding, "It is our responsibility to make them so." Palmer claimed, "The first and most obvious step is the elimination of the foreign language school." He proposed a campaign to explain Americanization and "why the foreign language schools are bad and seek their cooperation"; and he cautioned that ruthless, tactless methods could increase resistance to Americanization. Palmer suggested that pupils in the eighth grade or above should have opportunities to take any language in public school if there was sufficient demand.[68] The Ad Club later adopted Palmer's suggestion in its recommendations on "policy and program [for the] foreign language school question."[69]

Fred Makino, publisher of the *Hawai Hōchi* and leader of the 1909 sugar plantation strike, blamed plantation owners for reviving "the school agitation . . . again to cloud the higher wage movement among plantation laborers."[70] Makino and others in the higher wage movement perceived the planters' attack on Japanese language schools primarily as an instrument to distract attention from labor's plea for increased wages.[71] Makino ridiculed how the planters rationalized their act of abolishing language schools on the incredulous basis that "they are prompted by [the] patriotic motive" of Americanization. He correctly predicted that "abolition of the language schools would be unconstitutional."[72] In addition, the *Hawai Shinpō* warned sugar plantation owners that abolishing Japanese language schools would result in a shortage of plantation laborers, as it would encourage Japanese to leave Hawaii. On the other hand, the *Nippū Jiji* editor, Yasutarō Sōga, blamed Buddhist priests for the Japanese school agitation.[73]

Echoing anti-Japanese rhetoric, the *Advertiser* claimed not only that Japanese schools did not teach Christian religion but also that they taught a religion that "regards the Mikado as divine," incompatible with the principles of Americanism. Furthermore, the *Advertiser* asked readers, "Can we afford to have future American citizens brought up in the belief that the ruler of a foreign land is superior to the government of this country?" The editor also pointed out the prevailing use of "pidgin English" among the Japanese children and erroneously claimed that foreign language schools prevented them from learning English, and even worse, that "they quickly contaminate the children that come from English-speaking homes."[74]

While debate raged in Hawaii, Claxton received Bunker's first draft of what became the report's first chapter. He complimented Bunker's work on the "population situation," and replied with further instructions. Claxton, by that time fully aware of MacCaughey's beliefs on the Japanese schools, encouraged Bunker to "confer freely with MacCaughey about what should be done in regard to the Japanese language schools." However, Claxton cautioned, "Under the policies of the United States, it will be very difficult to prohibit schools of this kind unless it were definitely proven that they were teaching treasonable things." Claxton's own view of Hawaii's Japanese school situation, shared with Bunker before his departure, was that children should learn their parents' native tongue as a second language in the public schools just as other European languages were offered. He reiterated this view in his letter: "Of course, this [offering Japanese at public schools] would not prevent the organization and maintenance of religious schools of any kind—Christian, Mohammedan, Buddhist, or what not, but democracy and freedom must always assume the risks inherent in their very nature."[75] On one hand, Claxton had a rather liberal perspective on Americanization; he took an unpopular position by defending teaching German during World War I and according to his biographer, he had a reputation for never making "any religious distinctions in administrative policy."[76] On the other hand, that Claxton instructed Bunker to work with MacCaughey suggests he was more of a pragmatist than a civil libertarian, since Claxton must have understood MacCaughey's objective of closing Japanese language schools. In either case, Claxton's heeding seemed not to discourage Bunker's critique of the Japanese language schools.

The bureau's files reveal even more actors behind the scenes. Around the time the commission was engaged on the Hawaii survey, Claxton's office, the Bureau of Education, received a confidential Office of Naval Intelligence (ONI) memorandum regarding Hawaii's Japanese language school problem. The report was circulated among several other government agencies, including the army's Military Intelligence Division (MID) and the State Department.[77] As the United States and Japan competed for power in the Pacific, Hawaii became an important strategic location for America's commercial and military interests. This, combined with the Nikkei population and labor movement, and Japan's expanding military, led ONI and MID agents in Hawaii to become suspicious.[78] Umetarō Okumura, Reverend Okumura's son, an HSPA translator and ONI informant since at least 1918, was likely responsible for some of this "information" that influenced the federal survey.[79] An August 20, 1919, ONI report dealt with conflict within the Japanese community over the language school issue including the struggles over the foreign language school control bills. The report began with the line, "The Buddhist priests who hold that the advancement of Emperor worship must be put first and foremost in teaching and training of the American born Japanese children . . . won another victory in the Japanese Language School controversy." According to the report, the *Nippū Jiji*'s Sōga criticized Buddhists' inconsistent attitude on the school issue. He accused them of playing a double game, "though the mission emphatically tells the Americans that it favors the preaching of Americanism, as a matter of fact it is preaching and spreading the principles of Buddhism through its educational work." The report further "confirmed" the popular theory that "Buddhist schools are anti-American," writing "these Japanese themselves in Hawaii who have turned away from Buddhism to Christianity will not concede any possible harmony between Buddhist and American democratic ideals." The report cynically portrayed the Nikkei as gloating over the victory against the language bill, and praised "the wiser element" who "began at once to plan a reformation of the Language School policy" in response to growing public sentiment. We may never know the identity of this informant, but it is suggestive that Takie Okumura uses almost the identical language in his book, *Taiheiyō no Rakuen* [Paradise in the Pacific].[80]

The ONI conducted its own investigation of Japanese in Hawaii. Based on the May 1918 MID's Merriam Report, it identified three supposed sources of anti-Americanism: the Japanese government, Japanese schools, and Buddhists. The August 14, 1918, ONI report, produced by "a Japanese informant in Hawaii," was very similar to the one Claxton received dated August 20, 1919, charging, "Buddhist priests in Hawaii, while ostensibly loyal to the United States, are in reality doing everything in their power to undermine any American allegiance entertained by the Japanese in Hawaii."[81] Army intelligence also investigated perceived Japanese subversion in Hawaii and the means to terminate it. Governor McCarthy wrote to Claxton's superior, Interior Secretary Franklin K. Lane, to inform him that the Hawaiian Department of the MID had asked the 1919 territorial legislature to pass "an act providing for the regulation of foreign language schools."[82] These ONI and MID reports on "Japanism" and subversive agents labeled the Japanese language schools and Buddhist temples as centers of anti-Americanism.

Claxton received another letter appealing against Japanese language schools. In November 1919, Reverend Sidney L. Gulick rejoined the movement's chorus. When Claxton dispatched the school survey team to Hawaii, Gulick sent the commissioner a copy of his 1918 book, *American Democracy and Asiatic Citizenship*.[83] Gulick encouraged Claxton to read page 241, stating his observations on Japanese language schools in Hawaii, particularly those administered by Buddhist priests. In his letter, Gulick argued against the irrationality of unqualified, non–English-speaking teachers teaching "American born children who are citizens of the United States." In his 1915 book, Gulick had criticized Buddhists' negative influence on Nisei Americanization and called for government intervention, but his 1918 book specifically argued for government control over the schools.[84]

On December 23, 1919, Bunker informed Claxton that he soon would receive a draft of the second chapter of the report, an examination of the foreign language school situation. Bunker's letter exudes pride for completing what he called an "accurate study of the facts." However, "to be absolutely certain," Bunker claimed to have submitted his report to several "Japanese scholars." Bunker wrote Claxton that the "Japanese will make splendid American citizens" and cleared the Japanese government of "attempting to exercise any political control over her people in the Territory." Rather, he saw the Americanization problem as "a religious one[,] and the Buddhist and Shinto religions provide a mighty poor soil for the growing of American citizens." He was convinced that if the present Japanese language schools were wiped out, "thousands of Japanese parents . . . will be glad for their children to occupy their entire time with the English language alone." He believed these children attend those schools only out of "the fear which their parents have of Buddhist priests and teachers." Bunker predicted that once the Japanese schools were terminated, few would study Japanese even if the opportunity were offered at public schools.[85]

In the same December 23 letter, Bunker encouraged Claxton to confer with Governor McCarthy when he came to Washington, D.C., in January. Bunker was unsure of the governor's language school position since he had changed perspective on Nikkei issues. According to "a number of inquiries among confidants of the Governor," Bunker wrote, McCarthy was quite pro-Japanese and "rather inclined to let the language schools alone."[86] In fact, on August 5, 1918, the newly appointed Governor McCarthy had delivered an official address at the Hongwanji Temple and publicly endorsed the extension of their school system. He praised the Buddhist temple's two decades of teaching Hawaii-born Japanese children the language of their parents. The governor told Nikkei parents, "I believe you should educate your children to be good citizens of the United States, that they be taught the Japanese language and whatever religion their parents or guardians think proper."[87] However, Bunker had been informed that the governor had changed his perspective and become quite "as anti-Japanese as are the rabid agitators on the mainland coast." The letter continued that the governor implied an alarming situation had arisen between the United States and Japan and advised local newspaper editors to "begin, somewhat quietly, the policy of arousing public sentiment against the Japanese."[88] The change reflects how McCarthy was co-opted by the Big Five, white business leaders who started as agents for the sugar plantations and later organized the HSPA. They also expanded into insurance, utilities, and wholesale and retail merchandising monopolies as well as rail and sea transportation, thus controlling much more than simply the Territory's economy.[89] As governor, McCarthy was initially critical of the Big Five and gave them a hard time. He and his treasurer Delbert Metzger administered strict laws to the conglomerates' insurance subsidiaries, and also significantly raised assessments on their plantation lands. However, when McCarthy, who came from a poor Irish family and was unsuccessful in various businesses, was approached by one of the Big Five, Henry Baldwin, McCarthy enjoyed being flattered and became more "pliable and acquiesced."[90] McCarthy's statement during the U.S. Senate Immigration Committee's hearings in February 1920 proved Bunker's concern about the governor's attitude toward the Japanese language school issue during the survey.[91] McCarthy testified that when one territorial senator asked his opinion of the present Japanese language school bill, he responded, "Personally, I would have preferred that this bill would not be introduced; but now . . . there is nothing left for you to do but to pass it." McCarthy confessed, "He thought I did not know what I was talking about; possibly, I did not." But the governor now assured the senators that "I believe this strike would never have taken place if the foreign language school bill had been passed." McCarthy explained that during the 1907 strike, the planters fired Japanese strikers and punished their leaders by placing them in jail, and these Japanese leaders lost face in the ethnic community. But, McCarthy continued, these leaders again tried to challenge the status quo by strongly opposing the school control bill, and if it had passed "it would have discredited the leaders who were opposing it."[92] His 1920 testimony shows the course of his changed perspective on the Japanese language school controversy. McCarthy's public endorsement of language schools as a secondary system was before the revival of the Japanese higher wage movement.[93] But, later, he became even more anti-Japanese to the extent that he came out in favor of California Senator Phelan's proposal for a constitutional amendment to deny citizenship to Nisei.[94]

The role of the HSPA on the federal survey concerning the Japanese language schools was one of ambivalence. When Issei leaders fought several initial school-control measures in the early months of 1919, one of their strategies was to send resolutions to their plantation bosses requesting support for their defeat. At a March 1919 HSPA meeting in Hilo, planters unanimously agreed that if Lyman's bill passed, the legislature should delay its implementation for two to three years until teachers could be ready to meet the requirements.[95] The planters' attitude toward Japanese language schools was not to abolish them, but rather to maintain them. However, this was just before the higher wage movement, first organized by the Young Men's Buddhist Association members on the Island of Hawaii in October 1919.[96] As Japanese became the largest labor force and learned to organize themselves to improve their working conditions, planters endeavored to reassert control over Japanese. Governor McCarthy testified on the planter's eagerness to dominate Japanese during the aforementioned 1920 Senate Immigration Committee hearings. In response to Senator Phelan's implication that planters had opposed the bill because they were apprehensive of a Japanese uprising, McCarthy replied that the planters were fearful that Japanese strike leaders would regain standing in the community if they succeeded in defeating the bill.[97]

Education scholar John Hawkins suggested that planters held varying opinions on the Japanese language schools. Some thought a measure to eliminate these schools would bring undesirable consequences over the long run, since modern public education would raise Nisei as "too" American to stay at the bottom of the socioeconomic ladder. Granting Japanese their own education system would separate them from access to the mainstream and, in turn, from politics and the economy.[98] This echoes Gail Miyasaki's 1981 observation on how the oligarchy, or plantation owners, perceived public education. She criticized the irrelevance of historian Lawrence H. Fuchs' explanation for the planters' detachment from public education between the annexation and 1920. She argued that "it would be absurd for the oligarchy to bring such a [public education] system under its wing, finance it, empower it with the task of training and Americanizing the thousands of children of their labor force, and yet allow it to run itself as it pleased . . . as indeed, it did not."[99] The same theory applies to Japanese schools. The planters, who supplied land, constructed school buildings, and sometimes subsidized teachers' salaries, had no reason not to take advantage of these schools, thus attempting to retain some control over Japanese laborers. This split among the planters is a likely explanation as to why the Japanese school control bills initially did not become law. Another factor was the vehement protest from the Japanese community. This is consistent with Reverend Palmer's testimony at the 1920 hearings, claiming that "some of the larger sugar interests were not in favor of the Japanese-language school bill, and there was a hesitancy about it."[100]

After Kolbe and Kemp finished their work and left for home, Twiss finally arrived in Hawaii on December 23. Bunker's surviving Hawaii correspondence ended on January 6, 1920, reporting he was waiting for the next ship to return. Finally, on May 28, 1920, Bunker mailed 2,000 copies of the report for MacCaughey to distribute in the Islands.[101] The report was also serially published in the *Honolulu Star-Bulletin* throughout June 1920.[102]

The Report

The published federal survey report consists of eight chapters, and chapter 3, "The Foreign Language Schools," was written by Bunker himself.[103]

The report seems greatly influenced by Reverend Okumura's perspective on the Japanese language school situation in relation to his conflict with the dominant Buddhist sect. The first half of the chapter describes the origin of the Japanese schools, crediting much to early Japanese Christian missionaries brought over by the Hawaii Mission Board. The report introduces the now-famous narrative of why Okumura established what was the first Japanese school in Honolulu. The story tells of his encounter with a young Nisei girl who spoke an unintelligible mixture of English, Japanese, and Hawaiian words. This situation not only concerned Okumura but also gave him "a further opportunity . . . to advance the Christian faith in the goodwill of the people of their race." The school began under very poor conditions, but soon received contributions as the number of students multiplied, and Okumura erected a school building. However, worried that the success of his school would give Buddhists a pretext for starting their own schools, Okumura supposedly separated himself and religion from the school's administration.[104] In his memoir, *Seventy Years of Divine Blessings*, Okumura gave an account of his struggle to sever the relationship between religion and Japanese education. He wrote of discussing his concerns with Hongwanji Bishop Yemyō Imamura and reaching an agreement not to open Buddhist schools. However, Okumura claimed that Buddhists simply opened their own schools, and enrollment at his school plunged from 200 to 70. Okumura explained, "This was the real beginning of oft-repeated friction between religiously-independent and Buddhist schools."[105]

Bunker's report on the Buddhist schools focuses on the Hongwanji sect, emphasizing its scale: 75,000 members, 60 churches and substations, 30 Young Men's Buddhist Association chapters, 40 Young Women's Buddhist Association chapters, and 42 Japanese language schools, embracing some 7,100 children and 155 teachers in Hawaii alone. The report then stresses the sect's strength as an organization and power over its followers, invoking an image of a medieval and dogmatic cult. Bunker wrote that the head of the sect, the "Hoss," is seen as "a living Buddha," and his representative in the islands, the "Kantoku" (Bishop Imamura), "has absolute authority."[106] The report depicts the Hongwanji school teachers as anti-democratic agents of "Japanism," providing fuel for the anti-Japanese activists' charge that they taught "Mikadoism." The report cast suspicion on the schools' preference for teachers from Japan over Hawaii-born Nisei. It used the following quote, supposedly by a Buddhist priest, to show that this was not only because of the different language ability of teachers but also because:

Any man who is to teach Japanese language schools should not be a man with democratic ideas. The language school is not a place for a man with strong democratic ideas. A man of strong Japanese ideas should be its teacher.[107]

This episode is also found in Okumura's *Taiheiyō no Rakuen*. During a Maui Japanese Education Association conference, a Buddhist priest boasted that "democracy is an American philosophy," and "it would be our shame if we let a teacher who has democratic ideas instruct our children."[108]

The survey's overview of the Hawaii Japanese Education Association was written in an ambiguous manner, the result either of editing or of Bunker's hope that one would read between the lines to understand the survey's intent. Teachers established the association in 1915 to coordinate the affairs of the Japanese language schools. According to the survey, it was originally proposed to include members in addition to teachers, but this was rejected at the first meeting. Their meetings since "have had no representation from those outside the teaching corps."[109] This refers to Okumura's 1915 effort to revise the association's bylaws, restricting association membership to teachers in Hawaii.[110] Bunker's description suggests that the association, consisting exclusively of Japanese teachers, many of whom were Buddhist priests, had been administered without external oversight, although Okumura and other Christian teachers proposed opening it to public scrutiny in order to reduce public suspicion of these schools. The report also implied how Buddhist language schools were problems that required outside control. Bunker wrote, "Indeed, the association has so far found it very difficult to outline an educational policy which will command the support of the Hongwanji, the Jōdo, the Independent, and the Christian groups."[111]

The federal commission also examined the Japanese language textbooks originally written by the Monbushō but revised by the association in accordance with its policy of Americanizing the Nisei. The report was equally critical of their contents, including remarks such as, "There are no distinctly American subjects treated in this book, and only one Hawaiian subject"; "One only No. 16, entitled 'Washington's Honesty,'... deals with an American subject"; and, "Only two lessons [in Book Four] touch on matters in any sense American."[112] Translations or synopses of stories of loyal samurai, a famous Buddhist priest, and a Japanese folktale, plus the Japanese Imperial Rescript on Education, were included in the report. It even hinted at the Japanese government's involvement in the textbook revision as it used funds from the Prince Fushimi Memorial Educational Fund.[113]

The survey also included several anonymous comments by public school teachers and principals on Japanese language schools, in response to the commission's questionnaire. Almost all of the published responses were in opposition to Japanese language schools; for example, "It is too much physical and mental work on the children"; "retarding the children's progress on English"; "a large measure to counteract patriotism and Americanization"; and many simply said, "they have to go." Most of these opinions were likely influenced more by the media's portrayal of the Japanese schools than by personal experience. Many teachers claimed: "The Japanese schools, under cover of religious instruction, teach the children loyalty to their Emperor and country"; "The Japanese school at —— is under the control of priests whose religion opposes the making of real Americans"; "If the Japanese schools are continued we shall have a mongrel citizenship, both in language and customs"; "What compatibility is there between Mikado worship, ancestor worship and the teaching of democracy?" Their opinions also embodied ideas of assimilating a subordinate culture to the dominant society and notions of white supremacy. They stated, "We can eventually mold them into real Americans if we have no Japanese competition"; "We must help them to assimilate and to develop a true love and respect for our American ideals and ideas"; and "It is a lasting insult to every real American teacher to have to compete with this survival of medievalism and nationalism flaunted under our very noses."[114]

Another key section of the survey included the recommendations for legislative action of three civic organizations: the Daughters of the American Revolution, the Honolulu Chamber of Commerce, and the Ad Club of Honolulu. The report offers no explanation as to why these white civic organizations were labeled important or representative of public sentiment. Each of the three organizations had passed resolutions opposing the Japanese language schools. The Daughters of the American Revolution concluded that "foreign-language schools are not only unnecessary, but a menace to the unity and safety of our Nation." The Chamber of Commerce and Ad Club both recommended the schools be placed under DPI supervision. The Ad Club further proposed a policy for their gradual elimination "as rapidly as may be wise."[115]

The commission concluded its analysis that the language schools were "centers of an influence which, if not distinctly anti-American, is certainly un-American." Perceiving the foreign language school issue through religious lenses, they indicted these schools:

> Although the commission recognizes the inherent right of every person in the United States to adopt any form of religious worship which he desires, nevertheless it holds that the principle of religious freedom to which our country is unswervingly committed does not demand that practices and activities must be tolerated in the name of religion which make the task of training for the duties and responsibilities of American citizenship a well-nigh hopeless one. The commission, therefore, feels no hesitancy in recommending as a first and important step in clearing away the obstacles from the path of the Territorial public-school system that all foreign-language schools be abolished.[116]

The survey commission's recommendation was radically more severe than the measures by either the Chamber of Commerce or the Ad Club, which proposed allowing these schools to survive under DPI supervision. The commission also predicted that few Japanese parents would have their children learn Japanese once pressure from Buddhist priests was removed. The commission's most important recommendations on Japanese language schools were: (1) that the legislature abolish all such schools at its next session; (2) creation of a foreign-language division in the DPI; (3) takeover of the Japanese school buildings for the use of the public school system; (4) that public schools offer foreign language classes taught by teachers employed by the DPI at the pupils' expense; and (5) lengthening of the school day to add agricultural and vocational instruction.[117] The recommendations were largely drawn from the Ad Club's proposals, with the exception of recommending "immediate abolition," rather than the Ad Club's proposal of "gradual elimination." However, the most distinctive characteristic of the report was that it not only suggested the abolition of such schools but also offered specific instructions on how to do so. Japanese school buildings after closing were to be purchased inexpensively and utilized for public school use. It even went so far as to suggest how to conduct this project peacefully so that "it may be accomplished with good feeling and good will on the part of all."[118] The commissioners tried to project an air of objectivity and authority as a federal study without stating specifically what aspects of these schools the commission saw as "un-American" and should be abolished.

Reaction on the Islands was immediate. Lorrin A. Thurston, publisher of the *Advertiser*, criticized the commission's report and the subsequent school control bills as un-American, devoid of the spirit of freedom, and "inexcusably tyrannical . . . to make it a penal offense for a man to teach his own child his own language."[119] However, the power of a study conducted by the federal government was enormous and encouraged many organizations to endorse school control measures.[120] The federal report also led Japanese community leaders to yield to the dominant group's desire despite all their endeavors to protect their cultural and linguistic heritage. Rather than further aggravating hostile territorial legislators by defending Japanese language schools, a group of Japanese leaders drafted a compromise bill. With an endorsement by Honolulu's Chamber of Commerce, it easily passed at a special session of the Hawaii legislature and was immediately signed by Governor McCarthy on November 24, 1920.[121] Act 30, as it became known, was written following the guidelines recommended by the commission with only a few modifications. It placed foreign language schools under the DPI, "so that Americanism of their pupils would be promoted," and required their teachers to obtain certification from the DPI.[122] The effect of the report was not limited to the Islands. As we will see, it provided impetus for similar attacks within the contiguous United States.

CHAPTER 3

Closing a Loophole
California Exclusionists' Attack on
Japanese Language Schools

Land is the very life of the Japanese race in California. Land is the
foundation of our development.
   —Editorial, (San Francisco) *Nichibei*, June 5, 1920

If the Japanese were sure of a welcome here or at the least that they
would not be legislated out of the privilege of farming the land, . . .
there would very soon be no Japanese language schools.
   —Reverend Dr. Paul B. Waterhouse, 1920

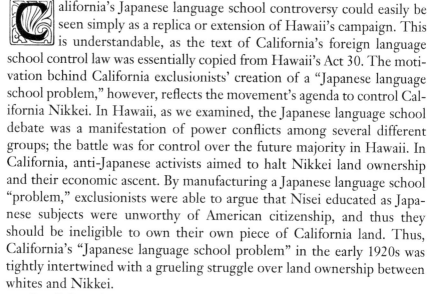alifornia's Japanese language school controversy could easily be
seen simply as a replica or extension of Hawaii's campaign. This
is understandable, as the text of California's foreign language
school control law was essentially copied from Hawaii's Act 30. The motivation behind California exclusionists' creation of a "Japanese language
school problem," however, reflects the movement's agenda to control California Nikkei. In Hawaii, as we examined, the Japanese language school
debate was a manifestation of power conflicts among several different
groups; the battle was for control over the future majority in Hawaii. In
California, anti-Japanese activists aimed to halt Nikkei land ownership
and their economic ascent. By manufacturing a Japanese language school
"problem," exclusionists were able to argue that Nisei educated as Japanese subjects were unworthy of American citizenship, and thus they
should be ineligible to own their own piece of California land. Thus,
California's "Japanese language school problem" in the early 1920s was
tightly intertwined with a grueling struggle over land ownership between
whites and Nikkei.

Paralleling the conditions that led to the Chinese Exclusion Act of
1882, anti-Japanese activists portrayed the growing Japanese population
as a threat of expanding Japanese economic power. Although a 1907–1908
accord between Japan and the United States, called the Gentlemen's
Agreement, ended the immigration of Japanese laborers, a variant of

Japanese traditional marriage known as "picture brides" allowed Issei bachelors to find a spouse who then could immigrate under a provision permitting family unification. To Japanese exclusionists, Issei multiplied their population exponentially. The number of Nikkei in California grew from 10,151 in 1900 to 41,356 in 1910, although this influx included laborers who remigrated from Hawaii after it was annexed by the United States. As some Issei shifted from being farm-sojourning laborers to land-owning farmers, they were increasingly perceived as competitors to white farmers. In response, California nativists passed the 1913 Alien Land Law to hinder Nikkei's rise in California agriculture. The law prohibited Issei from purchasing or leasing land for more than three years.[1] The Alien Land Law came as a blow to Issei, but many circumvented it by forming corporations or purchasing land as guardians for their American-born children who, as citizens, could not constitutionally be barred from purchasing land. In the six years following the law's passage, Nikkei landholding increased by more than four times.[2]

The anti-Japanese movement was largely quiescent during World War I, when both Japan and the United States fought Germany. However, after the armistice, the movement was revived on the West Coast. During the war, the government appreciated Nikkei farmers' productivity, but during the postwar recession, politicians and journalists considered that success as a domestic threat. Building from the foundation of the 1905 Asiatic Exclusion League in San Francisco, postwar anti-Japanese activists asserted that the Japanese were not assimilable since they worked long hours for lower wages and were largely non-Christian. Exclusionists propagated a fear that an unassimilable, mass Asiatic population with strong economic power would take over the West Coast and eventually devour the whole nation—the revival of the "Yellow Peril" fear.[3] Japan's military gains strengthened the exclusionists' argument that Japanese immigrants were sent as part of Japan's scheme to invade the United States. When the Japanese exclusion movement was revived in 1919, it naturally expanded its target to include Nisei, since they remained the primary obstacle to removing Nikkei from agriculture in the Golden State. Exclusionists challenged Nisei loyalty to America and sought to deprive them of their American citizenship. Meanwhile, exclusionists tried to accomplish this by proposing a tighter alien land law.

In this chapter, I will examine another aspect of the "Japanese problem" in California that Roger Daniels so carefully captured in his classic *Politics of Prejudice*, but from a slightly different angle: the manufacture of a "Japanese language school problem." Daniels writes, "For the rest of the decade [following the passage of the 1920 Alien Land Law] the legislature attempted minor harassments of the Issei," but he does not treat these issues in detail.[4] This chapter, however, focuses precisely on what happened after the 1920 Alien Land Law in terms of one of these "minor harassments" enacted by California's legislature as it attempted to control and then eliminate the state's Japanese language schools.

The Early Period of California's Japanese Language Schools

The origins of California's Japanese language schools were rooted in the universal desire of immigrant parents to impart their native tongue and cultural heritage to their children. Issei worried about their children's deficient Japanese, "rude behavior," and their future education in Japan, since many Issei parents still considered themselves as sojourners. As Nisei started attending public schools, Issei parents faced communication difficulties. A typical Nikkei nurseryman in Oakland explained that his wife felt separated from her two children because they used English exclusively, and she no longer understood what they said or thought. He forced his two children to speak Japanese at least during meals in order to keep their children close to them.[5] Parents also hoped that learning the language would help Nisei to advance their careers and to serve as bridges between Japan and the United States.[6] All over America, concerned Issei parents cooperated to build Japanese language schools and sent their reluctant children to study their parents' mother tongue.

Japanese language schools often played another indispensable role for immigrant parents as mediators between public school teachers and parents. Since most Issei parents did not speak English well, it was hard for them to communicate with their children's public school teachers, so Japanese language school teachers often went as their representatives.[7] According to the principal of a public school, some Nisei children could not tell teachers their ages or parents' names, and in some cases, even their parents could not provide necessary information regarding their children. Principals and teachers of the ethnic schools were often called in to mediate these problems.[8] Another important role for a Japanese language school was to provide opportunities for children to receive an American public education. Most Japanese agricultural communities were located far from public schools, and in some communities, transportation provided by Japanese schools carried children between home, public school, and the language school. Since some very early Japanese parents cared little about American education, without transportation they might not have sent their children to public schools. The principal of the Gardena Gakuen (California) explained that since the school began offering transportation, the number of students increased from around 50 students to 100. Although some pupils were somewhat older than school-aged children, this transportation enabled them to attend a public school as well as a Japanese language school after public school hours.[9] As was mentioned, they also functioned as daycare for immigrant parents who did not want to take their children with them to the fields or leave them alone at home. Of the twenty-six or twenty-seven Japanese language schools existing in Southern California in 1920, at least fifteen operated such kindergartens.[10] Some of these kindergartens also taught English to Nisei preschoolers.

Issei regarded Japanese language schools as the ideal solution to these problems, and with the help of clergy or community leaders, these concerned parents opened schools for Nisei.[11] Unlike language schools in Hawaii that were subsidized by sugar planters, Japanese schools in California largely depended on tuition paid by parents. This was especially the case for large schools, while entire ethnic communities in agricultural villages often supported rural schools.[12]

The first Japanese language school in California, the Nihon Shōgakkō (Japanese Elementary School) was established in 1902 by a Christian couple, Mr. and Mrs. Keizō Sano, in a San Francisco home.[13] The next year, Hongwanji Buddhist missionaries established their own Meiji Shōgakkō. It began with support from San Francisco Japanese Consul General Kisaburō Ueno, a branch manager of the Shōkin Bank, and local Nikkei community leaders. The Nihon Shōgakkō, between O'Farrell and Ellis streets, and the Meiji Shōgakkō, on Polk Street, were both located east of the area now called Japan Town. Another Hongwanji-affiliated school, the Sakura Gakuen (Sakura Institute), also opened in 1903 at the southern end of Sacramento's Japan Town. Since most Japanese immigrants of the time were bachelors, the Japanese community had few potential pupils, so teachers like Sano struggled to survive, often supporting themselves with a second job.[14] Despite the economic struggles of the schools and the lack of children in the communities, most Nikkei appreciated the language schools.

The San Francisco earthquake and fire of 1906 destroyed both Sano's Nihon Shōgakkō and the Meiji Shōgakkō, but they were rebuilt in new locations and played important roles in the 1906 San Francisco School Segregation Incident. The incident was a result of pressure from the newly formed Asiatic Exclusion League on the San Francisco School Board to classify Nikkei as "Mongolian" children and force them to join Chinese children in the segregated Oriental school on October 15, 1906. This order affected ninety-three Nikkei pupils (who attended twenty-three schools) out of a school system encompassing 2,800 students at seventy-two schools.[15] Until the school segregation order was reversed on February 15, 1907, the Zaibei Nihonjin Kyōgikai (later the Nihonjin Kai or Japanese Association) gave support to the Nihon Gakuin (formerly the Nihon Shōgakkō) to hire three white teachers so the displaced Japanese American children could continue their public education without the humiliation of segregation. Until the school closed in 1907, the Japanese Association also supplied school equipment to the Meiji Shōgakkō to support Japanese language education. The segregation order was lifted following pressure from the Japanese foreign ministry on the State Department, which approved a 1907 presidential order prohibiting Japanese migration from bordering nations and Hawaii, leading to the "Gentlemen's Agreement" of 1907–1908. When these children returned to their original public schools, their Nihon Gakuin grades were officially accepted by the San Francisco School Board.

As the population of Japanese immigrants increased on the West Coast, California had sixteen Japanese language schools by 1912 (see Table 2).[16] Unlike the situation in Hawaii, Buddhist temples began offering Japanese instruction to Nisei children in California before Christian churches were involved. All sixteen schools were located in either northern or central California, reflecting early Nikkei settlement, with only one exception—Los Angeles' Dai Ichi Rafu Gakuen. Besides these denominationally affiliated schools, some individuals also ran private schools, and several local Japanese associations sponsored Japanese schools in smaller rural communities. In the latter case, association leaders oftentimes were concerned that a school might become involved with religious conflicts between Buddhists and Christians, and they established a nonsectarian school. Under this policy, the two existing sectarian schools in Watsonville were merged in 1912 into the Watsonville Gakuen, a secular, independent school under the auspices of the local Japanese Association.[17]

In this formative period, each school functioned independently. According to Kinmon Gakuen Principal Takashi Suzuki, some schools stressed *nisshu beijū*, the primacy of Japanese education, considering American education as secondary, while others conducted curricula in the reverse order, *beishu nichijū*. Subjects taught at the schools, recalled Suzuki, included Japanese history and geography based on the Monbushō curricula. Although some schools also adopted *shūshin* (moral education), drawing, and arithmetic, others exclusively taught Japanese language.[18]

In May 1908, an editorial in San Francisco's Japanese daily, *Shin Sekai* (New World), questioned the role of Japanese schools for Nisei who were American citizens and attended public school. This opened prolonged discussion in the community on Nisei education. The newly established Zaibei Nihonjin Kai or Japanese Association of America, a community group connected to the Japanese consulate, conducted a survey that year to investigate the number of Nisei children in San Francisco. Responding to the results of the survey, which found a growing young Nisei population, several Issei leaders in 1909 formed the Mokuyōbi Kai or Thursday Club to discuss Nisei education. The Thursday Club drew a blueprint for Nisei education that emphasized American assimilation, supplemented

Table 2: Japanese Language School in California, 1912

School	Year Established	Affiliation	Location
Nihon Gakuin	1902	Independent	San Francisco
Sakura Gakuen	1903	Buddhist	Sacramento
Alviso Nihongo Gakuen	1904	Independent	Alviso
Ōfu Bukkyō Gakuen	1904	Buddhist	Oakland
Fushi Nihongo Gakuen	1905	Buddhist	Fresno
Sashi Nihongo Gakuen	1906	Buddhist	San Jose
Ashi Gakuen	1907	Christian	Alameda
Sushi Gakuen	1908	Buddhist	Stockton
Agnew Nihongo Gakuen	1909	Independent	Agnew
Florin Nihonjin Shōgakkō	1909	Independent	Florin
Berryessa Gakuen	1910	Christian	Berryessa
Penryn Nihongo Gakuen	1910	Independent	Penryn
Kawashimo Gakuen	1911	Independent	Walnut Grove
Kinmon Gakuen	1911	Independent	San Francisco
Dai Ichi Rafu Gakuen	1911	Independent	Los Angeles
Watsonville Gakuen	1912	Independent	Watsonville

Sources: Shinichi Katō, *Beikoku Nikkeijin Hyakunenshi* [A history of one-hundred years of the Japanese and Japanese Americans in the United States] (Tokyo: Shin Nichibei Shinbun Sha, 1961), 116; for affiliations, Hokka Nihongo Gakuen Kyōkai, eds., *Beikoku Kashū Nihongo Gakuen Enkakushi* [A brief history of the Japanese language schools in California] (San Francisco: Hokka; Nihongo Gakuen Kyōkai, 1930), 235–264; and Ken Ishikawa, *Beikoku Kashū Nihongo Gakuen ni Kansuru Kenkyū* [A study of Japanese language institutes in California] (n.p., 1923), 30–32; letter, San Francisco Consul General Unojirō Ōyama to Foreign Minister Nobuaki Makino, April 7, 1913, DRO 3.10.2.10.

with Japanese language education. Based on these objectives, the club created the Kinmon Gakuen (Golden Gate Institute) in San Francisco two years later. The organizers recruited a principal from Japan to lead the model school.

In order to unify California's Japanese schools, the Japanese Association sponsored the first meeting of Japanese teachers in 1912. Association leaders and teachers declared that the objectives of Japanese language schools are to "educate permanent residents of the United States," while recognizing that public schools were the primary schools and that the role of Japanese schools was to "provide supplementary instruction in Japanese and education about Japan."[19] At the same time, they also insisted that moral education for the Nisei should be based on the 1889 Imperial Rescript on Education. Language school teachers gathered again in 1913 to establish the Zaibei Nihonjin Kyōiku Kai or Japanese Teachers Association of America. At this conference, members decided not to provide specific classes on moral education, but rather to teach it through lessons in language, history, and geography.[20] This consensus, however, seems to have been at most a short-lived recommendation, because a survey of some sixty California language schools taken only five years later shows that moral education was still offered at thirty-four schools as a distinct course.[21] Japanese teachers suggested the creation of new textbooks at association meetings every year following the group's 1913 founding. Many of the objects, customs, and living circumstances described in the present Monbushō textbooks were unfamiliar to Nisei. Their contents were too advanced for nonnative speakers. Educators also saw some Japanese ideas, such as *bushidō* (the samurai code of behavior) or stories emphasizing Japanese patriotism, not only as inappropriate for American citizens but also as likely to provoke questions from critics of Japanese language schools. According to Japanese education historian Tomitarō Karasawa, Monbushō textbooks between 1910 and 1917 emphasized nationalism and imperialism, using such themes as the importance of family and ancestors in parallel with the relationship between Japanese subjects and the emperor.[22]

The Nikkei population in southern California rapidly increased by the end of the 1910s, in response to opportunities to be part of Los Angeles' booming market.[23] Issei farmers moved to acquire farmland and avoid discrimination prevalent in northern California.[24] Between 1911 and 1915, eight Japanese schools were established to meet the growing need for Japanese language education in southern California (see Table 3). In 1915, with the establishment of a Japanese consulate in Los Angeles, Southern

Table 3: Japanese Language School Affiliations in Southern California, 1911–1915

School	Year Established	Affiliation	Location
Dai Ichi Rafu Gakuen	1911	Independent	Los Angeles
Moneta Gakuen	1912	Independent	Moneta
Oxnard Gakuen	1912	Christian	Oxnard
Rafu Seikō Kai	1914	Christian	Los Angeles
Rafu Dai Ni	1915	Independent	Los Angeles
Seirin	1915	Christian	N/A
Maryknoll Gakuen	1915	Christian	Los Angeles
Montebello Dai Ichi	1915	Independent	Montebello

Sources: Japanese Chamber of Commerce of Southern California, *Japanese in Southern California: A History of 70 Years* (Los Angeles: Japanese Chamber of Commerce of Southern California, 1960), 283; for affiliations, Hokka Nihongo Gakuen Kyōkai, eds., *Beikoku Kashū Nihongo Gakuen Enkakushi*, 235–264; and Ken Ishikawa, *Beikoku Kashū Nihongo Gakuen ni Kansuru Kenkyū*, 30–32; letter, San Francisco Consul General Unojirō Ōyama to Foreign Minister Nobuaki Makino, April 7, 1913, DRO 3.10.2.10.

California Nikkei formed their own Japanese Association. This provided a stimulus for local teachers to form the Nanka Nihonjin Kyōiku Kai (Southern California Japanese Educators Association), making it independent of San Francisco's Japanese Teachers Association of America.[25]

By October 1919, Japanese language school teachers and others in the community may have foreseen trouble brewing. The *Rafu Shinpō*, Los Angeles' leading Japanese daily newspaper, reported news of anti-Japanese measures, including California exclusionists' plan to deprive Nisei of their right to acquire land.[26] At the annual association meeting in Stockton, anticipating intense public scrutiny of their schools, Japanese teachers again questioned the role of Japanese language education for Nisei. They redefined their mission as equipping Nisei to be American citizens, although they could not agree whether schools should teach only language or also cultivate the spirit of the Yamato (Japanese) race.[27]

The Pre-Initiative Movement

In California, the main issue for anti-Japanese activists was land. State Senator James M. Inman (Republican, Sacramento) tried to introduce a more stringent alien land bill during the 1919 legislature. After Califor-

Fig. 5. Japanese language schools were located throughout California, as this map from the early 1920s shows. Ken Ishikawa, *Beikoku Kashū Nihongo Gakuen ni Kansuru Kenkyū* [A study of Japanese language institutes in California] (n.p., 1923).

nia Governor William D. Stephens refused his demand to call a special session of the legislature, Inman and fellow exclusionists determined to pursue a ballot initiative campaign.[28] At the same time, the postwar Japanese exclusion movement began with the 1919 founding of the California Oriental Exclusion League, by leaders of the American Legion, the

Native Sons of the Golden West, the Native Daughters of the Golden West, the California State Federation of Labor, and the State Grange. Inman, a member of the Native Sons of the Golden West, was appointed president. The league's objectives were to cancel the Gentlemen's Agreement and to exclude picture brides and all other Japanese immigrants. Members also hoped to pass a constitutional amendment to remove the citizenship of Nisei born in the United States, and thus to close one loophole to the state's land law.[29] Exclusionists in California then made Nisei the focus of their anti-Japanese movement. It is within this context that exclusionists assailed California's Japanese language schools.

Politicians in all of California's parties also routinely used anti-Japanese rhetoric as part of their own election campaigns. For example, Governor William D. Stephens, a Progressive Republican, "investigated" Japanese landholding conditions under the guise of a 1919 study by the State Board of Control.[30] His report, *California and the Oriental*, was published on June 19, 1920, and was presented to Secretary of State Bainbridge Colby.[31] Beyond the original call to investigate Japanese farm ownership, the report turned out be a wide-ranging assault on the "Japanese problem" in California. Ten thousand copies were printed, in order "not only to influence voters for the 1920 initiative, but also to advance the whole exclusionist cause," and of course to bolster Governor Stephen's reelection.[32] Using his letter to Secretary Colby as a preface to the report, Stephens wrote that California's children attended schools "crowded with other children of a different race."[33] Although San Francisco city authorities once had attempted to separate their children from these Japanese students by mandating segregated schools for the latter, Stephens said this was ended by federal intervention in exchange for the promise that they would stop further Japanese encroachment by negotiating the "Gentlemen's Agreement" with Japan.[34] It had, Stephens argued, practically no effect; California's Japanese population increased regardless, since picture brides were permitted under the agreement and more were entering via Mexico. Stephens stressed further actions by the California legislature to solve this problem, such as the enactment of the 1913 Alien Land Law which was designed to completely shut off Japanese immigration. This too, he argued, had "been evaded and broken" through purchasing land under the names of corporations and Nisei children.[35] The report included a section on Japanese language schools, which reproached Japanese efforts to defeat a Japanese language school control measure in Hawaii. The report denied claims that Japanese language schools were "not intended to perpetuate the traditions and moral concepts of Japan."[36]

The *Rafu Shinpō* criticized Stephens' report, writing that although it implied that Japanese American students dominated public school classes, these cases were extremely rare among California's thousands of schools. The newspaper added that, in those areas, Japanese had developed and settled there first, and that a small number of whites came after the development; it was not the case that Japanese dominated communities developed by whites.[37]

The true force behind the exclusion movement was Valentine S. McClatchy, the retired publisher of the *Sacramento Bee* newspaper, and also a member of the Native Sons of the Golden West.[38] McClatchy claimed to have been against Japanese immigration since he visited Korea and witnessed Japan's brutal suppression of independence demonstrations. McClatchy strategically cast suspicion on the Nisei's education and their relationship with the Japanese government, thus challenging their loyalty to the United States. During the United States House of Representatives' Committee on Immigration and Naturalization hearing on Japanese immigration in July 1920, McClatchy testified against Nikkei, submitting more than sixty articles of "evidence" over two days. The hearings investigated "the Japanese problem" on the Pacific Coast, especially Japanese ownership of land and businesses at the very same time that California exclusionists were desperately trying to collect signatures for the initiative ballot to create a new land law.[39] At the hearings, McClatchy claimed that Japanese were unassimilable because they were subjects of the Mikado, or the Japanese emperor. McClatchy escalated his theory of the emperor's power over his subjects in America by stating the mere fact that under the Japanese constitution, Nisei were still Japanese citizens, and that only a handful had actually tried to expatriate. Moreover, he testified, according to San Francisco Vice-Consul Itarō Ishii, no such petitions to renounce Japanese citizenship had yet been approved.[40] The Japanese were now, McClatchy stated, desperate to secure American citizenship, not because of a desire to be good American citizens but to better serve Japan and their emperor. McClatchy cited an article translated from Sacramento's daily, *Ōfu Nippō*, advising not to report birth notices to the Japanese government, thus not registering Japanese citizenship for the time being in order to avoid unnecessary friction with whites. He implied there was a Japanese conspiracy to deceive the American public.[41] Contrary to McClatchy's portrayal, the referenced article merely encouraged fellow countrymen not to be afraid of cutting off Japanese citizenship for their children in order to avoid further conflict. Extending his attack to Nisei education,

McClatchy suggested the Japanese government was directly involved with Japanese language schools:

> Japan not only claims as her citizens all Japanese born on American soil, but she takes great care that they grow up really as Japanese citizens, with all the ideals and loyalty of the race, untouched by the notions prevalent in this country, which would weaken that loyalty.[42]

Japanese children born in America, argued McClatchy, were required to attend a local Japanese language school, located wherever a Japanese community existed. He claimed Japanese language school teachers usually spoke no English and had no knowledge of American civics, and that they taught "the language, the ideals, and the religion of Japan, with its basis of Mikado worship," using Monbushō textbooks.

McClatchy further critiqued Hawaii's Japanese language school problem, warning that Japanese schools in California followed the same policies, so that Hawaii's problem would soon become California's. Pointing at Hawaii's Japanese language school control bill, McClatchy argued that "the bill was defeated on the demand and through the influence of the Japanese," in order to protect the center for indoctrinating Mikado worship. He tried to prove his statement by directing the Immigration Committee's attention to the newly published report of the Federal Survey of Education in Hawaii, which concluded that these schools were, "if not anti-American, are at least not pro-American," and recommended their abolition.[43] To complete their indoctrination, argued McClatchy, 5,000 California-born Nisei were living in Japan. This meant, McClatchy elaborated, that about 20 percent of California's Japanese minors were now in Japan, "being thoroughly instructed in the religion and ideals of Japan." He continued, "they return here . . . as loyal subjects of the Mikado, to do his will and serve his interests."[44] He then illustrated education for girls at schools in Japan, based on a patently fictitious story from a Swedish publication from Portland, Oregon. The *Northman* article claimed that girls in Japan were taught to fulfill their duty to the emperor by becoming "picture brides" in America and raising as many children as possible "so that the foreigners' land may become in time a possession of Japan, through the expressed will of a majority of the people."[45] The committee reinforced McClatchy's testimony fostering the public's suspicion of Japanese language schools. In Sacramento, they visited Buddhist Japanese language schools and also inspected language schools in Florin and Penryn, where they requisitioned Japanese national textbooks.[46] The committee also followed Reverend Gulick's suggestion to summon the general secretary of the Japanese Association of America, Kiichi Kanzaki, to discuss Japanese language schools.[47] The hearings were part of the exclusionists' larger campaign to further a new land law initiative and also to focus national attention on their concerns.

Fig. 6. This caricature of a Japanese language school appeared in Sacramento's daily, the *Sacramento Bee*, in 1922. Valentine S. McClatchy, a leader of the anti-Japanese movement, published the newspaper before retiring. McClatchy's brother was publisher at the time this editorial cartoon appeared.

Two months after the House Immigration Hearings in California, Japanese language schools became a topic in the negotiations between the Japanese ambassador to the United States, Kijūrō Shidehara, and the United States ambassador to Japan, Roland Morris. Between September 1920 and the following January, the two ambassadors had more than twenty consultations in Washington, D.C., to seek a diplomatic resolution to critical problems, including revising the Gentlemen's Agreement and the 1911 U.S.-Japan Treaty.[48] In their sixth meeting on October 21, Ambassador Morris raised a very similar question to McClatchy's Immigration Hearings testimony. Morris voiced concern that Japanese were forming self-sufficient, internal communities that were independent from the rest of America, particularly in California. There, he argued, civic and religious organizations, headquartered in Japan, fostered Japanese culture and provided American-born offspring with education based on Japan's school curricula. Morris argued that these various religious and educational agencies maintained control over Japanese settlers and Nisei.[49] Ambassador Shidehara responded that he was aware of the fact that some of the Japanese schools were financially supported by those Japanese associations, but that there was no intention to keep children of Japanese immigrants removed from American life. He explained that these schools' curricula were vastly different from those of Japanese public schools, which should be obvious simply by comparing instructional hours. Shidehara responded that, considering their current living situation, the high levels of anti-Japanese sentiment, and the movement to deny Japanese immigrants' naturalization and even their children's American citizenship, it would be understandable that "profound unrest prevailed among Japanese residents who were beginning to look with grave concern upon the future destiny of their children, . . . and had sent their children back to Japan for education." Shidehara asserted that this fact also was evidence of the relative inefficiency of these language schools in America.[50]

On September 2, 1920, the Japanese Exclusion League of California was restructured in order to develop a unified nationwide movement.[51] The league's purpose was "to secure the passage, at the November election, of the [land law] initiative measure." The league also adopted a resolution to deny "the right of citizenship to all Asiatics."[52] The *Grizzly Bear*, the official monthly organ of the Native Sons and Native Daughters of the Golden West—important coalition members with the Exclusion League, and according to Daniels, "the most influential pressure group in the state"—then began agitating against Japanese language schools.[53] The movement followed McClatchy's theory of the Mikado doctrine and Japanese colonization. The monthly's editor argued that, as far as Nikkei tried to maintain these schools where "Japanese children are taken, everyday after the public school, and taught, by a Buddhist priest, loyalty and obedience to the mikado, who is the Japanese god!,"[54] it was "utterly useless to hope to assimilate the Japanese and make of him an American citizen entirely without divided allegiance."[55] The editor expanded the attack on the ethnic community and its supporters. He scornfully said, "The idea of the Japanese in this country, espousing the Christian religion is ridiculous" since, he claimed, there were more Buddhist temples in America than Christian churches in Japan. The editor insisted that the "wily Japanese will go [to] any length to enlist the services of influential churchmen in combating the anti-Japanese sentiment."[56] A June 1920 *Grizzly Bear* article by State Senator Inman elaborated on a peaceful invasion by Japanese through their "fertility," and he tried to "enlighten" Californians about the importance of the vote on the upcoming land initiative. Inman used statistics from the California State Board of Health that illustrated the growth of Japanese births, from 134 in 1906 to 4,378 in 1919, and stressed the line: "The increase of Japanese births in thirteen years, from 1906 is 3,000 percent." Inman argued that these babies, "approximately 29,556 Japanese" born in California since 1906, were all "entitled to own land outright, and will someday be voters."[57]

Inman manipulated Japanese birthrate statistics (see Table 4). First, he calculated the Japanese birthrate increase from 1906, when only a few Japanese women were in California, in order to magnify the increase. Second, while the 3,000 percent increase in birthrate between 1906 and 1919 is mathematically correct, the number was presented in a way that made it look more meaningful than it was. However, one can easily imagine that Inman's article was potent enough to draw readers' attention to the land law initiative.

In November 1920, the month of the initiative vote, the *Grizzly Bear* displayed several sample ballot forms, exclaiming "Vote 'Yes' on Proposition One—The Alien Land Law." It frantically pressed readers to "wake up," warning of a scheme of Japanese invasion and colonization of the West Coast. The *Grizzly Bear*'s editor claimed that in "Jap schools . . . their children born upon our soil are instructed in the language, government and traditions of Japan, to realize that the conquest of California . . . for the glory and expansion of the Yamato race." It escalated the attack using a racist remark that "a Jap is always a Jap at heart . . . his allegiance is everlastingly pledged to Japan, and though born upon American soil he is always a subject of Japan." The article concluded by challenging readers to question, "Are the people of this state willing to entrust the destiny of California to the subjects of Japan?" "That is the question involved in Proposition One," the paper argued, adding, "California's destiny may be placed for all time in the keeping of the White Race."[58]

Anti-Japanese activists also tried to disseminate their propaganda via films and popular novels in preparation for the alien land initiative and produced a pervasive and long-lasting impact among California's public. Wallace Irwin's *Seed of the Sun*—an example of "sentimental magazine romances with a political message inserted"—first appeared in an early October 1920 *Saturday Evening Post* serial, as well as in other papers, and was later published as a book in 1921, which remained popular in public libraries for decades.[59] McClatchy and other exclusionists gave Irwin $7,000 and information in order to have him produce such anti-Japanese propaganda.[60] In subplots, the novel depicted a Japanese language school as an institution controlled by the super-vicious Mikado and his "Beneficent Society," or portrayed a Japanese association that Japanese in California supposedly had no choice but to obey. The descriptions of Japanese and Japanese language schools left a powerful impression that likely prejudiced many readers. In the novel, protagonist Anna Bly visited a

Table 4: Registered Births in California by Ethnicity, 1910–1919

Year	White (% of total)		Japanese (% of total)		Black	Chinese	Indians	Total
1910	30,893	(96.13)	710	(2.24)	232	277	17	32,138
1911	33,245	(95.45)	995	(2.86)	258	307	23	34,828
1912	37,194	(94.57)	1,467	(3.73)	319	321	29	39,330
1913	40,864	(93.19)	2,215	(5.05)	343	381	49	43,852
1914	42,281	(91.89)	2,874	(6.25)	388	418	51	46,012
1915	43,874	(91.26)	3,342	(6.95)	392	429	38	48,075
1916	46,272	(91.38)	3,721	(7.35)	199	425	21	50,638
1917	47,313	(90.59)	4,108	(7.87)	328	419	62	52,230
1918	50,986	(91.17)	4,218	(7.54)	262	413	43	55,922
1919	50,898	(90.86)	4,378	(7.82)	256	432	55	56,019
TOTAL	459,044		28,037		2,977	3,822	388	459,044

Source: California State Board of Health, cited in U.S. Congress, House, Committee on Immigration and Naturalization, *Japanese Immigration Hearings, 66th Congress, 2nd session, 1921* (Washington, D.C.: GPO, 1921; reprint, New York: Arno Press, 1978), 84.

Japanese language school taught by the Japanese wife of a Christian parson. There, she saw little children as "quaint dolls," the girls with "their wiry black hair cut severely straight across the forehead," and the boys with "their heads close-cropped like German soldiers," reciting sentences from the primer that included the legend of Japan's creation by the sun goddess and the first emperor, Jinmu.

Answering Anna's questions, the parson's wife said that as a Christian, she did not believe all the stories in the primer. Neither did the "Gentlemen who are running Japan," she said, but the "Mikado makes [a] nice idol to set up and worship." Being honest and betraying the "presence of a secret she was loath to keep," the wife explained that since the Beneficent Society helped to establish the Japanese school, they had to use the same textbook used to teach children in Japan, "if we wish keep them Japanese here." When Anna and the teacher walked out of the school, they saw the church across the street, a rival Buddhist temple with an expensive altar. The teacher said that the majority of Japanese did not desire Buddhist temples, but "no sooner [does a] Christian church rise up nice [sic] than considerable money come[s] from somewhere to build [a] grand Buddhist temple so that we shall be choked off."[61]

Within the novel's few pages on a Japanese language school, it included almost all of the anti-Japanese arguments McClatchy raised in the hearings: the Japanese as an unassimilable race, Mikado worship, imperial control over subjects through Japanese associations, and Japan's colonization of California through Buddhism and Mikadoism. It even touched on Japanese women's prolific nature, an utterly inaccurate caricature created by exclusionists.[62] Anti-Japanese propaganda movies, such as *Shadows of the West*, produced and circulated by the American Legion, also reached mass audiences in 1920.[63] According to the *Nichibei*, California's Attorney General Ulysses S. Webb made speeches between several showings. The newspaper interpreted this as yet another effort to pass the upcoming initiative.[64]

Japanese Supporters

On most issues, Nikkei could count on a few defenders from outside of the community, primarily missionaries who wanted to maintain influence in the Nikkei community and Japan. At the Japanese Immigration Hearings, Reverend Paul B. Waterhouse, a representative of the American Missionary Association, who had lived in Japan for seven years, testified in support of Nikkei. Defending Japanese from accusations of a high birthrate, and the theory of Japanese plans to take over the United States, Waterhouse ridiculed the possibility, claiming that California's white population was also increasing by birth and through internal migration. He also criticized testimony that Japanese did not stay in one place and lived in unsanitary conditions. He explained that the alien land law prevented Nikkei from having more than a three-year lease, thus discouraging them from settling down and investing in nice homes.

However, contrary to his supportive stance on other Nikkei issues, Waterhouse called Japanese language schools "a hindrance toward full Americanization of the Japanese," and claimed that Japanese themselves recognized American education was appropriate for Nisei and disapproved of anything that countered this.[65] Waterhouse argued that many Issei still felt it necessary to maintain language schools because "the anti-Japanese attitude is fostered and aroused by politicians who twist and exaggerate the truth and do everything in their power to cause misunderstanding between Americans and Japanese." Waterhouse reasoned that "if the Japanese were sure of a welcome here or at least that they would not be legislated out of the privilege of farming the land, if they were sure of not being discriminated against, there would very soon be no Japanese language schools." In 1921, Waterhouse even encouraged House Immigration Committee Chair Albert Johnson to consider Hawaii's school law a solution for the "Japanese language school problem." Waterhouse sent Johnson a copy of Lorrin A. Thurston's 1920 address to the Honolulu Social Science Association, which argued for regulating Japanese language schools but opposed Territory Attorney General Harry Irwin's bill to completely suppress them. Waterhouse wrote Johnson that "since this address, the bill proposed by the Japanese themselves was adopted and is now the law in Hawaii. Does this law not work toward a real solution of that noted question?"[66]

Christian missionaries believed that Asian immigrants' maintenance of religious institutions to preserve tradition and attachment to native countries was the most serious barrier to what they called Americanization, as well as to their work. They, however, recognized parents' strong desire to teach their mother tongue to the second generation.[67] Missionaries then acquiesced to provide this within a "Christian environment," rather than dropping out of the competition over language schools with Buddhists.

In 1923, twenty-eight of California's fifty-five Japanese language schools were secular (independent or run by a local Japanese association), ten were Buddhist, and another six were run by Christians, whereas the

Table 5: Japanese Language School Affiliations in Northern and Central California, 1923

School	Teachers	Students	Affiliation
Alameda Gakuen	2	72	Independent
Alviso Gakuen	1	18	Independent
Berkeley Gakuen	3	60	Independent
Bowles Gakuen	1	38	N/A
Colusa Nihon Gakuen	1	19	Independent
Del Ray Gakuen	1	16	N/A
Florin Kindergarten	1	32	Buddhist
Fowler Nihongo Gakuen	2	45	Independent
Fresno Gakuen	3	49	Buddhist
Fushi Nihongo Gakuen	4	98	Buddhist
Futaba Gakuen	1	16	Christian
Gilroy Gakuen	2	17	Independent
Hanford Gakuen	1	26	N/A
Irvington Kokugo Gakkō	1	25	Independent
Isleton School	1	44	Independent
Kawashimo Gakuen	2	41	Independent
Kinmon Gakuen	5	196	Independent
Kyōwa Gakuen	2	29	Independent
Los Altos Gakuen	1	11	Independent
Marysville Gakuen	1	45	Independent
Mayfield Gakuen	1	39	Independent
Mii Gakuen	1	22	N/A
Minami Nihongo Gakkō	2	37	N/A
Morning Star Japanese School	3	46	Christian
Mountain View Mission School	1	57	N/A
Newcastle Nihongo Gakkō	1	27	Independent
Nihon Gakuen	1	62	Independent
North Fresno Gakuen	1	14	N/A
Oak Grove Nihongo Gakkō	1	20	N/A
Ōfu Gakuen	3	50	Christian
Parlier Gakuen	1	29	Independent
Prather Nihongo Gakkō	2	41	N/A

(continued on next page)

Table 5: Japanese Language School Affiliations in Northern and Central California, 1923 *(continued)*

School	Teachers	Students	Affiliation
Riverside Gakuen	1	43	N/A
Sakura Gakuen	5	185	Buddhist
San Jose Gakuen	2	30	Buddhist
San Juan Hoshū Gakkō	1	36	Independent
San Mateo Gakuen	1	21	Independent
Selma Gakuen	1	34	Independent
Sōkō Gakuen	2	65	Buddhist
Stockton Children's Home	2	133	Buddhist
Taishō Gakuen	1	27	Independent
Vacaville Gakuen	1	18	Buddhist
Watsonville Kindergarten	2	57	Independent
Yōlō Gakuen	1	23	N/A
Total	74	2,013	

Sources: "Japanese Language Schools, Northern and Central California, January 3, 1923," Papers of the Survey of Race Relations in the Pacific West, Hoover Institution Archives; for school affiliations, Hokka Nihongo Gakuen Kyōkai, eds., *Beikoku Kashū Nihongo Gakuen Enkakushi*, 235–264; and Ishikawa, *Beikoku Kashū Nihongo Gakuen*, 30–32.

affiliation of the remaining eleven is unknown (see Tables 5 and 6). The 2,884 Nikkei students (2,013 in northern and central California and 871 in southern California) who attended California's Japanese language schools in 1923 accounted for approximately 42 percent of all Nikkei students attending public schools (6,817 Nikkei students; 4,190 male and 2,627 female students).[68]

The Nikkei Community before the Initiative

In the face of the initiative vote on an alien land law, there was a ground-shaking debate on Japanese language schools at a special February 1920 meeting of the Pacific Coast Japanese Association Deliberative Council. This central organization consisted of the four West Coast regional Japanese associations: the Northwest American Japanese Association (based in Seattle), the Japanese Association of Oregon (Portland), the Japanese Association of America (San Francisco), and the Central Japanese Association of Southern California (Los Angeles), each of which was operated under the supervision of a Japanese consulate, providing a link to between ten to forty local Japanese associations underneath.[69] Toyoji Abe, representing the Oregon Japanese Association, proposed abolishing Japanese schools. He contended that the schools "contradicted" the association's policy of Americanization since the schools impeded Nisei's Americanization.[70] Their existence itself, reprimanded Abe, put Nisei in danger of losing their American citizenship to the exclusionists.[71] Proposing to go along with white demand for their elimination, Abe suggested the council recommend that the schools instead teach English to Issei. Opponents to Abe's stance emphasized the importance of the schools and argued that Nisei would need Japanese language skills to build a foundation between the two countries. Others pointed out that the council had no authority over these schools since most were not under its direct administration. In the end, however, Issei leaders at the council meetings could not come up with a resolution or reach any consensus, and the debate continued at its June regular session. These dialogues among Nikkei leaders illustrate how strong the public's anti-Japanese sentiment had become by that time and

Table 6: Japanese Language School Affiliations in Southern California, 1923

School	Teachers	Students	Affiliation
Rafu Dai Ichi	5	234	Independent
Rafu Dai Ni	2	53	Independent
Baldwin Park Nihongo Gakuen	1	26	Independent
Rafu Seikō Kai	1	20	Christian
Gardena Gakuen	2	88	Buddhist
Guadalupe Japanese Children's Home	1	28	Buddhist
Hollywood Nihongo Gakuen	3	78	Independent
Moneta Gakuen	2	60	Independent
Montebello Dai Ichi	2	68	Independent
Oxnard Gakuen	2	21	Christian
Seirin	9	195	Christian
TOTAL	30	871	

Sources: "Japanese Language Schools, Southern California" (January 3, 1923), Papers of the Survey of Race Relations in the Pacific West, Hoover Institution Archives; for school affiliations, Ishikawa, *Beikoku Kashū Nihongo Gakuen*, 30–32.

how it seriously affected them to the extent that some of the association leaders "entertained the idea of doing away with the schools."[72]

Japanese language school teachers gathered for their ninth annual conference in Fresno on October 15, 1920, in direct response to the central body's discussion on their future. This time, the situation differed from their 1919 conference, when they could not unite on whether Japanese language schools should only teach Japanese language or should also try to teach Japanese values and spirit. In this crisis atmosphere, members quickly moved to take their own countermeasures to fight the land law initiative.[73] The teachers redefined the mission of Japanese language schools to "be supplementary to effect the education of good citizenship of the American-born Japanese based upon the spirit of the public school instruction in the United States of America."[74] Following the decision of Hawaii educators five years earlier, California teachers decided to drop *shōgakkō* (elementary school) from the names of language schools and replace it with *gakuen* (institute) to remove the association with elementary schools. Issei educators also changed the association's name to Nihongo Gakuen Kyōkai (Association of Japanese Language Institutions).[75] They agreed to teach only language so that children could communicate with their parents. Following Hawaii's Act 30 provision, teachers also resolved to limit the operating hours to one hour after public school. The ongoing project of compiling a new textbook set to replace the Monbushō textbooks was also hastened with more specific plans.[76] The textbooks were aimed to focus on language education, and to teach language not only from literature but also from various sources to adjust children's social and psychological development. The content was selected from American and Japanese textbooks, as well as other foreign language textbooks used in the United States or Japan, anecdotes, geography, history, and children's stories. Learning from Hawaii's situation, California's Japanese teachers did everything they could think of to preempt intervention. These new policies were translated into English and submitted to California State Superintendent of Public Instruction Will C. Wood.[77] Upon receipt of this declaration from the Japanese Teachers Association, Wood publicly announced his position on the Japanese school issue in a report to the governor. He suggested California law should require all private school teachers to pledge their loyalty to the United States, adding California should not tolerate language schools whose loyalty belonged to a foreign country.[78]

In the fall of 1920, the *Ōfu Nippō* and *Nichibei* both reported that Hawaii Superintendent of Public Instruction Vaughan MacCaughey had arrived in San Francisco to attend the California Education Conference at the University of California on October 18. According to the papers, Mac-Caughey announced that he would report on the Japanese language school situation in Hawaii at the conference and stress the need for further action. The *Nichibei* predicted that exclusionists would use MacCaughey's presentation to stir up the Japanese school situation in California.[79]

Japanese language school teachers in the Golden State understandably became apprehensive in this atmosphere, and they responded immediately. Administrators of Florin's language school decided to temporarily close its school. This was also because 70 percent of Nikkei students failed their English final exams, and would not advance to the next grade. At a Japanese Parent-Teacher Association (PTA) meeting held at the Japanese Hall, twenty-five attendees blamed this failure on the Japanese language school and decided to close their ten-year-old school.[80] In nearby Sacramento, at a PTA meeting of the Sakura Gakuen, originally called Ōfu Nihon Shōgakkō (Ōfu Japanese Elementary School), 300 parents decided to follow public school practice and closed school on Saturdays and during summer vacation, eliminating classes in sewing, Japanese geography, and history. The Japanese Association and the Christian church also decided to provide a nursery school for preschoolers to learn English from white caretakers.[81]

The Land Law Initiative

For anti-Japanese activists, the land law ballot initiative was an important first step toward their goal of total Japanese exclusion. However, the California Japanese Exclusion League encountered difficulties in collecting enough signatures in the face of the majority's mood to maintain the status quo and belief that this was a federal issue. Although the league established local offices across the state and planned to secure 55,000 signatures by July 15, 1920, it had only gathered around 30,000 by that time. Considering this situation, San Francisco Consul General Tamekichi Ōta, the Japanese association, and many white politicians predicted that the initiative would not appear on the ballot. Ōta reported this to the Japanese Foreign Ministry. However, according to a *Nichibei* editorial, two separate incidents, one in Washington, D.C., and the other in California, energized the exclusionist movement and propelled it to victory. In Washington, D.C., Ambassador Kijūrō Shidehara was discussing California's "Japanese problem" with the Department of State and gave an unofficial "warning" that was leaked in a sensationalized United Press International story on July 25, 1920. Also around that time, anonymous pamphlets supporting Nikkei on the alien land law ballot were delivered all over the state. Exclusionists interpreted Shidehara's action as foreign meddling and the pamphlet campaign as alien subversion and used both to whip up their stagnant campaign. In San Francisco, the well-publicized July 12 commencement of the Japanese Immigration Hearings by the House Immigration Committee also greatly advanced the exclusion cause. By August 5, exclusionists had 85,000 signatures, enough to place the initiative on the November ballot.[82] A September 3 editorial in Sacramento's Ōfu Nippō predicted that the upcoming initiative would pass and encouraged fellow immigrants to purchase land while they still could.[83] The new alien land law gathered more than enough votes on November 2, 1920, and though the exclusionists had hoped to triumph by a margin of ten-to-one, they had to settle for a close victory instead.

Roger Daniels concludes that this 1920 Alien Land Law "was doomed to failure."[84] It prohibited Issei land leases, and blocked land acquisition by corporations if Nikkei owned the majority of shares. The law also barred Issei from owning land as guardians for their children. The 1920 Land Law caused problems and encouraged many to return to Japan.[85] However, its actual impact according to Daniels was "an attempt to lock the door after the horse had been stolen." Many Nisei by that time had already acquired land, while at the same time Nikkei were becoming more aggressive in defending their legal rights. Most importantly, the guardianship ban was later found to infringe on Nisei rights as American citizens protected under the Fourteenth Amendment.[86] The survival of this right gnawed at exclusionists, giving them a further motivation to escalate their attack on Nisei citizenship and education.

In November 1920, the Nichibei published a six-day series of articles analyzing the reasons behind the passage of California's anti-Japanese initiative law.[87] The newspaper blamed some Nikkei for overreacting to the initiative. In hindsight, the Nichibei suggested that rather than having launched a massive public relations campaign against the initiative, they should have simply explained to the public the provisions of the alien land law; shown that it was unfair; and explained how it would do nothing to cease further Japanese immigration. The newspaper also suggested correcting the exclusionists' fabrications about Nikkei. The editorial asserted, "We are Japanese, and from the American viewpoint, we are foreigners without suffrage or the rights to impose our voices in California's politics." However, continued the article, since "we foreigners" conducted a political movement, "it is understandable that we are identified as rebellious foreigners." The article insisted that their action was an inexcusable interference in California politics, and "it is understandable that we are called most unfavorable foreigners." The article especially condemned "some schemers" who took desperate actions, placing the Nikkei future in question. The newspaper pointed out that the anti-Japanese movement remained intense even after November 2, unlike the usual pattern with anti-Japanese moods normally dissipating shortly after elections. The newspaper interpreted this situation as the result of their "interference."[88] The *Nichibei*, projecting the assimilationist, settler, and Christian perspectives of its owner, Kyūtarō Abiko, suggested that the community should not protest further inevitable exclusion bills, but rather should endeavor to cultivate better relations with whites and patiently nurture a pro-Japanese environment.[89]

Japanese Language School Control Measures

By late November 1920, San Francisco's *Nichibei* claimed "by now everyone knows that a foreign language school control bill will be proposed this session" as one of the many anti-Japanese measures proposed in the 1921 California state legislature.[90] Immediately after the alien land law passed, Californians began paying increased attention to news of Japanese language school bills in Hawaii. After the strong resistance of Nikkei there against a series of school control bills, eighteen representatives of Hawaii's Nikkei community wrote a compromise bill. This immediately cleared the Territorial legislature and became Act 30 on November 24, 1920.[91] The *Nichibei* praised Hawaii's Nikkei leaders' decision to compromise rather than confront exclusionists, confirming their "misunderstanding" that these schools raised Nisei as subjects of Japan. The paper encouraged California Nikkei to follow Hawaii's lead. It also suggested that California's Japanese teachers should submit a similar proposal placing their schools under state supervision.[92]

The Japanese Teachers Association of America shared the view of the *Nichibei*. The association sent Vice Chair Keizō Sano (principal of San Francisco's Nihon Gakuin) to Sacramento to explain the Japanese school situation to the Department of Education. Sano explained that there were 1,900 students (1,426 school-aged children and 489 kindergartners in 1920) attending forty Japanese language schools in California, the primary purpose of which, he argued, was the Americanization of Nisei children and that they did nothing against fostering American spirit.[93] He said that Japanese language school administrators proposed that local public school superintendents should oversee the Japanese language schools.[94]

Nonetheless, as predicted, several private school control bills were proposed in the 1921 state legislature. After two such bills, proposed by Assemblyman Will R. Sharkey (Republican, Contra Costa and Marin) and Senator Charles W. Lyon (Republican, Los Angeles), were killed,[95] Assemblyman Ivan H. Parker (Republican, Nevada and Placer counties) introduced his bill on January 21. The bill, essentially a copy of Hawaii's language school control law, was designed to give the state control over teachers, schools, and curricula. The *Ōfu Nippō* criticized Parker's charge that Japanese language schools, especially ones administered by Buddhist temples, instilled Nisei with loyalty to Japan.[96] However, it endorsed Parker's bill, because the paper claimed that, like Hawaii's initial school control law, its purpose was not to abolish Japanese language schools but rather to sanction them with regulations.[97] After the bill had passed both houses and was waiting for Governor Stephens' signature, Superintendent of Public Instruction Wood informed the general secretary of the Japanese Association of America, Tamezō Takimoto, that he was concerned that Jews might protest against the bill since it supposedly would also affect Jewish schools, making it difficult to obtain the governor's approval.[98] Wood himself later publicly criticized Nikkei for the poor maintenance of their schools. He stated that this problem should be corrected by compelling the "Japs" to build and maintain schools for the education of their offspring, and that the Japanese government should be held fiscally responsible, since, he argued, it was "sending its subjects here to breed children with whom to evade California Alien Land Law."[99]

The Parker bill passed the legislature on June 3 and went into effect on August 2, 1921.[100] It required: (1) teachers and administrators at foreign language schools must obtain a license from the Superintendent of Public Instruction; (2) teachers and administrators must be able to demonstrate knowledge of American history and English language skills, and to pledge to make pupils good and loyal American citizens; and (3) classes could neither take place in the morning before public school hours, nor operate for more than one hour per day, six hours per week and thirty-eight weeks in any school year. In addition, the law granted the Superintendent of Public Instruction full control over the course of study, textbooks, and the right to issue and revoke teaching permits. The bill defined a foreign language school as "any school which is conducted in any language other than the English language except Sabbath schools." Because Parker's definition was loose, Wood's rationale for the governor's apprehension may have been understandable even though this bill clearly targeted Japanese language schools.[101]

Parker, a newspaperman, started his political career by serving as Placer County's Recorder for a dozen years and was later elected as an assemblyman by Nevada and Placer counties in 1917, 1919, and 1921. He rose to become chairman of the important Agriculture Committee.[102] Parker's bill was criticized by Colonel John P. Irish, a large landowner and the leading member of the American Committee of Justice, which had waged a campaign against the 1920 Alien Land Law initiative. Irish wrote Superintendent of Public Instruction Wood that the bill was an "expression of hatred and persecution, and is in violation of the treaty with Japan." Responding to Irish's criticism, Parker lambasted Hawaii's Japanese school situation in the March 22, 1921, *Sacramento Bee*. There, according to Parker, arrogant Japanese threatened a sugar plantation strike if the school control bill passed. Parker predicted that California would follow Hawaii's Japanese language situation and argued for "the urgent need of the measure regulating language schools." He wrote that he visited a Japanese language school in Placer County that displayed a large map of Japan, but nothing American. It was taught by a Buddhist priest who supposedly stated that "knowledge of Japan and Japanese ideals were the major things taught" to Nisei children.[103] Testifying at the 1920 Japanese Immigration Hearings in California, Parker had stressed the rapid increase of Nikkei population in his county and claimed that in less than a decade, Japanese children had become more than 10 percent of the school population. He criticized how Nisei receive benefits "enjoyed by every citizen" despite their dual citizenship. Parker also emphasized how quickly Japanese immigrants had gained an economic foothold in the state. He testified that there were only a few Japanese ten years ago, and they were happy to work for $1.50 per day, but that they had since learned horticulture and refused to work as petty laborers. Parker further claimed that Japanese farmers controlled over 17,146 acres out of the 20,000 acres possible of producing orchards in Placer County and had created twenty-four "dummy or alien land-law evading, land-holding corporations."[104] Parker's testimony clearly summarizes the Japanese exclusionists' connection between the land issue and a Japanese language school control measure.

In addition to Parker's Japanese language school control bill, Assemblyman Reverend Franklin D. Mather (Republican, Pasadena), a Methodist Episcopal minister, proposed a public school segregation bill, as did Assemblyman Carlton Green of San Luis Obispo.[105] Mather's bill originally had targeted Chinese and "Mongolian children"; however, at the bill's third reading in the House, a legislator suddenly proposed including Japanese American students in the bill.[106] San Francisco Consul General Shichitarō Yada telegraphed Foreign Minister Yasuya Uchida that "it is not hard to imagine that Inman and his group are behind the bill."[107]

Upon the enactment of the private school control law, Sam H. Cohn, California's assistant superintendent of public instruction, was placed in charge of monitoring the Japanese language schools.[108] Cohn told a newspaper reporter that state legislators believed that Japanese language schools threatened the very foundations of the United States government because they taught American-born children imperialism and loyalty to Japan. He argued that operation of these schools was equivalent to another country forming inside the nation.[109]

To comply with the law, local Japanese associations organized Teacher's Training Institutes.[110] In 1921, two-week workshops for Japanese teachers were offered in San Francisco, Fresno, and Los Angeles in order to prepare them for the Department of Education's certification examinations. Each workshop covered American history and civics. Guest lecturers included Colonel Irish, Reverend Dr. Waterhouse, Assistant Superintendent of Public Instruction Cohn, Superintendent of the Japanese Methodist Episcopal Mission Herbert Johnson, and Harvey Guy (professor at the Pacific School of Religion and an advisor to the San Francisco Japanese Consulate). In San Francisco, of the 131 teachers who participated, 108 passed (including 94 who passed conditionally), and 23 failed. Among the 25 examinees in Fresno, 17 passed and 8 failed.[111] The results were a disappointment to the Nikkei community, since it suggested that many Japanese teachers had minimal knowledge of American history or civics. However, the results of the 1922 examination were greatly improved.[112]

California's textbook compilation had not yet been completed when the school control measure was enacted. Japanese language teachers submitted the Monbushō textbooks and translations to the state's Board of Education. It allowed use of the textbooks until the new series could be ready, but only after exercising wholesale censorship.[113] Subjects excised included stories promoting nationalism and imperialism, such as those about Emperor Jinmu, the Yasukuni Shrine, historical samurai figures (such as Shōgun Hideyoshi Toyotomi), and military stories and figures, such as the Japanese navy and Lieutenant Tachibana.[114] These steps to comply with the 1921 private school control law cost the Nikkei community nearly $10,000. However, this effort became meaningless, as an amendment to the school control law was submitted to the 1923 legislature. A frustrated Takimoto wrote California Senators that Japanese "have done our part to the full." "Yet, in spite of this," he continued, "it seems that renewed effort is now being made to further restrict and ultimately to eliminate the Japanese language schools entirely."[115]

The Inman Bill

McClatchy resumed agitating specifically on the Japanese language school issue again in late 1922, referring to Hawaii's controversy. Although California already had adopted the private school control law, McClatchy again brought up the exclusionists' pet theory of the schools' teaching Mikadoism, in the *Sacramento Bee* on November 17:

> These Japanese language schools in Hawaii, as in California, while ostensibly maintained to keep Japanese children . . . in closer touch with their non-English speaking fathers and mothers, are really used to drill the Japanese youth . . . the views and the loyalty to subjects of the Mikado. The safety of the nation demands that we either cease to confer American citizenship on Japanese born under the Stars and Stripes, or suppress schools, which make Japanese citizens of them.[116]

McClatchy claimed it was important to revisit the Japanese language school issue based on the report of the Federal Survey of Education of Hawaii, which recommended Japanese language schools be "abolished as 'un-American if not anti-American.'" Following the publication of the report, McClatchy wrote, Japanese in Hawaii conceded and voluntarily proposed a bill requiring Japanese teachers to pass the necessary examinations. However, McClatchy indicted the school measure, stating that "a mere knowledge of English and American history will not necessarily force a Japanese Buddhist to make good American citizens of his young pupils." He then presented Hawaii's newest school control measures, including regulations to bar Nisei between kindergarten and the third grade from attending Japanese schools, thus eliminating the two lower grades and the kindergartens.[117] McClatchy predicted that the question of Japanese language schools would likely receive attention in the 1923 California State Legislature, since the foreign language school bill passed in June 1921 is "defective, . . . if the oath [on their efforts to Americanize students] was not effective in Hawaii it cannot be relied upon in California."[118]

Around the time when McClatchy commenced a campaign to amend the school control law, University of Hawaii Political Science Professor Karl C. Leebrick started corresponding with California's Assistant Superintendent of Public Instruction Cohn. On December 12, 1922, Cohn wrote Leebrick, who also served on the Joint Committee that revised the regulations curtailing the course of study at Japanese language schools, to request information regarding the new school regulations signed by Hawaii's Governor Farrington the month before. Cohn sent Leebrick a copy of a new Japanese school control bill before it was to be proposed in the January 1923 legislature. He also asked Leebrick to contact Hawaii Superintendent MacCaughey to obtain his suggestions, so that "I may have the benefit of your combined wisdom."[119] McClatchy and former Californian Leebrick also started exchanging information. Replying to McClatchy's letter of February 3, 1923, Leebrick sent a "statement of the recent language school agitation," prepared for the governor and Walter F. Dillingham of the Washington [D.C.] Labor Commission. Leebrick wrote that "it was prepared for this semi-confidential purpose, but I . . . see no reason why, if it will be of assistance to the people of California, it should not be published."[120]

As a part of McClatchy's efforts, on January 12, 1923, Inman introduced a Japanese school control bill, California Senate Bill No. 7.[121] The bill would require that beginning in September 1923, pupils would have to complete the first grade of public school before attending any foreign language school. In 1924, the bar would have been raised to the second grade, in 1925, the third grade. Inman's law would make these schools completely illegal by 1930.[122] California's second school control measure was again modeled after Hawaii's school regulations.

Facing Inman's school control bill, the *Ōfu Nippō* explained Hawaii's new school regulations, prohibiting pupils to enter Japanese language schools until their third grade of public school and condemning Hawaii Nikkei for taking the laws to court. On January 11, 1923, the newspaper questioned the benefit of having six- or seven-year-old children attend both Japanese and public schools. The editorial concluded that Japanese teachers and administrators were protesting this law, simply to protect their jobs, rather than doing what was best for the children. The editor regretted that this also applied to California, and that those trying to maintain Japanese language schools seemed to worry more about themselves than their children's future.[123] The more powerful *Nichibei*, however, encouraged readers not to be afraid of the new school bill and wrote that according to an investigation by San Francisco's Ōkawara Law Office, this measure would violate Section 1 of Article 9 of the California code of citizens' rights and freedoms. It would also infringe upon the Fourteenth Amendment of the United States Constitution, and thus was a "dead letter" law.[124] The next day, the *Nichibei* explained that the Ōkawara Law Office concluded the bill was like a "mad dog with no teeth, which barks but cannot bite," because the bill had "no sort of physical punishment, merely a fine of not less than $25, as the only penalty for a violation." Based on Ōkawara's analysis, the *Nichibei* suggested two options to resist the school law: to sue Superintendent Wood and apply for an injunction to halt the measure, or to simply ignore it and refuse the government's investigation on grounds of the rights protecting individual freedom, and once charged, take it to the court. The *Nichibei* encouraged schools to "continue teaching as usual without worry."[125] Three days later, the *Nichibei* reported the news of the Palama Japanese Language School's lawsuit in Hawaii.[126]

The *Grizzly Bear*'s editor was furious about the Nikkei reaction to the Inman Bill and spurred the legislature to take the "hunch" and put plenty of sound "teeth" in the proposed amendment to the present foreign language school law, emphasizing "the Jap Schools should be exterminated at once." Citing the *Nichibei* article, the indignant editor wrote, "This is veiled advice to the Japs to violate this law, and is similar to that which is continuously given by Jap papers and officials respecting all laws not to their liking."[127] On February 10, 1923, the Board of Grand Officers of the Native Sons of the Golden West unanimously endorsed Inman's language school bill.[128]

In this context, the ongoing project to produce a new Japanese textbook series officially conducted by California's Japanese Association since 1920, was greatly hastened. The textbook publication committee was supposed to have completed revising the entire sixteen volumes by the end of 1922, but in January 1923 it announced that they were only on the twelfth volume, and that it would take five to six months more to finish.[129] Meanwhile two representatives of a Japanese Christian group, Mr. Muraoka and Reverend Shibata, visited Cohn to try to mediate the conflict.[130] Cohn told them that he wished to eliminate not only Japanese language but also all ideas related to Japan and to educate children solely as American citizens. He told them, "By all means I'd like to abolish Japanese schools, and make public schools alone responsible for their education."[131] Continuing their lobbying efforts, Muraoka and Shibata visited McClatchy at the *Sacramento Bee* to discuss the Japanese language school problem on February 6.[132] Restating his view in favor of abolishing the Japanese language schools, McClatchy argued that the idea was not only his or that of Japanese exclusionists, but that it was shared by Japanese leaders themselves and by white advocates of Japanese Americans. McClatchy told the Issei representatives that he had exchanged opinions on this issue with Kyūtarō Abiko, Stanford University Professor Yamato Ichihashi, Reverend Kengo Tajima of the Japanese Church of Christ, and also Professor Guy, and they all agreed: (1) to absolutely oppose the existence of Japanese language schools, and (2) to disallow those who did not speak English from teaching Japanese to children who were still learning English.[133] Not coincidentally, all of these Issei leaders and friends were in the Christian minority.

Within one month of the proposal of the Inman Bill and its initial editorial encouraging resistance to the bill, the *Nichibei* did a complete about-face. The newspaper sternly stated that there were various opinions regarding the proposed Japanese language school law, but the editor believed that it would not violate either the Constitution or the treaty. The article explained this was because "the law is related to education of American citizens who were born in America, and thus is purely a matter of educational problem of America." Another reason, the article continued, was that the purpose of the law was to raise good American citizens, and this measure removed obstacles preventing it, and lastly, that it would be established through legal means. For these reasons, "there would be no chance to win the case." The editorial strongly encouraged Nikkei to focus on solving the misunderstandings between them and Americans, instead of insisting on their rights through the courts.[134]

Inman was quoted in the March 8, 1923, *Ōfu Nippō*, as publicly announcing that he was soliciting Japanese opinion on the bill, before his bill would be discussed in the House Education Committee two weeks later, but he dampened free expression by warning that "illegitimate objections could bring about the doubt of Japanese loyalty to America." Inman challenged Nikkei that "it is absolutely fine with me for them to explain their situation and hopes, but if anything goes beyond that level, I am afraid that it would put them in a very delicate position." Inman compared Californian Nikkei with Hawaii's counterparts, stating that "in Hawaii, Japanese considered progressive, advocate the abolition of Japanese language schools, and I strongly believe that Californian Japanese who are even more progressive would not be bothered by the passage of the bill."[135]

Consul General Yada reported to Foreign Minister Uchida that the proposed bill would practically mean the abolition of Japanese language schools. Yada personally believed that Japanese language schools would naturally die out over time, and that there was no need to support those schools. However, considering the present circumstances of Japanese in America, Yada admitted that no one could deny the need for these institutions to teach their children the Japanese language. Yada labeled the bill unreasonable because: (1) opponents to Japanese language schools proposed the bill based on their deliberate misrepresentation that Japanese language schools instill Japanese principles; and (2) opponents had already passed a harsh school control measure in the previous legislature, for which Japanese teachers and administrators were creating new textbooks, retraining teachers according to the superintendent's instructions, and sincerely trying to abide by the law. Yet, before evaluating its effects, legislators were passing another law to terminate the schools. Yada explained that "this bill is not based on serious thought, but was simply 'agitation.'" He suggested that the best strategy to block the bill would be to work on the California Governor through federal intervention.[136] Two days later, Foreign Minister Uchida (who had been the Japanese ambassador to the United States from 1909 to 1911)[137] replied to Yada that he did not oppose the policy of Americanization and that, considering Japanese living conditions in America, they would have to bear with some restrictions, such as cutting off kindergartens and the first two elementary years. Any effort beyond that level, however, such as completely abolishing the schools, should be resisted. Uchida wrote that this would not be tolerated either by California Nikkei or the public in Japan. Uchida agreed with Yada's suggestion to appeal to the American Secretary of State and gave Yada permission to proceed.[138] Responding to Yada's inquiry, specifically as to what extent he should ask the bill to be modified, Uchida commented on the passage of Hawaii's school control law. He wrote that it took into account that a too-severe law would produce Japanese objections, and also harm diplomatic relations between Japan and the United States.

Therefore, continued Uchida, the measure was discussed between Japanese and Hawaii authorities before being taken to the legislature. Although, Uchida continued, the present California foreign language school law did not take such a procedure ("secretly the Japanese side gave an approval, however"), the content of the bill itself was almost identical to Hawaii's law. Uchida concluded that therefore, "when you negotiate the degree of a school control law, you should ask to maintain the present level and not exceed it." Uchida further instructed Yada to stress the difference between an acceptable level of restrictions in Hawaii and in California; cutting kindergarten and two elementary years might be acceptable in Hawaii, but this would financially mean the end for smaller schools in California.[139]

To prepare for the Education Committee's hearing, Reverend Johnson and Professor Guy, following Yada's instructions, lobbied committee members. They explained that the Inman Bill would cause tremendous difficulties for schools to sustain enough revenue to maintain school buildings and pay teachers' salaries, and that consequently it would bankrupt many schools. They also tried to convince members that they should wait until the outcome of the present school control law could be evaluated.[140] In addition, Yada's collaborators had a secret meeting based on Johnson's conversation with committee members, and decided on a strategy to: (1) work with the "dry elements (prohibitionists)," who made up more than half of the House Education Committee and had strong connections with religious groups; (2) send committee members a statement with Japanese and other perspectives (such as Chinese) to appeal to Americans' sense of justice (to be signed individually by lobbyists); and (3) select, as lobbyists, those who had never lent their signatures to "Japanese problems," including representatives of religious groups with connections to foreign language schools, and the Catholic Church.[141] Professor Guy visited McClatchy, ostensibly to comfort him after his car accident; however, in actuality he went there to discuss the bill, since Takimoto of the Japanese Association of America had confirmed that McClatchy was behind the bill.[142] Guy also played the role of contact person between Paul Scharrenberg, representative of the California State Federation of Labor, and Consul General Yada. Scharrenberg confessed to Guy that the "real intent" of the Japanese school control bill was to attract the attention of the federal government, and that because of this, the bill was deliberately unfair. According to Guy, Scharrenberg hoped both Japan and the United States would "take advantage of this opportunity" to negotiate a new treaty;

otherwise, they threatened to continuously propose new Japanese exclusion laws and wage other crusades to force federal intervention. The State Federation of Labor, explained Scharrenberg, would be satisfied and cease all exclusion efforts once a new treaty was established. Scharrenberg added that he was planning to go to Washington to discuss the matter with American Federation of Labor President Samuel Gompers, as well as the Secretary of State. He asked Yada to learn Ambassador Masanao Hanihara's opinion on the matter and to secure an appointment for him.[143]

On March 29, 1923, the Senate Education Committee discussed the Inman Bill. Unlike other bills directly affecting Nikkei life, only a small crowd attended, including Johnson and Guy. Following Inman's explanation of his bill, Assistant Superintendent of Public Instruction Cohn testified, on the basis of his "study," that teaching Japanese to children who had not mastered English produced unfavorable results, and that it would not be too late if they began studying Japanese in high school or later. Reverend Johnson advocated Japanese language schools, arguing they were not harmful to society, but rather helpful. Senator Dennett of Stanislaus County insisted that prohibiting foreign language schools would be unfair to Japanese. In the end, though, the bill passed unanimously with the exception of one absentee member.[144] According to Yada's report, during the hearing Cohn suddenly revealed the nature of his discussions with Japanese Association General Secretary Takimoto, and used his statements to attack Japanese language schools, which led the committee to pass the bill.[145] Inman's bill was later discussed in the Senate Finance Committee since one of the bill's provisions required an appropriation of $10,000 to supervise these schools, and was then sent to the Senate where the bill was passed on May 9, and to the House which passed it on May 19, 1923.[146] However, before California Governor Richardson signed the bill, Robert T. Meyer won his lawsuit against the State of Nebraska in the United States Supreme Court on June 4, 1923, protesting his arrest for teaching in German to a ten-year-old boy. Governor Richardson announced that he wished to sign the bill, but that according to Attorney General Webb, this bill would have wider effects; it would supposedly impact foreign language programs at Mills College and Santa Clara and Stanford universities. As such, he regretted that he could not sign the bill.[147] Another explanation behind Governor Richardson's veto was a petition of church groups sent by Edward L. Parsons, bishop coadjutor of California, warning that anticipating consequences of such a measure would entail a closure of "American language" schools abroad, and hamper Christian mission work among Asian Americans. The petition also requested the governor to review fairly the new Japanese Association's "Americanization" textbooks.[148]

Conclusion

As the final step to comply with the 1921 school control law, the Japanese teachers finally finished compiling their textbook series, *Beikoku Kashū Kyōiku Kyoku Kentei, Nihongo Tokuhon* [the Japanese Reader, approved by the California State Board of Education] in August 1923 and submitted it to the Board of Education for approval.[149] Before the board issued its official imprimatur, it sent the textbooks to the American Legion for approval.[150] This illustrates how heavily Japanese exclusionists pressured the California Department of Education, and as this chapter has shown, how California's Japanese school controversy, ostensibly following the pattern of Hawaii's model, actually followed the agenda of the Golden State's exclusionists. Exclusionists persistently advanced their ultimate objective of completely halting Japanese immigration by pressuring Nikkei, using the threat to abolish Japanese language schools in order to force Japanese government involvement to rescind the Gentlemen's Agreement that permitted some immigration. To achieve this, exclusionists developed a well-calculated plan, using their Hawaii contacts and powerful allies to orchestrate events to their liking.

In 1935, Stanford Professor Reginald Bell wrote that California's 1921 school control bill passed without strong opposition from the Japanese, unlike the resistance of Hawaii's Japanese.[151] While there is some truth to this, and indeed California's Nikkei could celebrate the court battle led by Hawaii's Japanese community, this study shows the situations were quite different. California's Nikkei community was much smaller and had its hands full with the aftermath of the passage of the new land law. They were also busy seeking possibilities to litigate against the state and to mobilize the federal government to defend their rights on the basis that the law violated the U.S.-Japan Treaty.[152] California's Nikkei were overwhelmed and exhausted from the battle and defeat on the alien land law; some felt that expanding the struggle would be in vain. They had also lost their final hope that Ambassador Kijūrō Shidehara would negotiate a new treaty with Secretary of State Colby to resolve California's "Japanese problem."[153] Psychological exhaustion, combined with Hawaii's precedent, would understandably have been more than enough to make them acquiesce and avoid conflict over the Japanese language school bill. Although California's Issei gave up fighting the language school law, they never conceded to abolishing the schools; rather, they made a deliberate choice to adapt and to forsake autonomy in exchange for survival. On this issue, Japanese schoolteachers even came forward and submitted themselves to state surveillance.

We have seen that different social factors triggered the Japanese language school controversies in Hawaii and California, but there were some commonalities in their experience of Japanese language schools that reflected early Japanese immigrants' processes of struggle with Americanization. The religious conflict between Buddhists and Christians deepened the Japanese language school debate in Hawaii. In California, Christian missionaries were antagonized by Buddhists' continued influence in the Nikkei community and Japanese language schools, and they took advantage of public hearings to assault Buddhist Japanese schools.

While the earlier Japanese consuls general in Hawaii and California avoided involvement, San Francisco Consul General Shichitarō Yada took an active role intervening in the 1923 school control bill. Behind his actions were negotiations between the Foreign Ministry and the Monbushō to determine an education policy for overseas Nisei. In 1922 when the Japanese school problem in Hawaii could no longer be ignored by the Japanese government, Vice Foreign Minister Masanao Hanihara wrote Vice Education Minister Takaichirō Akaji that the education policy on Japanese emigrants' offspring had been conducted on the basis of an official letter from Vice Education Minister Seitarō Sawayanagi back in 1906. However, Hanihara wrote, as the international political climate changed, each region had a different situation, and in some places, such as Hawaii or California, it was almost impossible to follow this education policy. If, continued Hanihara, they tried to maintain the Imperial Education Policy, it would provide Japanese exclusionists with ideal ammunition. This policy, he explained, was creating a situation whereby, if maintained, "where it is impossible to maintain, continuing to persevere might bring about a serious diplomatic incident." Hanihara finally suggested that:

> Fortunately, Japanese residents in each place are seriously studying an educational policy appropriate to their own situation. Under these circumstances, the government should not try to apply a uniform policy for every location, but under the leadership of the local consul general and according to their situation, local Japanese should be able to establish their own policy, which could deviate from the official one.[154]

Akaji approved Hanihara's proposal on August 24, 1922.[155]

As seen in chapter 1, the Japanese government deliberately tried to minimize its public involvement in the education of the offspring of Japanese emigrants during this period of American history. Once a situation arose with a plea from the local consular official, they reluctantly selected a policy that Tokyo felt resolved the problem with the least possible effort. This revised 1922 directive allowed Yada to approach the State Department to conduct bilateral negotiations as directed by Foreign Minister Uchida. However, Tokyo's new policy on educating Nisei again reflected the Foreign Ministry's continued emphasis on international prestige and harmony over the interests of its overseas nationals. With such intentions, it seems doubtful that the Japanese government seriously championed Yada's appeal for the federal pressure on California's state leaders. As the 1920 Japanese Immigration Hearings in California moved to Washington State, the nature of the Japanese language school controversy changed in Seattle and other Nikkei communities.

CHAPTER 4
A Transplanted Attack
Japanese Language Schools in Washington State

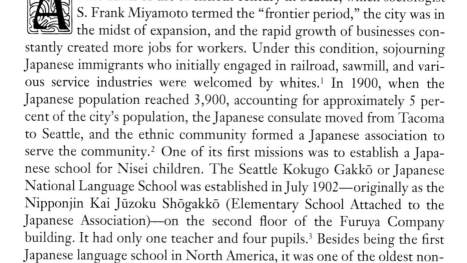

CONGRESSMAN BOX: Do you attend the Japanese-language school?
MR. SAKAMOTO: Yes, sir.
CONGRESSMAN BOX: What do they teach you there?
MR. SAKAMOTO: Japanese.
—Hearings on Japanese immigration, Seattle, July 26, 1920

t the dawn of the twentieth century in Seattle, which sociologist S. Frank Miyamoto termed the "frontier period," the city was in the midst of expansion, and the rapid growth of businesses constantly created more jobs for workers. Under this condition, sojourning Japanese immigrants who initially engaged in railroad, sawmill, and various service industries were welcomed by whites.[1] In 1900, when the Japanese population reached 3,900, accounting for approximately 5 percent of the city's population, the Japanese consulate moved from Tacoma to Seattle, and the ethnic community formed a Japanese association to serve the community.[2] One of its first missions was to establish a Japanese school for Nisei children. The Seattle Kokugo Gakkō or Japanese National Language School was established in July 1902—originally as the Nipponjin Kai Jūzoku Shōgakkō (Elementary School Attached to the Japanese Association)—on the second floor of the Furuya Company building. It had only one teacher and four pupils.[3] Besides being the first Japanese language school in North America, it was one of the oldest non-religious Asian language schools in the United States.[4]

The 1907–1908 Gentlemen's Agreement, terminating Japanese laborer immigration, helped transform Nikkei society into a settler period. This spurred interest in building up the community.[5] In 1907, the Kokugo Gakkō was separated from the Japanese Association, and an *ijikai*, or support group, consisting primarily of parents, took over the school's operations. They decided to run the school on donations rather

Fig. 7. The Seattle Kokugo Gakkō picnic at Alki Point, Washington (1912). (Courtesy of the University of Washington Libraries, Special Collections [UW 6314])

than charging tuition.[6] When in 1913 Seattle Issei built a new school building at Weller and 16th streets, they raised $10,282 from countrymen in Seattle and abroad, including from such Japanese dignitaries as Prince Fushimi, Foreign Minister Jutarō Komura, and heroes Admiral Heihachirō Tōgō and General Tamemoto Kuroki.[7] In 1917, the school built an extension to allow the admission of over 100 Nisei.[8] In 1920, Jimmie Sakamoto, who testified about his Japanese language school experience at the United States House of Representatives Committee on Immigration and Naturalization Hearings on Japanese Immigration, was one of the 251 Nisei attending the Kokugo Gakkō.[9] Another 238 Nisei students attended 11 other Japanese language schools in other parts of the state. These 489

Table 7: Japanese American Children Attending Japanese Language Schools in the State of Washington

	Students	Teachers
1916	178*	9
1917	208	11
1918	313	14
1919	397	16
1920	489*	20

Source: The 1920 Japanese Immigration Hearings of House of Representatives, U.S. Congress, House, Committee on Immigration and Naturalization, *Japanese Immigration*, 1177–1178.

* Numbers for these years were retabulated by the author to remove errors.

Table 8: Japanese American Pupils and Teachers at the Seattle Kokugo Gakkō, 1902–1930

	Students	Teachers
1902	4	1
1915	140	4
1920	251*	7
1925	485	11
1930	1,080	24

Source: Myron E. Powers, "Telic Attempts of Two Racial Groups to Retain Their Social Inheritance," master's thesis, University of Washington, 1932, 26.

* The 1920 data was taken from statistics from the 1920 Japanese Immigration Hearings of the House of Representatives because Powers did not cite 1920 data.

pupils represented approximately 30 percent of the 1,623 Japanese Americans attending public schools that year in Washington.[10]

In this chapter, the Japanese language school "problem" in Washington State will be examined and compared to California's. Ever since the Japanese exclusion movement began on the Pacific Coast in the early 1900s, Washington's legislature "invariably copied" California's anti-Japanese measures.[11] As was examined in chapter 2, California's foreign language school law was part of exclusionists' scheme to halt Japanese land ownership: the problem was highlighted during the 1920 Japanese Immigration Hearings. In Washington, exclusionists did not wait for the hearing's arrival in Seattle to create a Japanese language school controversy, but they began collaborating with Californian exclusionists one year earlier in congressional hearings held in Washington, D.C.

The 1919 Japanese Immigration Hearings in Washington, D.C.

Exclusionists in Seattle revived their post–World War I anti-Japanese movement during the 1919 hearings conducted by the House Immigration and Naturalization Committee chaired by Albert Johnson (Republican, Washington) in Washington, D.C.[12] The focus of the hearings was Reverend Sidney L. Gulick's proposal that the government give Asian immigrants, who were not allowed to become citizens, the same naturalization rights it gave white immigrants.[13] The hearings also included a debate about Hawaii's Japanese language schools. The committee invited anti-Japanese activists to participate, and they emphasized the growing political power of Nikkei in the territory and the nationalistic nature of Japanese language education.

Valentine S. McClatchy, the retired publisher of the *Sacramento Bee* and the anti-Japanese movement's leading propagandist, dramatized the power the Nikkei community had over white politicians in Hawaii by exaggerating the community's resistance to the territory's 1919 foreign language school bill. To instill paranoia, McClatchy claimed that children "imbibe Japanese principles and ideas" in the schools and accused the Japanese government of lurking behind Nisei education. He argued that the government needed to begin supervising the schools before it was too late and the Japanese were controlling the government.[14] Senator James D. Phelan, a Democrat from California, supported McClatchy's conspiracy theory by citing the Japanese family registration system—which required Issei parents to register their American-born children with the

Japanese consulate—as evidence of Nisei disloyalty.[15] The motivation behind his action, besides crass election campaigning, was that he hoped to close a loophole in California's 1913 alien land law. The law restricted leases of land to Asian immigrants to a maximum of three years and prohibited Asian immigrants from buying land. Issei bypassed the law by purchasing land in their children's names.[16] Gulick was invited to the hearings supposedly to defend the Nikkei position. However, on the subject of language schools, he testified that "it is not right for the Buddhist priests and the Shinto priests who know no English or nothing of our American history [to] give instruction to the Japanese children" and insisted that the schools should be under government supervision.[17] After Gulick's testimony, Albert Johnson declared that the federal government needed to take over the supervision of language schools in Hawaii before the American-born Japanese were "in control" and could prevent it from doing so.[18]

Two Washingtonians were also invited to the hearings: Miller Freeman, publisher of the *Pacific Fisherman*, and Reverend Ulysses Grant Murphy, the pastor of Seattle's Methodist Church, who had been a missionary in Japan for fourteen years. Freeman was not the most prominent Pacific Coast exclusionist, but the Seattle-based activist had been on the attack since 1905, when he began protesting the intrusion of Japanese fishing boats into Alaskan waters.[19] As secretary of the Washington Veterans' Welfare Committee, Freeman testified that returned servicemen were unable to find work, because while they had been fighting for America, Japanese had "found the door open to come in and colonize and engage in all kinds of business activities."[20] The Washington department of the American Legion reinforced this idea, arguing that Nikkei farmers occupied the best land on the Yakima Indian reservation and thereby prevented veterans from taking advantage of a state program to assist those wishing to enter agriculture. At its 1920 state convention, the Legion passed a resolution urging the Bureau of Indian Affairs not to allow Asians to lease reservation farmland.[21] The people of Seattle, Freeman contended, believed that maintaining good relations with Japan "would encourage trade and help to make a great world seaport," but, he argued, that country had violated the Gentlemen's Agreement by bringing "women in for breeding purposes and enabl[ing] the Japanese, then, through their children, to own property."[22] Freeman's solution to the problem was "to deny the right to citizenship to those who come here and possibly those who are born here."[23]

Murphy, the other Washingtonian, disagreed with Gulick about language schools and praised the schools' positive influence on Nisei children. According to him, the superintendents of both the Seattle and San Francisco public schools stated that Nisei who attended the Japanese schools "made better students" than Nisei who did not, because the schools taught etiquette as well as language. Murphy also argued that Issei parents, who he asserted were illiterate, naturally hoped their children could acquire sufficient Japanese to write letters home for them.[24] He also submitted a resolution on behalf of the Seattle Ministerial Federation in support of the Gulick bill "to permit the naturalization of all aliens on an equal footing."[25]

Exclusionists testified at the hearings about the increasing number of Japanese and their economic advancement. However, that testimony was based on inflated numbers. The 1920 census showed that in reality there were only 17,387 Japanese Americans in Washington, representing 1.3 percent of the state's population.[26] Most of the Nikkei population, 7,874 people, lived in Seattle, representing only 2.6 percent of the city's population.[27] Washington Nikkei owned 928 acres and rented, leased, or managed another 24,413 acres, which accounted for only 0.19 percent of the state's farmland.[28] The 1919 hearings demonstrate that the language school issue was deeply rooted in exclusionists' efforts to curtail Japanese land ownership and business success. The hearings also marked a significant transition for the exclusionists. They had expanded the focus of their attack from Issei to Nisei and identified the schools as the primary target in their campaign to contest Nisei American citizenship. These hearings helped shape the postwar exclusion movement and gave exclusionist leaders from California an opportunity to share a new agenda with Washington comrades. They created models that they hoped other states would emulate.

The Formation of the Anti-Japanese League

In Seattle, while the congressional hearings were still in progress, Washington's American Legion and the Mutual Business Club organized a "civic mass meeting" on August 11, 1919. The meeting was in response to Congressman Johnson's announcement that he and other members of the House Immigration and Naturalization Committee would visit Seattle before the summer recess to investigate Japanese immigration.[29] The announcement served as a rallying cry to revive the anti-Japanese movement in Washington State, which had been dormant during the war. The meeting was called to protest the recent Nikkei advancement in business, to end Japanese immigration, and to gather evidence on Washington's "Japanese problem" for Johnson's committee to take back to the Capitol. Only a few days before the meeting, the *Star* announced that Johnson's committee had cancelled its visit to Seattle because the House did not recess.[30] But Seattle's mass meeting went on as planned. Its organizers asked Washington's governor, Louis F. Hart, to investigate and report on Japanese businesses in the Northwest, but according to the *Star* he was unable to attend the meeting.[31] Following Freeman's advice, organizers also asked the state's attorney general, L. L. Thompson, to report on Japanese ownership of land and property and to investigate legal means of prosecuting violations of Washington's Alien Land Law, which predated statehood and prohibited alien land ownership. Thompson did attend the meeting, where he reported that the laws were full of loopholes and in need of "stringent congressional action or an amendment of the state constitution."[32]

One of the exclusionists' main arguments, voiced at an earlier meeting by Frank E. Kannear, the secretary of the Business Club, was that "the Japanese cannot be assimilated" and that they "will eventually gain control of the Coast and sweep eastward over the whole country." Murphy had countered this argument, stating that "America can assimilate a large number of Japanese" and that "American-born Japanese children respond to American ideas." He had also claimed that unrestricted immigration had ceased and that "the Gentlemen's Agreement is the best observed contract between the two nations."[33] Despite his efforts, the meeting ended with a resolution asking the House Immigration and Naturalization Committee to investigate the Japanese situation in the Northwest.

In an attempt to manufacture an anti-Japanese mood in Seattle, the *Seattle Star* conducted a ten-day publicity campaign for the meeting. Afterward, it reported that 250 people, including representatives of "practically every civic organization," had attended the meeting.[34] However, one of Seattle's other major newspapers, the *Seattle Daily Times*, did not even mention the gathering. Freeman had also done his best to stir up racial animosity. Ten days before the meeting, he gave a speech to a Seattle crowd titled, "This Is a White Man's Country." Trying to instill the fear that the Japanese would soon overrun the West Coast, Freeman falsely claimed that Japanese women bore five times more children than white women did.[35]

The Seattle meeting replayed what had been demonstrated in the

Washington, D.C., hearings in the setting of Washington State. This meeting was the prologue to an organized exclusion movement that built on a history of anti-Chinese and anti-Japanese incidents in the state dating back to the turn of the century.[36] Only ten days after the meeting, two of its organizers, Kannear and Jack Sullivan, the president of Washington's American Legion, founded the Seattle Anti-Japanese League.[37] The League claimed that the Japanese had become a sizable threat because of their supposed inability to assimilate, strong economic power, and growing population, an argument that was similar to the yellow peril myth used against the Nikkei community in California.[38] The League consisted of members of the Retail Grocers Association, the Seattle Laundrymen's Association, the Veterans of Foreign Wars, the Retail Clerks Union, and, according to the partisan *Star*, other "middle class elements" concerned about Japanese economic competition.[39]

Seattle Consul General Naokichi Matsunaga reported to Foreign Minister Yasuya Uchida about Freeman and other exclusionists' anti-Japanese activities. Matsunaga wrote that from July 1919, Freeman collaborated with the *Seattle Star* to conduct an anti-Japanese crusade for about two months. Seattle businessmen, especially leaders of Seattle's chamber of commerce who perceived Freeman's act as a local scandal, tried to remonstrate with Freeman, but he ignored them. Matsunaga also explained that the *Star*, "Seattle's only yellow paper," was seeking a chance to regain subscriptions among white laborers since the paper had criticized their 1919 general strike. Struggling to gain a footing, according to

Table 9: Japanese Businesses in Seattle, 1920

Business	Number	Percentage
Hotels / apartments	338	25.87
Barber shops	70	22.70
Dye works / cleaners	48	26.00
Grocery stores	80	12.64
General merchandise stores	75	N/A
Restaurants	38	13.20
Tailors	29	16.80
Secondhand stores	45	15.00
Laundries	12	12.60

Source: U.S. Congress, House, Committee on Immigration and Naturalization, *Japanese Immigration* (1920), 1179.

Matsunaga, Freeman held an anti-Japanese campaign meeting under the sponsorship of the "Mutual Business Club"—a front organization created by Freeman, which disappeared shortly thereafter. They finally formed the Anti-Japanese League after receiving support from the grocers' union. Matsunaga reported that although the League tried to mobilize the press to reach the public, Seattle's two big newspapers, the *Post-Intelligencer* and *Times*, were not interested, and labor unions had rather good relations with Japanese. According to Matsunaga, the majority just ignored the League's campaign, and its efforts failed miserably.[40]

Contrary to Matsunaga's report, the League's attempts were not entirely in vain. The meeting inspired Washington educators to start speaking out against the Japanese language schools. Shortly after the meeting, Pierce County's superintendent of public schools, Minnie Bean, wrote a letter to Thompson requesting assistance.[41] She claimed to be troubled by several Japanese schools housed in old school buildings in her county, especially one at Firwood, which Nisei attended after regular school hours and on Saturdays. Bean had scoured school laws for an act that would enable her to prohibit the schools, but had come up empty-handed.

Bean, born in 1881 in Michigan to Canadian immigrant parents, eventually moved to Tacoma with her family and started teaching there in 1904. She married a laborer, Nelson H. Bean, who died just a few years after their wedding. Bean had taught in several rural schools "from the remote one-room school to the principalship" of a school in the Tacoma area, including a Puyallup grade school for three years.[42] Since Puyallup at the time contained Firwood, which was home to many Japanese farming families, it is likely that she taught some Nisei pupils.[43]

On September 2, 1919, the *Star* published Bean's letter and then went on to claim, "First steps have been taken to oust Japanese schools that are being maintained in the valley land between Seattle and Tacoma." Two days later, Thompson replied to Bean, advising her to consult the county's legal counsel but adding, "unofficially," that he had not found any laws that could prohibit such schools.[44] Bean likely came up with her scheme to ask Thompson for a legal means of closing down the Japanese schools because of the publicity surrounding Seattle's mass meeting. Bean's letter was written just two days before she was to take office as superintendent, suggesting that she (or someone sharing her intentions) leaked the letter to the *Star* to declare that her first priority as superintendent was to close the Japanese schools.[45] Bean's efforts to "oust Japs' schools," as the *Star* headline read, were aimed at the Firwood and Fife schools, which together had only thirty-five students and two teachers.[46] In an attempt to demonize the schools, the article in the *Star* reported that they operated even when American schools were closed for summer vacation. The *Star* claimed that Nisei children were enrolled so that they could be "Japanize[d]" by "Oriental teachers." They were then sent to Japan to complete the "Japanization process." The article then unfurled the yellow peril story of how these children of picture brides were enrolling in ever-increasing numbers and warned that within ten or fifteen years they would take political control of Washington State. The next day, the *Hokubei Jiji*, Seattle's leading Japanese-language daily, printed a translation of the *Star*'s article along with news about the efforts of Freeman and his group to abolish the schools.[47]

Bean did not limit her campaign to Pierce County. As chair of the Americanization Committee at the 1919 state convention of superintendents, Bean led fellow committee members in strongly opposing foreign-language schools and demanding that they be placed under the supervision of the Washington State Board of Education. The committee also requested a survey to investigate "the number of aliens, alien sympathizers and disloyal inhabitants of the country."[48] Although Bean seemingly never found a legal justification for closing the schools, she pressed the

Fig. 8. Minnie D. Bean, the new president of the Washington Education Association. (*Washington Education Journal* 3 [November 1921])

Fife school board not to allow the local language school to renew its lease. The school board ignored her, but parents closed down the language school to avoid further trouble.[49] Bean's letter prompted other public school teachers and administrators to take actions against Japanese language schools in their districts.

The Tacoma Japanese Language School

Tacoma's Nikkei had different opinions on building a local ethnic school. While some families expressed a desire for a Japanese school in Tacoma,[50] others in the Japanese Association feared that a school would become too financially burdensome for the community.[51] The situation was resolved when the Japanese consul gave permission for the association to use a portion of the fees it received for certificate issuance,[52] and parents supplemented this with donations and tuition.[53] The school began in May 1911 with thirteen students and one preschool teacher, Kuni Yamasaki, who had taught at a girls' high school and elementary school in Fukushima Prefecture before she embarked for Seattle in 1910.[54] Her husband, Masato Yamasaki, was hired six months later as the principal. He taught language, history, and ethics there as well.[55] Also a Fukushima native, he graduated from the Tokyo Special School in literature in 1902 and taught at the Fukushima Teachers School before emigrating to Seattle in 1908.[56] The Yamasakis introduced many learning opportunities, such as speech competitions, storytelling contests, an orchestra, athletic meetings, and school excursions including swimming trips to the Pacific.[57] Mr. Yamasaki taught history and ethics based on the Japanese moral code and had children memorize Meiji-era poetry while Mrs. Yamasaki taught calligraphy and weaving in addition to Japanese language. In the school's second year, twenty-eight students crowded the small school, half of whom were born in Japan while the other half were Washington-born Nisei.[58]

In 1913, the Tacoma Japanese Association foresaw the possibility that its Japanese language school might be used as a political target by anti-Japanese activists, and they divorced the school from the association.[59] For the same reason, ever since the school's inception, it maintained the school as a secular institution, even turning down an offer from the Japanese Methodist Church for the free use of its building.[60] Seven years later these policies would prove extremely prescient.

In 1920, the principal of Tacoma's Central Elementary School, George A. Stanley, asked Yamasaki to close down his school.[61] Although most of the more than sixty students had above average grades, some of the Nisei first graders apparently were failing their reading class.[62] Yamasaki refused to close, but in May he and a group of Nisei high school students and bilingual adults organized a Saturday school to tutor pupils in subjects taught at public school and to teach English to preschoolers. The Saturday school helped the students improve their grades markedly and was very popular; most of the language school students also attended the Saturday school.[63]

Meanwhile, overcrowding at the language school had become a serious problem—the number of students had increased from twenty-six in 1914 to sixty-two in 1920.[64] The school's board of directors wanted to build a new school but encountered difficulties securing land for a new building because of Washington's alien land law. To circumvent this problem, lawyer Joseph H. Gordon, Baptist missionary Electa A. Snyder, and accountant Jonathan M. Walker, along with two Issei, formed a school corporation, the Tacoma Yōchien (Kindergarten). The corpora-

Fig. 9. Tacoma Japanese Language School, Washington (ca. 1920). Masato Yamasaki, principal, is in the back row, second from the right; next to him is his wife, Kuni. (Courtesy of the Washington State Historical Society, Tacoma [E2717])

tion bought lots at 1713 and 1715 Tacoma Avenue, where the school building still stands, for $1,600 and then spent another $9,000 on construction. In January 1922, the acting consul, Toshihito Satō, presided over the opening ceremony.[65]

At about the same time, Mr. Yamasaki started receiving complaints from public school teachers that they were having a hard time communicating with incoming Nikkei students because of the children's poor English. Over the previous five years, many Issei men had sent for either their wives or picture brides from Japan. Consequently, a large group of young Nikkei who had socialized more with Japanese speakers than with English speakers had entered the public schools in the 1920s. Yamasaki responded to the complaints by asking Snyder to teach English to preschoolers on Tuesdays and Thursdays. The program, started in 1925, was so successful that some of its graduates skipped the first half of first grade upon entering public school.[66]

Mr. Yamasaki probably took these preventive measures because of the assault on foreign-language schools that had occurred elsewhere on the Pacific Coast and in Hawaii and that had been covered frequently by Japanese-language newspapers. Seattle's *Hokubei Jiji* had reported in December 1918 that the teachers' association in Hawaii had passed a resolution asking the territorial legislature to close the Japanese language schools.[67] Two months later, the first act to regulate foreign-language schools in Hawaii had been proposed; it mandated that public and private schoolteachers pass a certification exam on American government and in English proficiency.[68] In February 1919, Oregon's legislature had prohibited German-language instruction in public schools.[69] In April of that year, the California State Assembly had revived the idea of segregating Nisei students and had called the Japanese a "Mongolian race" who should attend segregated schools along with Chinese, Korean, and Indian children.[70] Mr. Yamasaki may have been even more concerned about events that had occurred closer to home. On October 4, 1920, the Seattle school district had decided to segregate foreign students. This action stemmed from an incident at Franklin High School in which students from Mercer Island had been denied admission to the school because of a lack of room. Irritated islanders had then discovered that twenty-six Japanese-born students were attending the school and accused the city of not having room for native whites. The school district, perhaps convinced by arguments made by the Japanese Association of North America and Seattle's Japanese consulate, soon recognized that segregation would be both difficult and costly and dropped its plans.[71]

Debate inside the Japanese Community

Many educators, like Mr. Yamasaki, sought to protect the schools by making them seem less offensive to whites. Some prominent Nikkei leaders, however, continued to question the merit of maintaining the schools. For instance, as early as 1918, *Hokubei Jiji* ran a series of articles reporting a two-hour speech by the Seattle business leader Ototaka Yamaoka.[72] Yamaoka was an important community voice. He established the Oriental Trading Company, one of the three major labor contractors in the Pacific Northwest in 1899, and later worked for Furuya Company, the largest Japanese enterprise in the Northwest.[73] He also served as the second president of the Japanese Association of Washington State.[74] Yamaoka blasted the language schools' nationalistic curricula, use of Monbushō textbooks, and observance of the emperor's birthday. He argued that the schools not only hindered Nisei from being accepted as American citizens but also elicited reasonable suspicion and disapproval from the American public. According to Yamaoka, simply maintaining a Japanese language school could be interpreted by Americanizers as a challenge to the United States government.[75] Seattle's consul general, Chūichi Ōhashi, also publicly declared Japanese language education useless and argued that all Nikkei should use English.[76] In 1923, he called for abolition of all the schools to alleviate friction with whites.[77]

Mr. Yamasaki replied to Yamaoka's speech in the Japanese-language monthly *Hankyō*. Yamasaki criticized Yamaoka's narrow concept of "nationalism," and defended Japanese schools as an educational institution raising Nikkei to be productive American citizens. Yamasaki stressed Nikkei children's dual citizenship. He further argued that, if providing Japanese language education to Japanese American students was considered disloyal to the United States, as Yamaoka claimed, sending them to American public school would be equally disloyal to Japan. Yamasaki claimed that language schools did not offer Japanese national education nor was that their purpose. Regarding celebrating the emperor's birthday at language schools, Yamasaki explained that at the ceremony, they read telegrams from the U.S. president and American ambassador in Japan to celebrate the occasion. These actions were, Yamasaki argued, regarded as diplomatic politeness, but not as disloyal behavior to their country. Yamasaki questioned, then, why only little American citizens attending Japanese language schools celebrating the Japanese emperor's birthday had to be disgraced as displaying disloyal behavior.[78] It "created sensations in the literary circles of the Northwest Japanese community."[79]

Other bold Issei leaders urged against yielding to outside pressure and blindly succumbing to Americanization. On March 12, 1919, an editorial in the *Hokubei Jiji* titled "Freedom of Education" criticized Japanese educators and leaders alike who too easily assimilated into the dominant culture. It argued that the state government's attempt to control individual thought was imperialistic and that Nikkei had the right to establish schools and educate their children as they saw fit. Another opinion piece contended that, unlike schools in Japan, Washington's language schools neither inculcated nationalism nor undermined American public education.[80]

Educators and Issei leaders also sought to protect the schools by revising the textbooks. Nikkei community leaders and Japanese language teachers in Washington had discussed the need for new textbooks at a 1918 regional meeting of Japanese associations.[81] Unlike in Hawaii and California, there was no central organization for Washington's Japanese language teachers, so the association was the central forum for discussing educational issues.[82] They considered the old books inadequate because they were the same as those used in Japan, designed to raise children under the Japanese imperial education policy.[83] When the language schools later became one of the exclusionists' targets, the texts were used to inflame the public against the schools. For instance, at the 1919 House Immigration and Naturalization Committee hearings, Valentine McClatchy had testified that a Nisei child "absorbs Japanese ideals and patriotism and that contempt for all other nations which is the spirit of every Japanese school textbook."[84] After a long delay, the Northwest American Japanese Association established a committee to create its own textbook series and to solve the problems that confronted the schools. First, the committee resolved that the new series would teach the Japanese language in a way that would not interfere with the Americanization of Nisei and to clear up misperceptions about the language schools. Second, the committee would eliminate content unfamiliar to Nisei, most of whom had never visited Japan. Finally, the committee would adjust the language to meet Nisei students' abilities and needs.[85] In the years 1920–1921, it published the first Japanese-language textbook series written in the contiguous United States.[86] The series, *Nihongo Tokuhon* (Japanese reader), consisted of eight volumes designed to instruct Nisei children at the elementary school level in the Japanese language.[87] The project, which cost $6,000, was financed entirely by Nikkei communities in Washington, Montana, and the Territory of Alaska through their local Japanese associations.[88] Six thousand textbooks were printed: 1,000 books each for grades one through four and

500 each for grades five through eight.[89] On April 1, 1921, the approximately 500 Nisei students in a dozen Japanese communities throughout Washington, ranging from 7 students in Spokane to 251 in Seattle, began the school year with the new textbooks.[90]

The 1920 Japanese Immigration Hearings in Seattle and Tacoma

The House Immigration and Naturalization Committee held its long-awaited hearings on Japanese immigration from July 26 to August 3, 1920, in Seattle and Tacoma. Johnson returned to his home state before the hearings to warm up anti-Japanese agitation. He declared in front of members of Tacoma's Wild West Post of the Veterans of Foreign Wars, just two days before Independence Day, that he would make the next Congress enact more rigorous immigration laws against Japanese than those currently in effect. He implied that the Japanese government was behind a political takeover of Hawaii and exhorted the veterans to do their best to create an anti-Japanese environment in Washington when the immigration committee arrived. He spurred on the former servicemen: "Wherever the Oriental has been kept out of our western states it has been in the communities that have taken local action. . . . That is where you will win." To encourage them to support his policies, Johnson guaranteed the passage of a veteran's "bonus bill," with benefits such as land allotments, during the next Congress.[91] Daihachi Matsumi, president of the Northwest American Japanese Association, submitted to the committee information on Washington's Japanese language schools, along with statistics on the Nikkei population and Japanese businesses and farming. During Matsumi's testimony, Congressman John E. Raker asked about the textbooks the schools used and requested that Matsumi submit a full set of the old textbooks as well as drafts of the new series.[92] On August 4, one day after the hearings in Seattle, Johnson and Raker continued their own "personal investigation," visiting various Japanese businesses and educational and religious institutions in the city.[93] In his history of Japanese immigrants in the United States, the journalist and community leader Kōjirō Takeuchi recalls that the congressmen visited the Seattle Japanese Language School and received drafts of all the volumes of the new textbooks. Contradicting the transcript of the hearings, Takeuchi claims that it was the Japanese Association that suggested that the committee examine the new textbooks:

We believed that this was a good opportunity to sweep aside suspicion of the American public towards the Japanese language schools, and requested them to visit the Seattle Japanese Language School for observation (August 3, 1920), and submitted drafts of all the volumes of the Japanese textbooks. . . . We acknowledged that they understood the facts about the Japanese language schools, which had been causing misunderstandings. [Therefore,] the mission of the new textbooks was already accomplished before its real publication.[94]

In any case, the Northwest American Japanese Association's mission was somewhat successful, because students started the school year with the new textbooks. The group had failed, however, in its larger mission to eliminate the dominant society's misperceptions about Japanese language schools.

Washington's Japanese Language School Control Bill

In February 1921, William Bishop, a Republican from Jefferson County and a real estate agent, introduced Bill 140 in the state senate to prohibit aliens and disloyal persons from teaching in public and private schools.[95] That bill, as well as California's school control bill, was modeled on Hawaii's school control law, Act 30, which the Hawaiian legislature had passed on November 24, 1920.[96] The Washington Education Association had called for such a bill at its annual meeting in October 1920.[97] Approval of the bill in the Washington state senate, by a vote of 37 to 2, prompted Japanese Association officers and Issei parents to voice their opposition at a special meeting. The bill, if enacted, would have affected 489 Nisei students attending Japanese language schools,[98] but for unknown reasons, it failed to emerge from the House Education Committee.[99] In Fife, however, the Japanese community responded to the conflict by again closing its school.

Unlike Hawaii and California, Washington never passed a bill to control Japanese language schools. In 1923 Bishop proposed a slightly revised version of the bill he had submitted two years earlier, but it neither passed nor drew much attention.[100] However, Washington did pass an alien land law in 1921, which scholars have suggested was modeled on California's 1920 alien land law.[101] As we have seen, exclusionists in both states ran their attack on Nisei education parallel to their attack on alien land ownership. California's first law controlling foreign-language schools passed in June 1921, just six months after its 1920 land law was enacted. Bishop introduced his second foreign-language school bill in February 1923, just when the Washington legislature was debating an amendment to the 1921 alien land law that would prohibit Issei from purchasing land in the names of their Nisei children.[102] Why did Washington pass an alien land law but not legislation controlling Japanese language schools, as California had done? There is no simple or definite answer; however, we can come closer to answering the question by analyzing the movements for alien land laws in California and Washington. Exclusionists in California supported legislation against language schools primarily as a way to challenge Nisei citizenship rights, as a step toward closing the loophole in the alien land law that allowed Issei to buy land in their children's names. For California exclusionists, passing an alien land law was critical to arresting the economic ascent of Japanese Americans. Because it would decrease competition with Nikkei farmers, this law appealed to members of California's chapter of the Grange—an activist agricultural association. The law was also an attack on California Nikkei in general because their economy centered on agriculture.

California's alien land laws were strongly supported by a coalition of anti-Japanese groups, including Progressive politicians, white craft labor unions (such as the American Federation of Labor), Grangers, nativists, and American Legionnaires, who shared the goal of stopping Japanese immigration. After passing the laws, however, they soon realized that California could not end Japanese immigration alone, because the federal government intervened when state laws infringed on foreign treaties or the rights of Nisei citizens. So California exclusionists tried to form a national anti-Japanese movement in order to force the federal government to prohibit Japanese from entering the country. California exclusionists attempted to disseminate their agenda across the nation, even reaching progressives, Grangers, and Legionnaires in the Midwest, encouraging them to pass alien land laws in their states.[103] Exclusionists received the most support on the Pacific Coast, especially from the American Legion, which made Japanese exclusion part of its national platform. Exclusionists in Washington State were strong allies, although they were much smaller in number than in California. Washington exclusionists adopted California's strategy of pursuing an alien land law, even though such a law may not have been the most strategic solution to the state's "Japanese problem." Washington had a law prohibiting aliens from owning land that predated statehood; consequently, far fewer Nikkei in the state were engaged in agriculture compared with California. Only 3.9 percent of Washington's Japanese farmers in 1920 owned land; 95.4 percent were tenants and the remaining 0.7 percent were farm managers.[104] Except for truck farmers, Nikkei were not as significant a threat to Washington farmers as they were to California farmers. Another important source of anti-Japanese activism in California was trade unionists; however, few Washington laborers joined the exclusionist campaign because of the influence of the Seattle Central Labor Council. During this period, the council embraced the ideas of the Industrial Workers of the World, which celebrated the solidarity of all workers, including blacks and immigrants. Nikkei workers even participated in the council's 1919 general strike through the Nihonjin Rōdō Kumiai (Japanese Labor Union).[105] The Seattle *Union Record*, a labor council publication, was a solitary voice in defense of Nikkei rights and often editorialized against anti-Japanese legislation.[106] Progressive farmers were active in the Washington Grange at that time, and so it cooperated with the council rather than with the nativists in the American Legion. Washington's strongest anti-Japanese contingent was comprised of owners of small enterprises like grocery stores and other businesses that were in direct competition with those owned by Nikkei, such as laundries, hotels, and restaurants. These businesspeople were part of the group that founded the Seattle Anti-Japanese League. Although the *Seattle Star* gave the movement much publicity, the League had a hard time recruiting members outside of these groups and the American Legion.[107] The Seattle chamber of commerce resisted the exclusionist campaign and admonished Freeman, a member of the League, for threatening the region's trade with Japan.[108] Regardless, the League followed the national exclusionist agenda, which meant supporting an alien land law, even though the law would not have decreased the small businesses' competition with Japanese markets. The land law passed but remained peripheral to most anti-Japanese activists in Washington, who were more concerned with fighting Japanese businesses locally.[109] Though Washington passed an alien land law in 1921 and an amendment to the law in 1923, it did not have a diverse coalition that considered land ownership the most pressing issue in the state. Thus, there was little interest in legislation to stop Japanese land ownership by campaigning for a bill to control the Japanese language schools.

Other factors may have prevented passage of a language school bill in Washington. One such factor may have been Seattle's school superintendent, Frank B. Cooper, a strong advocate of progressive education, who curbed the oppressive surge of Americanism during his 1901–1922 administration. People like him treated immigrants and their children with sensitivity and sympathy. Cooper resisted what he considered mindless patriotic exercises, such as flag rituals at schools mandated by a 1915 state law and the school board's proposal for segregated education of nonnative students. His resistance often led to conflict with the Daughters of the American Revolution, the Minute Men, and other nativist groups that tried to dictate school curricula.[110] Education historian Yoon Pak argued that Cooper's fairness toward minority students and his belief in progressive education "set the stage for how the Seattle Public Schools would approach citizenship education and Americanization." According to Pak, the instruction at Seattle schools was nationalistic and progressive at the same time, reflecting the city's mix of fundamentalism and political radicalism.[111] Progressive teachers may also have played a part in discouraging the antiforeign campaign among educators like Minnie Bean and the public.

The most important of all factors, however, were Japanese parents and educators, who actively defended their interests and refused to accept any social injustice that would diminish opportunities for their children's education. Their resistance was manifested in various ways: debating opponents of Japanese language schools inside the Nikkei community, adjusting the schools' curricula to fit public policies, circumnavigating laws to build schools, and participating in the democratic process by lobbying against a school control law. Not all of these acts of resistance were highly visible, but together they may have helped educators like Cooper understand the community's faith in their schools.

Conclusion

The 1919 congressional hearings and Seattle's mass meeting against Nikkei can be seen as the beginning of the exclusionists' shift from aiming at Japanese immigrants to aiming at their American offspring. Some public school administrators also blamed the language schools for delaying Nisei pupils' mastery of English and assimilation into American society. In spite of these sentiments, however, the number of Japanese language schools grew, especially after passage of the Immigration Act of 1924.[112] The act, which completely barred Japanese immigration, made Issei uneasy about an American future, and indeed many thought about returning to Japan. Their Nisei children would need proficiency in Japanese if they "returned" with their parents to Japan, so the importance of the language schools grew. A more likely cause, however, for the continued growth of the schools was that many of the immigrants decided to remain in America.[113] As Miyamoto explains in his classic study of Japanese Americans in pre–World War II Seattle, the dominant society greatly restricted career opportunities for Nisei. According to Miyamoto, the "ability to speak the language is an absolute necessity for the second generation, . . . because their economic relationships are in large part with the first generation."[114] Most important, Issei parents felt that ethnic pride, heritage, and morals were needed to protect Nisei from a sense of racial inferiority and to boost their self-confidence.[115]

These were the ideas behind the creation of the first Japanese language school in the Yakima Valley, the Wapato Nihongo Gakuen (Japanese Language Institute), in 1926. After passage of the 1921 alien land law and the Immigration Act of 1924, attendees at the 1925 Yakima Japanese Association annual meeting decided to educate Nisei as Americans with the best traits of the Yamato, or Japanese race.[116]

Japanese schools in Washington did not close down, but educators such as Masato Yamasaki and his students had to endure minor harassment and strive to improve the learning environment, despite the racism and political turmoil around them. With the growing Nisei population, Seattle's and Tacoma's schools survived and thrived, as did twenty-two other Japanese language schools in Washington State before the dawn of World War II.[117]

CHAPTER 5

Conclusion

If the Department of Public Instruction is going to curtail years of
study at Japanese language schools, we must fundamentally solve the
Japanese language school problem, or this would be used every year
as a political and exclusion tool, and we would struggle to fight it.
—*Hawai Hōchi*, August 14, 1922

ive months after the June 1920 publication of the Federal Survey
of Education, a group of Nikkei community leaders in Hawaii
drafted a compromise bill on Japanese language schools. With
the endorsement of the Honolulu Chamber of Commerce, the bill was
presented to the Territorial House by Henry J. Lyman (Republican, Hilo),
and a similar bill was proposed by Harry A. Baldwin (Republican, Maui)
in the Senate in November 1920.[1] Both bills passed their respective houses
and were signed into law as Act 30 by Governor McCarthy on November
24, 1920. The law regulated language schools' operating hours and
required permits for both schools and teachers. The law also empowered
the Department of Public Instruction (DPI) with complete authority
over the textbooks and curriculum at Japanese language schools.[2] A companion bill, Act 36, prescribed language school teacher's qualifications.[3]
In order to prepare for the teaching license examination, Japanese teachers attended Americanization classes held at the public library. The ethnic community spent more than $6,000 on the three-month workshop.[4]

Japanese Language School Lawsuit

On November 18, 1922, the DPI changed gears and headed in the direc-
tion of wiping out these schools by enforcing stricter regulations closing
kindergartens and the first two grades of Japanese language schools.[5] The
Nikkei leaders who submitted the original draft of Act 30 felt betrayed.

The Japanese community was split on how to react to the DPI's harsh rules. Some advocated resistance. Others wanted to comply rather than rock the shaky boat of race relations. *Hawai Hōchi* publisher Kinzaburō Fred Makino challenged the constitutionality of the school laws. With his "dynamic and aggressive editorial style," Makino urged Nikkei to file a lawsuit, emphasizing that they should fight to protect their rights as Americans.[6] On the other hand, Hawaii's Consul General Keiichi Yamazaki, University of Hawaii Professor Tasuku Harada, board members of the Japanese Association, the *Nippū Jiji*'s Sōga, and other Nikkei leaders strongly cautioned against battling with authorities. On December 9, 1922, Consul General Yamazaki invited thirty Nikkei to a meeting in order to produce a public statement against the lawsuit. The statement claimed that a lawsuit against Japanese language school control laws would worsen relations between Japanese and Americans, and could cause problems for Japanese American children.[7] Of the thirty Nikkei in attendance, only fourteen signed the statement, primarily Christians and businessmen with close relationships with the Territorial government.[8]

On December 28, 1922, the Palama Japanese Language School, along with three others, filed suit in the Territorial Circuit Court (see Fig. 10). This led to the celebrated test case known as *Farrington, Governor of Hawaii, et al. v. Tokushige et al.* It questioned the constitutionality of Act 30 and the subsequent DPI ban on kindergartens and lower grades. This was unbearable to these schools since it would ruin them financially, forcing many to close.[9] According to a *Nippū Jiji* estimate, of the 5,708 enrolled students in Oahu's twelve Japanese language schools, 1,918 students or 34 percent would be immediately expelled from their schools. This tally did not count students at the over 140 other Japanese schools in the territory.[10]

On February 2, 1923, Territorial Circuit Court Judge Banks ruled that Act 30 was constitutional, but that the DPI's regulations were invalid.[11] Both sides appealed this ruling to the Territorial Supreme Court on the next day. Meanwhile, the legislature upped the ante codifying the DPI's regulations into law as Act 171 on May 2, 1923.[12] Act 171 prohibited Nisei from attending a Japanese language school until they successfully passed the second grade of public school, forcing the closure of kindergartens and the first two grades of Japanese language schools. It also mandated the use of textbooks written in English and levied an annual $1-per-pupil fee to defray the DPI's costs to oversee foreign language schools.[13] After Act 171 was enacted, sixteen additional Japanese language schools joined Palama's suit.[14] These schools filed a petition in the Territorial Circuit

Court for an injunction against Act 171. Judge Andrade granted it on May 10, 1923.[15] Furious territorial legislators responded with Act 152 to amend Acts 30 and 171 on April 29, 1925, adding a provision to execute civil action against any school that did not pay the fee as well as any person involved with such a renegade school. The act also denied the right of a petition for an injunction.[16] It involved 163 foreign language schools, including 9 Korean and 7 Chinese language schools.[17]

In June 1925, the state and Palama Language School decided to discontinue their court battle without prejudice since the Territorial Supreme Court had stalled for more than two years. This left standing Judge Banks' decision that Act 30 was constitutional, but the DPI could not enforce its abridgement regulations.[18] Although the DPI commissioners conceded to rescind the regulations, the Japanese language schools took their case directly to Honolulu's Federal District Court. There, Judge DeBolt granted an injunction against Act 152 to halt the collection of fees from Japanese language schools and suggested forwarding the question of the constitutionality of the school laws to the San Francisco

Fig. 10. Palama Gakuen, Oahu (1912). It was established in 1910. This Hongwanji school joined the litigation in 1923—seven months after the Palama Japanese Language School and other schools sued the Territory. (Courtesy of the Bernice Pauahi Bishop Museum)

Ninth Circuit Court of Appeals in July 1925.[19] The higher court affirmed DeBolt's decision on the injunction and declared Act 30 unconstitutional on March 22, 1926.[20] The territorial government appealed this to the United States Supreme Court on July 8, 1926. Judge Walter F. Frear, former governor, wrote the brief defending the territorial government. Frear's brief echoed the 1919 Federal Survey's recommendation to "abolish the Japanese language schools," labeling them as "if not distinctly anti-American, [then] certainly un-American."[21] His brief argued that:

> It would be a sad commentary on our system of government to hold that the Territory must stand by, impotent, and watch its foreign-born guests conduct a vast system of schools of American pupils, teaching them loyalty to a foreign country and disloyalty to their own country, and hampering them during their tender years in the learning of the home language in the public schools, . . . to hold that the Territory could not by mere regulatory measures even alleviate these evils.[22]

The Supreme Court, however, did not allow the Territory to submit the Federal Survey report as evidence, although it was "extensively referred to in Frear's brief."[23] The court agreed with Joseph Lightfoot, attorney for the Japanese language schools, that Nikkei were given "no opportunity of being heard."[24] Lightfoot claimed that nothing "un-American was taught in the foreign language schools, and that Americanization of the pupils was promoted by the schools."[25] The Supreme Court supported the lower courts' decisions, finding Hawaii's foreign language school laws unconstitutional on February 21, 1927.[26] The court vindicated both Nikkei parents' and children's rights under the Fourteenth Amendment: no state shall "deprive any person of life, liberty or property without due process of law," fundamental rights that are further guaranteed by the Fifth Amendment. Federal Supreme Court Justice James C. McReynolds, speaking for the majority, wrote that "the Japanese parent has the right to direct the education of his own child without unreasonable restrictions; the Constitution protects him as well as those who speak another tongue."[27] The overturning of Hawaii's foreign language school control laws benefited Japanese Americans beyond the Islands. California also had to nullify its foreign language school laws.[28]

Hawaii's Japanese language school litigation, *Farrington v. Tokushige*, was decided on the basis of *Meyer v. Nebraska* and Oregon's *Pierce v. Society of Sisters*. Today, these three cases are usually presented as one unified chapter of the "Americanization Period." The Meyer and Society of Sisters cases were victims of the Americanization movement. They were based on nativists' attempts to assimilate immigrants, and their belief that compulsory public English-language education was the only way to unify the nation and alleviate the fear of foreign elements. These cases were clearly further motivated by anti-Catholic and anti-German sentiment.

Meyer's case involved German-language instruction at Zion Lutheran Church in Hampton County, Nebraska. The Zion congregation challenged Nebraska's 1919 Simon Law, prohibiting the teaching of "any subject to any person in any language other than the English language . . . in any private, denominational, parochial or public school" for the first eight grades.[29] Robert Meyer was convicted on the charge of teaching Raymond Parpart, a fourth-grader, the Old Testament in German. After both the Hamilton County Court and the Nebraska Supreme Court found Meyer guilty and upheld the law's constitutionality, the United States Supreme Court reversed the lower courts' decisions on June 4, 1923.[30] Justice McReynolds delivered the court's majority opinion, recognizing both Meyer's right to teach and parents' right to engage him to teach their children.

While the Meyer case repealed school control laws related to non-English language instruction in some states, an even more coercive law, championed by the Ku Klux Klan, to control foreign language education was passed in Oregon in 1922. The Society of Sisters, who ran Roman Catholic parochial schools, decided to challenge the constitutionality of the law, mandating all children of ages between eight and sixteen to attend public schools.[31] Justice McReynolds made his decision based on the Meyer case in *Pierce v. Society of Sisters of the Holy Names of Jesus and Mary*. McReynolds emphasized the law's dogmatic nature, dealing with children as "mere creature[s] of the state," and safeguarded parents' liberty to "direct [their] destiny."[32]

Many researchers portray *Farrington v. Tokushige* and the anti-Japanese language school legislation merely as extensions of the Meyer and Society of Sisters cases. They ignore the critical differences between the cases—the undercurrents of context and catalysts for each law. For example, legal historian Kenneth O'Brien summarizes the Hawaii case thus: "Even though the problem of assimilation was more pronounced in Hawaii, the Supreme Court, in line with the Meyer and Oregon opinions, had to rule in favor of parental and private school rights."[33] Hawaii's Japanese language school laws obviously shared a similar social background with the precedents, with the exception of the question of religious freedom and competition between Christians and Buddhists. However, as we have examined, what differentiated it from these other cases was that it was also rooted in the complexity of Hawaii's social, economic, and political setting, including the power conflicts between the white ruling class and Asian immigrant laborers. Moreover, in California and Washington, the Japanese language school controversy was used as a political tool to seal Japanese Americans' future development and to exile them all.

Legal historian William Ross recognized the value of the Supreme Court decision on the Nebraska and Oregon cases, calling them a "turning point in American constitutional history." This, according to Ross, was the "emergence of the Supreme Court as a persistent guardian of personal liberties."[34] For Japanese Americans, the *Farrington v. Tokushige* decision, however, not only seemed to assure their personal liberties and rights to education, but also vindicated their social position as an ethnic group in the United States, as unhyphenated Americans.

Why did so many Issei insist on defending Japanese language schools during the five years of court battles after years of attack from the dominant society? What did these language schools mean to the ethnic community? As was examined, Japanese language schools were originally established to provide immigrants' children with Japanese education based on the assumption that they would eventually return to Japan. The language schools, however, blossomed when many Issei determined to settle in the United States. According to Nikkei sociologist S. Frank Miyamoto, for Issei who were born in Meiji-era Japan, American schools and culture could not provide "a kind of training that the schools in Japan and Japanese society necessarily infused in children." Issei believed only a society based on a solid history and traditional values could teach children important elements of human life and create the foundation required to be members of society. Miyamoto portrays early 1900s Seattle, one of the most civilized cities in Western America at that time, as a city "barely coming out of the Wild West frontier." It was a "relatively undisciplined, highly individualistic, traditionless, and ahistorical society."[35] Even for Seattle Issei, the society was "deficient" in providing their children with proper discipline; we can imagine how keenly Issei in Hawaii and California felt that American public education alone would be unreliable for raising Nisei, so they felt a need to provide their own educational institutions.

A second reason, according to Miyamoto, was difficulties in communication between Issei parents and their children. This situation was not unique to Nikkei but common among immigrant parents and their English-speaking children. However, unlike European languages, there is no linguistic or cultural common ground between Japanese and English. This communication gap in Nikkei families was "really never overcome."[36] When Issei parents wanted to have a serious conversation beyond everyday talk, the frustrations and sorrow caused by their inability to express thoughts in either Japanese or English must have been indescribable.

Thirdly, there was no inherent conflict for Issei between raising Nisei as American citizens and teaching them Japanese. Issei truly believed that Nisei who inherited the old country's moral values, combined with the philosophy of democracy and social justice, would make them ideal Americans. They hoped Nisei would be the generation who could create a bridge between Japan and the United States. This Issei aspiration is frequently seen in many statements on Japanese language school policy announced to the American public. Japanese language schools underwent attacks from Americanizers, Japanese exclusionists, politicians, and public educators; yet, Nikkei maintained their stance, insisting that teaching the Japanese language would provide the best asset for their American offspring. Miyamoto claimed that Nikkei aspired to the high principles that were manifested in the Declaration of Independence, the Constitution, and the Gettysburg Address, and Nikkei made strenuous efforts to adapt themselves to the system.[37] However, the Issei interpretation of assimilating Nikkei to American society was incompatible with the dominant society's belief—the only acceptable assimilation pattern was absolute conformity to the Anglo-Saxon society.[38] The same American society that propagated democracy and freedom also demanded that immigrants shed old customs and adopt the host society's customs.

Lastly, Nikkei never completely gave up on Japanese language schools because the schools were a cultural symbol of the ethnic community and a physical tie with their home country. Many language schools, established by a local Japanese association, were a concrete expression of the ethnic community's collective will. The schools were supported by tuition and community members' monthly donations when funds were insufficient. The language schools embodied the psychological and material unification of the Nikkei community. Through participation in various ceremonies and events held at the schools, Issei and Nisei cemented a sense of community and oneness. The schools hosted athletic meetings, school plays, festivals, and celebrations of the emperor's birthday. When Japanese warships or dignitaries came to town, the proud Nikkei community, including language schools, welcomed them and conducted festive receptions. Miyamoto recalls that Seattle's Kokugo Gakkō "had overwhelming support in the [Japanese] community," regardless of which region of Japan they came from or whether the families were Buddhist or Christian.[39] In segregated communities, this made schools the only public space for Japanese Americans.

Does this mean that the Nikkei experience of dealing with Japanese language schools produced an introverted force that confined members within the community and hampered their assimilation in American society? On the contrary, Miyamoto claims that an ethnic social force, which he calls "voluntary association," propelled Nikkei assimilation. Voluntary associations are organizations established by people sharing a common interest, for the purpose of seeking to advance their common interests. Japanese American communities possess a strong tendency of organizing voluntary associations, such as Protestant churches, business associations, farmers' cooperatives, and sports and cultural clubs. Miyamoto claims, because they are organized "associationally, . . . they have actually aided them in their assimilative process," in that these associations directed their members to orchestrate their efforts to achieve common goals and became "important platforms from which Japanese Americans could launch themselves into participation in the larger society."[40]

How then did Japanese language schools as "voluntary associations" increase the chances of Nikkei assimilation? For Issei, the entire process of establishing Japanese language schools involved interactions, cooperation, and negotiations with the dominant society. When California and Washington alien land laws prevented Nikkei from securing school land, white friends lent their names to purchase land. Missionaries also taught English to Issei and Nisei children at Japanese language schools so as to make it easier for them to adjust to American society and public schools. After the schools' curricula came under the scrutiny of Americanizers and exclusionists, Issei parents and teachers tried to explain the schools' purpose and policies in order to solicit approval from the outside community. The culmination of Nikkei experience in communicating with the larger society was when Hawaii Nikkei fought *Farrington v. Tokushige* and claimed the right to educate their children. These incidents support Miyamoto's argument that the schools, "while seemingly promoting identity with Japan and retarding entry into the larger society, were in fact a valuable stepping stone in the Japanese American process of gaining a significant role in American society."[41]

This book has focused on the role of Japanese language schools for anti-Japanese activists as well as Issei. However, another important question—

not explored in this study—is how the Japanese language school experience helped construct Nisei identity. The literature of Japanese American history suggests Japanese language schools were far from effective in terms of importing language ability.[42] This narrative also emphasizes that Nisei were far from serious about learning Japanese and were far more susceptible to American ideas taught in public school than to Japanese traditional values that Issei parents wanted them to learn in language school. Most Nisei who studied at a language school could not develop enough ability to express complex ideas in Japanese. Moreover, when asked, most claim that the Japanese national events held at the schools, such as the celebration of the emperor's birthday, "had no real meaning."[43] However, most had warm memories of group activities, playtime, and cultural events at Japanese language schools. For example, reflecting on his experience in the 1920s, Miyamoto himself recalls "it was the socializing that I especially enjoyed in connection with the language school, whereas the language learning, I have always felt, was almost a total loss." With a careful probe, however, one can see this dominant narrative of Japanese language schools is an overgeneralized picture, and that there were many diverse experiences. Various factors, such as the period, location, school, and teacher, could have created completely different experiences.

As the chapters on Hawaii, California, and Washington have demonstrated, the social milieus of Japanese language schools differed greatly in each location. One striking difference was the rate of attendance. In Hawaii, over 20,000 Nisei, or 97 percent of the school-aged Nisei population, attended Japanese language schools in 1920.[44] In contrast, only approximately 3,000 California Nisei, or 42 percent of all Nisei students in public schools, attended Japanese language schools,[45] and only 489 pupils in Washington, representing approximately 30 percent of Japanese Americans attending public schools, also went to Japanese language school in 1920.[46] These statistics simply demonstrate the differences in needs and expectations for Japanese language learning. In Hawaii, attending Japanese language school was regarded by both students and parents as the norm, if not mandatory.[47]

Japanese language school experiences also varied among Hawaii Nisei. Unlike in rural Japanese plantation camps, one Nisei described that flag hoisting or Kyōiku Chokugo recitation was not practiced in her Honolulu Japanese school, even during the 1910s. Teachers' perspectives toward Nisei education created completely different experiences. Some teachers modified Monbushō textbooks so as to deemphasize Japanese nationalistic values and to differentiate Nisei from Japanese in Japan.[48] Others tried to create democratic textbooks for both genders. On the other hand, Senator Daniel Inouye recalls his nationalistic Japanese language school teacher in 1939 teaching pupils that "when Japan calls, you must know that it is Japanese blood that flows in your veins."[49]

Japanese language school experiences must be fundamentally different for Hawaii Nisei, who attended before the mid-1910s, and those who attended after this period. Students in the former period attended schools that aimed to provide Japanese national education. In the latter period, however, the Hawaii Japanese Education Association reoriented language school teaching to conform to public school education, although the precise goal of Nisei education was an everlasting and fluctuating topic at their meetings.

Mere examination of Hawaii's conditions alone displays considerable differences in individuals' experience of Japanese language schools: needless to say, there would be even more differences among situations in Hawaii, California, and Washington. It is still a premature exercise to try to generalize the Nisei Japanese language school experience or even attempt to analyze its effect on the construction of Nisei identity.

There is a need for revisionist research on the role of Japanese language schools for both Issei and Nisei. Historian Franklin Odo argues that the role of Japanese language school has been deliberately and effectively downplayed. In *No Sword to Bury*, Odo explores a group of Hawaii Nisei men, who after rejection by the American military during World War II, formed the Varsity Victory Volunteers (VVV), a civilian group supporting America's war effort with volunteer labor. Odo claims that there was a feeling of "disconnect" between Nisei and their parents, their ancestors' country, and their cultural heritage, but that there is compelling evidence that "Japanese-language learning was more effective and more appreciated than other studies have reported." According to Odo, the most significant manifestation of this is the outstanding work of the 3,000 Nisei in the Military Intelligence Service.[50] Odo argues that a "post–World War II mythology" stressed Nisei acculturation as part of an effort to present themselves as ideal Americans. "This narrative," Odo continues, includes Nisei identity "untouched by their years of language schooling." Odo claims that by creating a narrative of Japanese language school ineffectiveness early in their lives, Nisei stressed their rebellion against the influence of linguistic heritage, cultural values, and also their Issei parents.[51] This strategy stemmed from the fact that the ethnic minority's "success depended on a thoroughgoing assimilationist stance, including the rejection of ethnic-based associations and of languages other than Standard English."[52] Odo deconstructs this narrative of Japanese American successful "assimilation," including the 442nd Regimental Combat Team and its heroic contributions, as well as its connection to the model minority myth. The model minority thesis, originally used by media in the early 1950s, suggests that Asian Americans were minorities others should emulate because they were able to advance in society despite racism and discrimination. Odo challenges this, explaining that the model minority myth was characterized by "an ahistorical attribution of upward mobility to cultural values embracing education, children or both; deferring gratification; stoic passivity; and a penchant for disciplined work," but according to Odo these were not the only factors controlling or contributing to ethnic mobility.[53] Odo's challenge suggests real difficulties in determining the relationship between Japanese language school experiences and Nisei identity. It is, however, ironic that this minority success has been attributed to Nisei possession of Japanese traditional values, which they intentionally denied. It was precisely these values that Issei wanted to transmit most, and it was their very raison d'être for the creation of Japanese language schools.

Odo's observation of Nikkei community in Hawaii echoes Miyamoto's explanation of an environment prone to promoting "voluntary associations." One Nisei interviewee recalled growing up in a real community, which "protected you against outside forces, but within it, if you don't behave, they'll let you have it . . . physically keep you in line." Almost all of Odo's interviewees expressed this sense of community: "No one locked doors; kids ate at each other's homes; it was very difficult to avoid the close and compelling sense of belonging." Odo argues this sense of community, presumably including Japanese language schools, "may have contributed to the young men's ability to form the VVV in 1942."[54]

Miyamoto observes that for most Nisei who were young teenagers in the 1930s, democracy or other political principles had little concrete meaning, but "in the rarefied atmosphere of school life, [Nisei] came away believing strongly in the American way of life," although they knew the reality might be quite different. Perhaps simply attending Japanese language schools, and experiencing "the associational and organizational functions," had much more impact than what the ethnic schools actually taught them. This culture was likely reinforced at home and seems to remain a part of the experience of modern Japanese American communities.[55]

The Japanese Government's Role in the Japanese Language School Controversy

Japanese immigrants wanted to bring up Nisei as American citizens, but were equally eager to pass down Japan's traditions and firm moral values by teaching Japanese. Issei hoped that their children could serve the United States as useful citizens who someday could also repay the ancestors' country by promoting understanding of Japan. However, as was examined, the host country absolutely rejected Nikkei intentions. Their mother country also gave them the cold shoulder.

One factor that fanned the Japanese language school controversy was the Japanese government's direct and indirect involvement in Nikkei life in the United States through consulates and Japanese associations. Japanese exclusionists argued for abolishing language schools, claiming the Japanese government was secretly controlling these schools. According to exclusionists, Japanese schools functioned as institutions to raise Japanese subjects; while Issei parents advanced economically, Nisei with a "Japanese mind" were numerically growing in order to take over the United States from within. Japanese language schools played an important role in the exclusionists' yellow peril myth.

In reality, however, perceptions toward education of overseas Nikkei varied among Japanese officials over time. There actually was one political minority, during the early Meiji period, which advocated utilizing Japanese emigration to advance the Yamato race. Its followers envisioned migration abroad and colonization as a solution to such domestic problems as overpopulation, economic depression, and acute poverty in rural Japan. However, even if some in the government had this perspective, a little over two decades after the 1885 government-organized emigration, the 1907–1908 "Gentlemen's Agreement" between the United States and Japan completely ended mass migration of Japanese laborers. Thus, the idea of emigration as colonial expansion targeted to America surely had rescinded.

As many Nisei reached school age, their education became Issei parents' concern. Responding to Issei requests on various questions regarding Nisei education, the Monbushō, which was enthusiastic to control overseas Japanese education especially in China and the rest of Asia, also became interested in taking Japanese language schools in America under its control. This caused a conflict with the foreign ministry's agenda. Facing exclusionists' attacks on Japanese language schools, the foreign ministry encouraged Nikkei to educate their children as American citizens.

The ministry's concern was to arrest friction with the American public and to halt the growth of anti-Japanese sentiment. However, even among consuls general, opinions on Japanese language schools varied. For example, Los Angeles Consul General Unojirō Ōyama valued the existence of Japanese language schools, and in 1919 he proposed that the foreign ministry provide Nisei students with opportunities to continue their studies in Japan. It was essential, he argued, for Japan's diplomatic relations to train people with foreign language abilities. He suggested Nisei who were native English speakers could become ideal candidates, if admitted to an appropriate school in Japan and if they developed the Japanese that they learned in language schools in America.[56] This shows that between the ministries, and even among diplomats, perspectives on Japanese immigrants in America varied, suggesting there probably was no absolute government policy. At any rate, according to correspondence between local consuls general and foreign ministers during the 1920s, Tokyo overall decided to retreat from Nisei education at this point. It is thus very ironic that the Japanese government provided fuel for exclusionists' attack on Japanese language schools.

Other Ethnic Language Schools

We have looked at language school experiences for Japanese Americans in the 1920s. However, it would be a mistake to generalize Japanese Americans' foreign language school experience for other ethnic or even Asian American groups. Chinese were the largest nonwhite minority in California in the 1900s.[57] They endured great suffering and anti-immigrant movements, which culminated in the Chinese Exclusion Act of 1882. They were also excluded from land ownership, voting, litigation, certain professions, interracial marriage, and naturalization.[58] Chinese American children had also been discriminated against and even were occasionally deprived of public school education, since an 1860 California school law ordered them to attend segregated schools, and an 1870 amendment temporarily removed the right to attend segregated, publicly financed schools.[59] As a result, California's Chinese language schools in the 1870s were established as "alternative avenues for receiving an education."[60] In 1884, a Chinese language school was established by the Chinese Consolidated Benevolent Association, known as the Six Companies. The school fostered traditional Chinese education: "it attempted to operate as if it were located in China."[61] Even after the opening of a public Chinese primary school in 1885,[62] Chinese American children living in Chinatown were accustomed to attending Chinese language schools for two hours every afternoon to learn languages, history, geography, and calligraphy.[63] Considering the origins of these Chinese language schools, the existence of such schools probably caused less conflict with the Americanizers, since the Chinese language schools were the products of whites' exclusion of Chinese Americans from mainstream education, and were thus perceived as an off-track education for "foreigners."

In 1919 Hawaii, the fourth-largest Asian ethnic group following Japanese, Chinese, and Filipinos was Koreans.[64] Like Japanese language schools in Hawaii, most of the Korean language schools were on sugar plantations. A typical Korean language school offered Korean language, history, customs, and ethics, taught by Methodist pastors in the afternoon or evening following public school.[65] Korean language schools also served indispensable roles for the Korean immigrant communities, teaching social conduct and raising ethnic solidarity for improved employment opportunities and communication with parents. Nonetheless, according to historian Wayne Patterson, "Korean language schools in Hawai'i never really flourished."[66] Part of the reason was that in 1910, the majority of Koreans were still bachelor plantation workers, so that the school-aged Korean population was very small—only 164 children were registered in the public schools. By 1920, however, the number of Korean schoolchildren grew to 4,950 and by 1930 to 6,461, but the number of Korean language schools only increased from eight schools in 1921 to nine in 1925 and ten (with 520 students in attendance) in 1930.[67] As Patterson explains, Koreans seemed less eager to retain their mother tongue than did Japanese or Chinese. First, many of the Koreans in Hawaii were urban Chris-

Table 10: Chinese American, Japanese American, and Korean American Students in Language Schools in Hawaii, 1922–1934

	1922	1924	1926	1928	1932	1934
Chinese	1,314	1,162	2,220	2,176	2,478	2,714
Japanese	21,448	15,687	26,768	33,607	40,017	41,192
Korean	126	225	468	732	522	646

Source: The data is from biennial reports of the Department of Public Instruction of Hawaii. The figures for 1924 might not be accurate because the foreign language schools were in litigation, and did not report to the DPI. From William Carlson Smith, *Americans in Process: A Study of Our Citizens of Oriental Ancestry* (Ann Arbor, MI: Edwards Brothers, 1937; reprint, New York: Arno Press, 1970), 328.

tians who already had a better English faculty, acquired through their contact with missionaries in Korea. They were thus more susceptible to the new culture and quickly changed their perceptions of themselves from sojourners to settlers. Secondly, after leaving the plantations, Koreans geographically scattered more and did not create a large community, so that they had more contact with whites and other Asian immigrants. All of these characteristics of Korean American life decreased the importance of passing down native language skills to their offspring. Patterson also pointed out that "A larger percentage of the Korean second generation than their Japanese or Chinese counterparts never attended a language school."[68]

In many ways, it would seem that Japanese language schools played a more important role for Japanese Americans than did language schools for Chinese American or Korean American communities during this interwar period. It is also true that Japanese language schools engendered more hardships for Japanese Americans than foreign language schools did for other Asian ethnic groups.

Following in the footsteps of the Chinese, the Japanese faced much discrimination. However, anti-Japanese actions differed from anti-Chinese attacks in that they took place under the social milieu of "100 percent Americanizing" foreign elements. To some extent, this Americanization crusade took Japanese immigrant children into the mainstream education system, instead of segregating them into ethnic schools. In Hawaii, however, the crusade was not motivated by the public school's advertised mission: producing socially contributing, future members of society and providing them equally with chances for upward mobility. Rather, the education system was used by a small group of business elites to mold children of the largest ethnic immigrant group. Through public education, these elites tried to control Nikkei children's educational opportunities so that they could confine Nikkei to the bottom rung of the social structure. Nikkei were inspired by Western ideas taught at public schools and tried to demonstrate their acceptance, but they were dismayed by the host society's self-serving response.[69]

Educational issues for immigrant groups involve power dynamics among members of the minority group and the larger society. As we have seen, perspectives on Nisei education differed within the Nikkei community. While conservative Issei leaders and Christians sided with the white elite and fanatically promoted assimilation and Americanization, cultural preservationists, such as some newspapermen, questioned blind acceptance of assimilation. On the other side, some Buddhists and rural Nikkei had greater psychological attachment to old traditions. When dealing with Japanese language schools, each group had its own political, cultural, and economic agendas.

For host societies, educational issues for Japanese immigrants were translated into political issues. In Hawaii, the Japanese language controversy emerged as a religious battle within the ethnic community, but it was used as a harness by a small, apprehensive, white hegemonic class to retain the mass of laboring aliens under its control. In California, the "Japanese language school problem" was an adaptation of Hawaii's problem; however, it was used as an attempt to deprive Nisei of their American citizenship in order to block Japanese land ownership and eventually remove them from California's profitable agricultural business.[70] With the third-largest Nikkei population, Washington State had a long history of anti-Japanese sentiment, and local exclusionists were susceptible to anything that might contest Japanese economic growth.

The history of the Japanese language school controversy was a long, painful process for Issei, and it raised the question of what Nikkei wanted the future generation of Japanese Americans to be like. This controversy also can be seen as central to the Japanese immigrants' struggle to establish a niche for themselves in the United States.

Education for minorities has been and always will be a central issue shaping the relationship between newcomers and older members of American society. My research highlights Japanese immigrants' resistance to preserve their patrimony and their efforts to foster traditional values in their Japanese American children. I hope that this book sheds light on the question of minority education, which challenges the very concept of education in the context of American diversity and multiculturalism. This remains an important question in America during this ethnocentric era with its rampant suspicion of immigrants.

Appendix
1921 California State Examination for Japanese Language School Teachers

History

1. Name two men permanently connected with each of the following periods of United States history. Give briefly the reasons for your selections; discovery and exploration; settlement and colonization; revolution and organization; expansion and development; civil war and reconstruction; present days.

2. What two questions were definitely settled by the Civil War?

3. Discuss the territorial expansion of the United States from the original 13 colonies, explaining how each acquisition was made.

4. Outline briefly the history of California.

5. Discuss the compromise of 1850.

6. What was Washington's policy in foreign affairs? How has it affected the foreign policy of America?

7. What is meant by the Monroe Doctrine?

American Institutions

Select any five

1. Compare the form of government of the United States with that of Japan in regard to similarities and differences. Point out the strength and weakness of each.

2. In instructing Japanese children in their relation to American institutions what point would you consider most needful of emphasis?

3. What weaknesses in the Articles of Confederation were remedied by the Constitution?

4. Why is it essential that a teacher should be familiar with the institutions of the country in which he resides? Illustrate.

5. Discuss briefly four of the causes for deportation of an immigrant.

6. Name four political parties in the United States. Tell what the leading principles of each are.

7. What can you, as an individual, do to secure better housing conditions? What can you do as a teacher?

Source: Report on the Japanese Language School, prepared for the Japanese Association of America by S. Kitasawa. Reel 762. JMFA/LC. There were regional variations on the test in each site. This seems to be the San Francisco examination.

Notes

Preface

1. Min Yasui's experience of attending the Hood River Japanese Language School was obtained from personal communications with Homer Yasui, M.D., July 11, 12, 2002.

2. Reverend Isaac Inouye went to a Methodist seminary in Kōbe, Japan before coming to America. He earned his A.B. and M.A. at Emory University. He also earned his M.R.E. at Boston University and his M.A. in education at Harvard University. See Linda Tamura, *The Hood River Issei: An Oral History of Japanese Settlers in Oregon's Hood River Valley* (Urbana: University of Illinois Press, 1993), 304.

3. Personal communications with Homer Yasui, M.D., July 11, 12, 2002.

4. Peter Irons, *Justice at War: The Story of the Japanese American Internment Cases* (Berkeley: University of California Press, 1983), vii.

5. Irons, *Justice Delayed: The Record of the Japanese American Internment Cases* (Middletown, CT: Wesleyan University Press, 1989), 74.

6. Irons, *Justice Delayed*, 60.

7. Ibid., 39. The interior quote is by Gordon Hirabayashi.

8. Yoshihide Matsubayashi, "The Japanese Language Schools in Hawaii and California from 1892 to 1941" (Ph.D. diss., University of San Francisco, 1984).

9. Ann L. Halsted, "Sharpened Tongues: The Controversy Over the 'Americanization' of Japanese Language Schools in Hawaii, 1919–1927" (Ph.D. diss., Stanford University, 1989).

10. Mariko Takagi, "Moral Education in Pre-War Japanese Language Schools in Hawaii" (master's thesis, University of Hawaiʻi, 1987).

11. Eileen H. Tamura, *Americanization, Acculturation, and Ethnic Identity: The Nisei Generation in Hawaii* (Urbana: University of Illinois Press, 1994).

12. Yukuji Okita, *Hawai Nikkei Imin no Kyōikushi* [Educational history of Japanese immigrants in Hawaii] (Tokyo: Minerva, 1997).

13. Toyotomi Morimoto, *Japanese Americans and Cultural Continuity: Maintaining Language and Heritage* (New York: Garland Publishing, 1997).

14. Teruko Kumei, "Nichibei 'Shinkō no Rensa': America no Nisei Kyōiku to Gaimushō" [America and Japan's "chain of relationship": Nisei education in America and the Japanese foreign ministry], in *"Zaigai Shitei" Kyōiku no Kitei Yōin to Ibunkakan Kyōiku ni kansuru Kenkyū* [A study of stipulation factors for the education of "Japanese children overseas" and and crosscultural education], ed. Masaru Kojima (n.p., 2000), 39–54.

15. Kumei, "'The Twain Shall Meet' in the Nisei?: Japanese Language Education and U.S.-Japan Relations, 1900–1940," in *New Worlds, New Lives: Globalization and People of Japanese Descent in the Americas and from Latin America in Japan*, eds. Lane Ryo Hirabayashi, Akemi Kikumura-Yano, and James A. Hirabayashi (Stanford: Stanford University Press, 2002), 108–125.

16. Yoon K. Pak, *Wherever I Go, I Will Always Be a Loyal American: Schooling Seattle's Japanese Americans during World War II* (New York: RoutledgeFalmer, 2002). Several dissertations explore the schools inside the concentration camps where 120,000 Japanese Americans from the West Coast were sent, including a few by former War Relocation Authority teachers and principals. Thomas James' 1987 monograph devotes some attention to schools in the Tule Lake Segregation Center, but he pays little attention to the Japanese language schools there or in the other concentration camps. Thomas James, *Exile within the Schooling of Japanese Americans, 1942–1945* (Cambridge, MA: Harvard University Press, 1987).

17. Yuji Ichioka, "A Historian by Happenstance," *Amerasia Journal* 26 (2000): 47.

1: Immigration, Education, and Diplomacy

Epigraph: Takie Okumura, *Seventy Years of Divine Blessings* (Honolulu: n.p., 1940), 35–36.

1. Gary Y. Okihiro, *Cane Fires: The Anti-Japanese Movement in Hawaii, 1865–1945* (Philadelphia: Temple University Press, 1991), 21.

2. Eileen H. Tamura, *Americanization, Acculturation, and Ethnic Identity: The Nisei Generation in Hawaii* (Urbana: University of Illinois Press, 1994), 11; Yuji Ichioka, *The Issei: The World of the First Generation Japanese Immigrants, 1885–1924* (New York: Free Press, 1988), 41; Okihiro, Cane Fires, 23–25.

3. Ichioka, *Issei*, 40–45.

4. Tamura, *Americanization*, 11.

5. Ichioka, *Issei*, 12.

6. Okihiro, *Cane Fires*, 59.

7. Ichioka, *Issei*, 51–57.

8. Hawaii's Japanese migration was made possible by the United States' annexation of Hawaii in 1898, and also by the 1900 Organic Act.

9. Gijo Ozawa, *Hawai Nihongo Gakkō Kyōikushi* [Educational history of Japanese language schools in Hawaii] (Honolulu: Hawai Kyōiku Kai, 1972), 14.

10. Fusa Nakagawa, *Tosa kara Hawai e* [From Tosa to Hawaii] (Kochi, Japan: Committee of Okumura Takie to Hawai Nikkei Iminten, 2000), 75.

11. Reverend Shigefusa Kanda was born in Kyoto in 1872. After graduating from Dōshisha University, he followed Reverend Sidney L. Gulick's advice to come to Hawaii in 1893. Yukuji Okita, *Hawai Nikkei Imin no Kyōikushi: Nichibei Bunka, Sono Deai to Sōkoku* [History of Japanese immigrant education in Hawaii: Encounter and conflict of Japanese and American culture] (Tokyo: Minerva Shobo, 1997), 133. Rev-

erend Kanda's school was later closed when he moved to Maui. Nakagawa, *Tosa kara Hawai e*, 78.

12. Takie Okumura was born in 1865 in Kōchi prefecture. He visited Hawaii in 1894 once, and settled there in 1896. Ozawa, *Hawai Nihongo Gakkō Kyōikushi*, 21; Okita, *Hawai Nikkei Imin*, 104.

13. The definition of a *terakoya* is from Ronald P. Dore, *Education in Tokugawa Japan* (Berkeley: University of California Press, 1965), 252; also see Richard Rubinger, *Private Academies of Tokugawa Japan* (Princeton, NJ: Princeton University Press, 1982); Okumura, *Taiheiyō no Rakuen* [Paradise in the Pacific] (n.d., n.p.), 217.

14. Ozawa, *Hawai Nihongo Gakkō Kyōikushi*, 21.

15. The report of the Federal Survey on Education described the "Japanese Imperial Rescript on Education" as "epitomizing Japanese morals." The U.S. Department of the Interior, Bureau of Education, *A Survey of Education in Hawaii*, Bulletin 1920, no. 16 (Washington, D.C.: GPO, 1920), 121. The 1916 Japanese Consular Guidebook instructed local consulates to provide a copy of the "Japanese Imperial Rescript on Education" upon request from Japanese language school officials. Japanese Foreign Ministry, *Ryōjikan Shitsumu Sankōsho* [Consular guidebook] (Tokyo: Japanese Foreign Ministry, 1916), 557. Copy in the Diplomatic Record Office, Tokyo (hereafter DRO).

16. Hawaii Education Association, *Hawai Nihongo Kyōikushi* [History of Japanese education in Hawaii] (Honolulu: Hawaii Education Association, 1937), 5.

17. Yemyō Imamura, *Hawai Kaikyōshi* [History of missionary work in Hawaii] (Honolulu: Honpa Hongwanji, 1918), 46.

18. Honpa Hongwanji, *Honpa Hongwanji Hawai Kaikyō 35-nen Kiyo* [Thirty-fifth bulletin of the Honpa Hongwanji Mission in Hawaii] (Honolulu: Honpa Hongwanji, 1931), 14; Imamura, *Hawai Kaikyōshi*, 46.

19. Sadanobu Washimi, "Hawai Jōdoshū to Nihongo Gakkō" [Hawaii Jōdoshū and Japanese language schools], in *Bukkyō Kyōka Kenkyū* [Study of Buddhist teachings], ed. Committee of Celebrating Mizutani Kōshō's Seventieth Birthday (Kyoto: Shimonkaku, 1998), 489.

20. In the early 1900s, 1.3 pounds of coffee cost 50 cents. Ozawa, *Hawai Nihongo Gakkō Kyōikushi*, 50.

21. Ozawa, *Hawai Nihongo Gakkō Kyōikushi*, 79.

22. Oftentimes, a school had already decided who it wanted to recruit. This tedious process became an official procedure.

23. Okumura, *Taiheiyō no Rakuen*, 222–223.

24. A passport belonging to Tomisaburō Makino, one of the *gannenmono*, contained the line, "Never convert to another religion," showing that the centuries-old custom of prohibiting Christianity continued into the first wave of immigration. Publication Committee of "A History of Japanese Immigrants in Hawaii," *Hawaii Nihonjin Iminshi* [A history of Japanese immigration in Hawaii] (Honolulu: United Japanese Society of Hawaii, 1964), 226.

25. Imamura, *Hawai Kaikyōshi*, 26–27, 29.

26. Chie Honda, "Dai Niji Sekai Taisen-zen no Hawai ni okeru Jōdoshinshū Honpa Honganji no Nihongo Gakkō" [Jōdoshinshū Honpa Hongwanji's Japanese language schools in Hawaii before World War II], in *America no Nikkeijin—Toshi, Shakai, Seikatsu* [Nikkei in America—Cities, society, life], ed. Toshio Yanagida (Tokyo: Dōbunkan, 1995), 193.

27. Imamura, *Hawai Kaikyōshi*, 42.

28. Ozawa, *Hawai Nihongo Gakkō Kyōikushi*, 31–35.

29. Roger Daniels, *The Politics of Prejudice: The Anti-Japanese Movement in California and the Struggle for Japanese Exclusion* (Berkeley: University of California Press, 1962), 50.

30. Hawaii Education Association, *Hawai Nihongo Kyōikushi*, 6.

31. The Monbushō sent the secretary of Education Minister Mosuke Matsumura to inspect Hawaii's situation. He was in the United States at that time on government business and stopped in Hawaii on his way home. Okita, *Hawai Nikkei Imin*, 107–108.

32. Okita, *Hawai Nikkei Imin*, 108–111.

33. Okihiro, *Cane Fires*, 43–44.

34. See Tomoe Moriya, "Amerika Bukkyō no Tanjō: Imamura Yemyō Ron" [The birth of Americanized Buddhism: A historical study of acculturation of Japanese Buddhism with special reference to Bishop Yemyō Imamura] (Ph.D. diss., Meiji Gakuin University, 1999), 97, for her insightful analysis of Imamura's change in attitude toward Japanese strikes.

35. Louise H. Hunter, *Buddhism in Hawaii: Its Impact on a Yankee Community* (Honolulu: University of Hawai'i Press, 1971), 71.

36. Letter, Bishop Yemyō Imamura to Vice Foreign Minister Kikujirō Ishii, April 11, 1910, DRO 3.10.2.10–3.

37. Ozawa, *Hawai Nihongo Gakkō Kyōikushi*, 45.

38. *Hawai Shokumin Shinbun*, June 2, 1909; cited in Okita, *Hawai Nikkei Imin*, 113.

39. *Hawai Shokumin Shinbun*, August 20, 1909; cited in Okita, *Hawai Nikkei Imin*, 114. Kazutami Eguchi was a pseudonym for Sadajirō Okumura.

40. *Hawai Shokumin Shinbun*, September 16, 1910; cited in Okita, *Hawai Nikkei Imin*, 122–123.

41. The English pamphlet listed Imamura as the superintendent and Ryūsaku Tsunoda as the president of the school. Tsunoda later created the foundation of Japanese study at Columbia University. Moriya, "Amerika Bukkyō no Tanjō," 98.

42. Letter, Hongwanji Bishop Yemyō Imamura to Vice Foreign Minister Kikujirō Ishii, April 11, 1910, DRO 3.10.2.10–3. The request to recruit a principal for the Honolulu Junior High School was placed by the current Consul General Ueno. Letter, Consul General Senichi Ueno to Foreign Minister Jutarō Komura, March 18, 1910, DRO 3.10.2.10–3.

43. Letter, Ueno to Komura, July 25, 1911, DRO 3.10.2.1; *Nippū Jiji*, June 5, 1911.

44. Letter, Kealakekua Japanese Association, Kainaliu Office President Shigeo

Aoki, and School Director Yasuzō Itō to Foreign Minister Kaoru Hayashi and Education Minister Nobuaki Makino, July 12, 1906, DRO 3.10.2.10–3.

45. Publication Committee of "A History of Japanese Immigrants in Hawaii," *Hawaii Nihonjin Iminshi*, 234.

46. Letter, Hawaii Consul General Hisakichi Nagataki to Foreign Minister Nobuaki Makino, March 6, 1913, DRO 3.10.2.10.

47. Publication Committee of "A History of Japanese Immigrants in Hawaii," *Hawaii Nihonjin Iminshi*, 234.

48. Washimi, "Hawai Jōdoshu," 489.

49. Okita, "Maui Kyōiku-Kai no Chowa Seishin to Nihongo Gakkō" [Maui Teachers Association's harmonious spirit and Japanese language school], in *Hawai Nikkei Shakai no Bunka to sono Henyō* [Hawaii Nikkei Society's culture and transfiguration], ed., Okita (Kyoto: Nakanishiya Shuppan, 1998), 7.

50. Nikkei students accounted for 37 percent of Hawaii's 36,529 entire student population. There are no statistics as to what percent of Japanese American public school students also attended a Japanese language school in 1915. However, in 1920, of the 20,651 Japanese students enrolled in public schools, 20,196 (or 97.8 percent) went to a Japanese language school. Koichi G. Harada, "A Survey of the Japanese Language Schools in Hawaii" (master's thesis, University of Hawai'i, 1934), 102.

51. The teachers agreed that additional subjects could be offered as necessary, such as sewing, singing, physical education, and abacus-use. Hawaii Education Association, *Hawai Nihongo Kyōikushi*, 63–64.

52. Hawaii Education Association, *Hawai Nihongo Kyōikushi*, 62, 70, 76. In 1916, they wrote a new textbook series specifically designed for the educational needs of Hawaii's Nikkei children.

53. In 1915, there were 122 Japanese schools in Hawaii. Ozawa, *Hawai Nihongo Gakkō Kyōikushi*, 31–33, 49–50.

54. Imamura, *Hawai Kaikyōshi*, 54.

55. Ibid., 54–57.

56. Hongwanji Bishop Imamura successfully challenged their detention in 1920 after several court battles. Ozawa, *Hawai Nihongo Gakkō Kyōikushi*, 79.

57. Sidney L. Gulick, *Hawaii's American-Japanese Problem* (Honolulu: Honolulu Star-Bulletin, 1915), 5.

58. Daniels, *Politics*, 79.

59. Gulick, *The American Japanese Problem* (New York: Charles Scribner's Sons, 1914), 304.

60. Gulick, *Hawaii's American-Japanese*, 24–25.

61. Ibid., 20.

62. Gulick, *American Democracy and Asiatic Citizenship* (New York: Charles Scribner's Sons, 1918), 241.

63. Ibid., 241.

64. Gulick, *Hawaii's American-Japanese*, 40.

65. *Pacific Japanese Mission of the Methodist Episcopal Church (North) 26th Annual*

Session (1925), 71; cited in Brian Masaru Hayashi, *"For the Sake of Our Japanese Brethren": Assimilation, Nationalism, and Protestantism among the Japanese of Los Angeles, 1895–1942* (Stanford: Stanford University Press, 1995), 103.

66. Sandra C. Taylor, *Advocate of Understanding: Sidney Gulick and the Search for Peace with Japan* (Kent, OH: Kent State University Press, 1984), 22.

67. Letter, Education Minister Seitarō Sawayanagi to Vice Foreign Minister Sutemi Chinda. October 9, 1906, DRO 3.10.2.10–5; Teruko Kumei, "Nichibei 'Shinkō no Rensa': Amerika no Nisei Kyōiku to Gaimushō" [America and Japan's "chain of relationship": Nisei education in America and the Japanese foreign ministry], in *"Zaigai Shitei" Kyōiku no Kitei Yōin to Ibunkakan Kyōiku ni kansuru Kenkyū* [A study of stipulation factors for the education of "Japanese children overseas" and cross-cultural education], ed. Masaru Kojima (n.p., 2000), 40. The *Shōgakkō Rei* (Primary School Order) of 1886 was introduced when the Meiji government tried to adopt a Western education system. Under it, primary education consisted of two steps. The first stage, primary schools, required four years of mandatory schooling; the second tier provided an additional two years. Yoshihisa Godo and Yūjiro Hayami, "Accommodation of Education in Modern Economic Growth: A Comparison of Japan with the United States," http://www.adbi.org/PDF/wp/wp4/wp4.pdf Asian Development Bank. Accessed June 14, 2002.

68. The Japanese Foreign Ministry, *Ryōjikan Shitsumu Sankōsho* [Consular guidebook] (Tokyo: Japanese Foreign Ministry, 1916), 557.

69. According to Kumei, the Monbushō does not retain any records on what was the first educational policy for Japanese children overseas or how Sawayanagi's policy became policy. See her "Nichibei 'Shinkō no Rensa'" to understand the Monbushō's involvement with Nisei education from the 1930s until World War II.

70. Letter, Sawayanagi to Chinda, October 9, 1906, DRO 3.10.2.10–5; Kumei, "Nichibei 'Shinkō no Rensa,'" 40.

71. Letter, Sawayanagi to Chinda, March 5, 1908, DRO 3.10.2.31; Kumei, "Nichibei 'Shinkō no Rensa,'" 41.

72. Letter, Hōten Consul General Motoshirō Katō to Foreign Minister Kaoru Hayashi, October 30, 1907, DRO 3.10.2.31; letter, Vice Foreign Minister Sutemi Chinda to Sawayanagi, January 27, 1908, DRO 3.10.2.31.

73. Letter, Sawayanagi to Chinda, March 5, 1908, DRO 3.10.2.31.

74. Shintarō Satō, Secretary to the Foreign Minister, indicated that in 1937, the government provided ¥1,980,000 to Japanese schools overseas that year, with the exception of ones in America and Canada. Satō, "Kaigai Hōjin Gakkō no Genjō ni tsuite" [Conditions of Japanese schools overseas], *Teikoku Kyōiku* (August 1938): 23; Kumei, "Nichibei 'Shinkō no Rensa,'" 41.

75. Letter, Ueno to Foreign Minister Komura, September 14, 1909, DRO 3.10.2.31. Consuls general of New York and Chicago also responded that a government subsidy was unnecessary because there were few schools in their districts. San Francisco's and Seattle's reports were not found in the file; Kumei, "Nichibei 'Shinkō no Rensa,'" 41.

76. In 1922, Vice Foreign Minister Masanao Hanihara wrote Vice Minister of Education Takaichirō Akaji to explain that this 1906 educational policy had served as guidelines for consul generals to determine local educational problems. Letter, Hanihara to Akaji, July 17, 1922, DRO 3.10.2.54.

77. *Hawai Shokumin Shinbun*, October 18, 1911, cited in Okita, *Hawai Nikkei Imin*, 132.

78. Okita, *Hawai Nikkei Imin*, 133.

79. Ozawa, *Hawai Nihongo Gakkō Kyōikushi*, 65.

80. *Nippū Jiji*, August 7, 1916, cited in Okita, *Hawai Nikkei Imin*, 210.

81. Okita, *Hawai Nikkei Imin*, 210.

82. Hawaii Consul General Yada to Foreign Minister Uchida, September 28, 1920, DRO 3.8.2.288-14.

83. Uchida to Yada, October 8, 1920, DRO 3.8.2.288-14.

84. Yada to Uchida, October 31, 1920, DRO 3.8.2.288-14.

85. Uchida to Yada, November 9, 1920, DRO 3.8.2.288-14.

86. San Francisco Consul General Tamekichi Ōta to Uchida, February 11, 1919, DRO 3.10.2.54.

87. Ōta to Uchida, February 11, 1919, DRO 3.10.2.54.

88. *Hokubei Jiji*, February 13, 14, 1919.

89. Ibid. February 13, 14, 1919.

90. Ōta to Uchida, July 30, 1919, DRO 3.10.2.27.

91. At least no reply is on file at the Diplomatic Record Office of the Japanese Foreign Ministry.

92. Okita, *Hawai Nikkei Imin*, 171.

93. Ichioka, *Issei*, 204-206; Toyotomi Morimoto, *Japanese Americans and Cultural Continuity: Maintaining Language and Heritage* (New York: Garland, 1997), 40.

94. U.S. Congress, House, Committee on the Territories, *Proposed Amendments of the Organic Act of the Territory of Hawaii*, 66th Congress, 2nd session, *1920* (Washington, D.C.: GPO, 1920), 20.

2: Mandating Americanization

Epigraph: Letter, Claxton to Bunker, December 6, 1919, RG 12, Records of the Office of Education, Records of the Office of the Commissioner, Historical Files, 1870–1950. File 501: Local School Surveys. Box # 56, Folder: "Hawaii," National Archives at College Park, Maryland. Hereafter this file is referred to as the "Hawaii Survey File" or HSF.

1. *Territory of Hawaii Session Laws*, 1917, 509–510; quoted in Ann L. Halsted, "Sharpened Tongues: The Controversy Over the 'Americanization' of Japanese Language Schools in Hawaii, 1919-1927" (Ph.D. diss., Stanford University, 1989), 81–82. School surveys, which flourished from the late 1910s to the 1920s, were both an instrument of progressive educators and a reflection of the movement's values. As historian Diane Ravitch and others have demonstrated, progressive education was a

"complex series of related movements." One of the tenets of progressive education was to examine the whole educational environment surrounding a school using "objective" methods in order to discover the "facts" and offer recommendations for educators to "base action on evidence rather than on tradition or speculation." Surveys were supposed to bring local educational issues and facts into the public sphere. Diane Ravitch, *Left Back: A Century of Failed School Reforms* (New York: Simon & Schuster, 2000), 102–107.

2. The classic study on the Americanization movement is Edward G. Hartmann, *The Movement to Americanize the Immigrant* (New York: Columbia University Press, 1948). Eileen H. Tamura presents an insightful treatment relevant to Hawaii in her work, *Americanization, Acculturation, and Ethnic Identity: The Nisei Generation in Hawaii* (Urbana: University of Illinois Press, 1994), 55–57, passim.

3. Frank V. Thompson, *Schooling of the Immigrant* (New York: Harper & Brothers, 1920), 288–289. For more recent studies, see William G. Ross, *Forging New Freedoms: Nativism, Education, and the Constitution, 1917–1927* (Lincoln: University of Nebraska Press, 1994); Frederick C. Luebke, "Legal Restrictions on Foreign Languages in the Great Plains States, 1917–1923," in *Language in Conflict: Linguistic Acculturation on the Great Plains*, ed. Paul Schach (Lincoln: University of Nebraska Press, 1980), 1–19.

4. Hilary Conroy, *The Japanese Frontier in Hawaii, 1868–1898* (Berkeley: University of California Press, 1953); Gary Y. Okihiro, *Cane Fires: The Anti-Japanese Movement in Hawaii, 1865–1945* (Philadelphia: Temple University Press, 1991); Ronald Takaki, *Strangers from a Different Shore: A History of Asian Americans* (New York: Penguin, 1989).

5. Lawrence H. Fuchs, *Hawaii Pono: A Social History* (New York: Harcourt, Brace & World, 1961), 43.

6. Ibid., 21.

7. See chapter 5 of John E. Van Sant, *Pacific Pioneers: Japanese Journeys to America and Hawaii, 1850–80* (Urbana: University of Illinois Press, 2000).

8. Roger Daniels, *Asian America: Chinese and Japanese in the United States since 1850* (Seattle: University of Washington Press, 1988), 127; Tamura, *Americanization*, 58.

9. Tamura, *Americanization*, 30. Japanese traditionally met their marriage partner through relatives and acquaintances. Often the hard life and the cost of transportation to Japan discouraged Issei men to go home and find a wife; instead, they asked fellow villagers to find a suitable spouse for them.

10. Ibid., 146.

11. Louise H. Hunter, *Buddhism in Hawaii: Its Impact on a Yankee Community* (Honolulu: University of Hawai'i Press, 1971), 93.

12. Ibid., 96. From 1921 to 1930, Okumura and his son Umetarō conducted a campaign to Americanize the Japanese community in Hawaii. See Noriko Shimada, "Okumura Takie to Shibusawa Eiichi: Nichibei kara Mita Hawai ni okeru Hainichi Yobō Keihatsu Undō" [Takie Okumura and Eiichi Shibusawa: A movement to Amer-

icanize Japanese to prevent anti-Japanese sentiment in Hawaii from the perspective of Japan-U.S relations]; *Nihon Joshi Daigaku Kiyō* 43 (1994): 39–56.

13. See Daniels, *The Politics of Prejudice: The Anti-Japanese Movement in California and the Struggle for Japanese Exclusion* (Berkeley: University of California Press, 1962) on the anti-Japanese movement in California. See Akira Iriye, *Pacific Estrangement: Japanese and American Expansion, 1897–1911* (Cambridge, MA: Harvard University Press, 1972) on the colonial visions of the Pacific held by Japan and the United States.

14. The 20,651 also includes a small number of Japanese students who attended private schools in Hawaii. Kōichi G. Harada, "A Survey of the Japanese Language Schools in Hawaii" (master's thesis, University of Hawai'i, 1934), 102. The entire enrollment of the public schools was 41,350 students in 1920, and according to Tamura, 47 percent of those were Nisei students. Tamura, *Americanization*, 30.

15. Gijo Ozawa, *Hawai Nihongo Gakkō Kyōikushi* [Educational history of Japanese language schools in Hawaii] (Honolulu: Hawai Kyōiku Kai, 1972), 84. For more on the Imperial Rescript on Education, see Herbert Passin, *Society and Education in Japan* (New York: Teachers College Press, 1965), 226–228.

16. Tamura, *Americanization*, 96. Also see John E. Reinecke, *Language and Dialect in Hawaii: A Sociolinguistic History to 1935*, ed. Stanley M. Tsuzaki (Honolulu: University of Hawai'i Press, 1969).

17. Tamura, *Americanization*, 96.

18. Benjamin O. Wist, *A Century of Public Education in Hawaii* (Honolulu: Hawaii Educational Review, 1940), 161; Riley Allen, "Education and Race Problems in Hawaii," *American Review of Reviews* (Dec. 1921): 616; quoted in Tamura, *Americanization*, 108.

19. Tamura, *Americanization*, 107–108.

20. Fuchs, *Hawaii Pono*, 274.

21. Tamura, *Americanization*, 110. In response to these parents' complaints, the DPI experimentally introduced an English examination to enter Central Grammar School in Honolulu at the end of World War I, and the parents appealed to have more of such "English standard schools" in 1920. See Tamura, *Americanization*, 108–115, for more details of what was essentially student segregation by ethnicity.

22. Halsted, "Sharpened Tongues," 69.

23. Okihiro, *Cane Fires*, 130–131.

24. Judd was a lawyer who had served as a representative of the Hawaiian Sugar Planters' Association in its 1906 effort to secure Filipino laborers. He served in the Hawaiian Senate from 1911 to 1913, but he was not a legislator when he campaigned for the Japanese language measure. John William Siddall, *Men of Hawaii* (Honolulu: Honolulu Star-Bulletin, 1917), 155.

25. Judd's definition of "teachers" also included administrators in "all schools in the Territory," except "Sabbath" schools. *Honolulu Advertiser*, January 4, 1919. When the Judd bill was introduced, there was a rumor that Okumura's son, Umetarō had a close relationship with Judd, and that father and son were the source of the bill in order

to retaliate against Hongwanji schools. Hawaii Education Association, *Hawai Nihongo Kyōikushi* [History of Japanese education in Hawaii] (Honolulu: Hawaii Japanese Education Association, 1937), 168; Report from Hawaii, attached to telegram, Consul General Rokurō Moroi to Foreign Minister Yasuya Uchida, March 13, 1919. The Diplomatic Record Office (hereafter DRO), 3.10.2.1, Tokyo. Hunter, who studied Okumura's personal papers, did not find Okumura's direct involvement with the bill. She concluded, however, "his peripheral activities and his later 'projects' for Americanizing the local-born Japanese were motivated by the desire to liquidate Buddhism and all Buddhist institutions." Hunter, *Buddhism in Hawaii*, 113.

26. Halsted, "Sharpened Tongues," 93–95. A consular report from Hawaii on March 20, 1919 suggests that Andrews solicited a bribe from the Hawaii Japanese Education Association, but did not succeed. The anonymous author of the report assumed that this was the motive behind his bill, DRO 3.10.2.1.

27. Ozawa, *Hawai Nihongo Gakkō*, 97–106.

28. Reinecke, *Feigned Necessity: Hawaii's Attempt to Obtain Chinese Contract Labor, 1921–1923* (San Francisco: Chinese Materials Center, 1979), 52. Secretary of State Robert Lansing sent a cablegram to the California legislature, requesting "no anti-Japanese action" in 1919. Daniels, *Politics*, 82.

29. *Honolulu Star-Bulletin*, April 30, 1919; cited in Yoshihide Matsubayashi, "The Japanese Language Schools in Hawaii and California from 1892 to 1941" (Ph.D. diss., University of San Francisco, 1984), 111.

30. Letter, Penhallow to Lane, June 10, 1914, HSF. The College of Hawaii later became the University of Hawai'i.

31. Letter, Claxton to Penhallow, June 30, 1914, HSF.

32. Letter, Weaver to Claxton, August 28, 1916, HSF.

33. Letter, College Club to the Governor of the Territory of Hawaii, Superintendent of Public Instruction, and Commission of Public Instruction, November 15, 1916, copy sent by Weaver to Claxton, HSF.

34. Reinecke, *Language*, 80–81. According to Reinecke, the percentage of teachers of Portuguese and Spanish ethnicity combined was 8.5 percent, while the percentages of Chinese, Japanese, and Korean teachers were 4.7 percent, 2.0 percent, and 0.2 percent, respectively. The number of students with Portuguese, Spanish, Chinese, Japanese, and Korean ethnic backgrounds were tabulated from the Department of Public Instruction's *Biennial Report 1923–24*, 113.

35. Letter, College Club to the Governor of the Territory of Hawaii, Superintendent of Public Instruction, and Commission of Public Instruction, November 15, 1916, copy sent by Weaver to Claxton, HSF.

36. Letter, Weaver to Claxton, December 18, 1916, HSF.

37. Edgar Wood was the Superintendent of the Normal Schools from 1897 to 1921. Tamura, *Americanization*, 198.

38. Letter, Weaver to Claxton, December 18, 1916, HSF. After sending off the letter, Weaver immediately sent a cablegram as well as another letter to Claxton to

express her regret for being so personal, and asked Claxton to destroy her first letter. Letter, Weaver to Claxton, December 21, 1916, HSF. However, a public high school teacher (who happened to confer with one of the federal survey committee members, and was asked about the schools in Hawaii) also informed of similar problems in her letter to Claxton, writing, "so many of their principals and teachers are old, inefficient, [who] smoke cigarettes and live immoral lives." She also pointed out corruption among school administrators, such as positions given to friends. Letter, R. H. Wallin to Claxton, January 2, 1917, HSF.

39. Letter, Pinkham to Claxton, December 15, 1916, HSF.

40. Although Pinkham used the governor's official letterhead, Pinkham underlined the word "Personal" to emphasize it was not an official invitation. Letter, Pinkham to Claxton, March 8, 1917, HSF.

41. Letter, Pinkham to Claxton, March 8, 1917, HSF.

42. Pinkham had his stenographer transcribe their December 5, 1916 interview, and sent a copy to Claxton with his March 8, 1917 letter, HSF.

43. Letter, College Club to Claxton, May 8, 1917, HSF.

44. Letter, Kinney to Claxton, January 22, 1918, HSF. Claxton originally planned to send H. W. Fought, Bureau of Education Specialist in Rural School Practice, and Willis E. Johnson, President of Northern Normal and Industrial School, South Dakota, to undertake the survey in the fall of 1918.

45. Reinecke, *Feigned*, 621; Letter, McCarthy to Claxton, November 8, 1918, HSF.

46. Letter, Claxton to McCarthy, November 23, 1918, HSF.

47. Daniels, *Politics*, 81–83. California's exclusionists at this time were preoccupied with establishing a revised alien land law, and a Japanese language school was not on the agenda until the initiative vote for the 1920 alien land law passed in November 1920.

48. MacCaughey was born in Huron, South Dakota in 1887. He graduated from Cornell University and was a member of Four-Minute Man, American Defense League, and Chautauqua Institution Summer Schools. He was a Congregationalist and chairman of the Religious Education Committee at Central Union Church. Marquis Who's Who, *Who Was Who in America*, vol. 3 (Chicago: Marquis Who's Who, 1963), 540.

49. Letter, MacCaughey to Claxton, April 8, 1919, HSF. MacCaughey was appointed Superintendent of Public Instruction for the Territory of Hawaii by Governor McCarthy, and took office on April 1, 1919.

50. Letter, MacCaughey to Claxton, July 25, 1919, HSF.

51. Vaughan MacCaughey, "Some Outstanding Educational Problems of Hawaii," *School and Society* 9 (January 1919): 99–105. The illiteracy rate was based on the 1910 census.

52. MacCaughey, "Some Outstanding," 100–101.

53. *Hawai Hōchi*, July 12, 1920. Sugar planters ended their subsidies following the

resolution. Publication Committee of "A History of Japanese Immigrants in Hawaii," *Hawaii Nihonjin Iminshi* [A History of Japanese immigration in Hawaii] (Honolulu: United Japanese Society of Hawaii, 1964), 229.

54. Shortly after Kinney resigned, he expressed his opinion on Japanese language schools in the *Pacific Commercial Advertiser*, based on his investigation of these schools and examination of their textbooks during his term. Kinney reported that he found no evidence suggesting Buddhist language schools instilled emperor worship or contradicted Americanization. It was a groundless claim, continued Kinney, who found the schools were working to promote Americanism. He implied that this accusation against Japanese language schools stemmed from a minority religious denomination's efforts to damage the Japanese language schools run by a competing religious group. *Jiji Shinpō* (Tokyo), April 15, 1919. Kinney visited Japan several times and learned Japanese from a Buddhist priest and also sent his children to a Japanese language school. Hawaii Japanese Education Association, *Hawai Nihongo Kyōikushi*, 261–262. Hawkins, however, describes Kinney as being against Japanese schools. John N. Hawkins, "Politics, Education, and Language Policy: The Case of Japanese Language Schools in Hawaii," *Amerasia* 5 (1978): 47. A March 20, 1919 report by the Hawaii consulate reported a rumor that Kinney's unexpected resignation was forced because of his handling of the Japanese language school controversy, DRO 3.10.2.1.

55. Hunter, *Buddhism in Hawaii*, 108.

56. *Pacific Commercial Advertiser*, October 11, 1919.

57. Letter, Bunker to Claxton, November 20, 1919, HSF.

58. Letter, MacCaughey to Claxton, September 4, 1919, HSF.

59. Letter, Bunker to Claxton, October 13, 1919, HSF.

60. Letter, Bunker to Claxton, October 14, 1919, HSF; letter, Bunker to Claxton, October 28, 1919, HSF.

61. Letter, Bunker to Claxton, October 28, 1919, HSF; and letter, Bunker to Claxton, November 20, 1919, HSF.

62. Bunker recommended Twiss. Letter, Bunker to Claxton, October 30, 1919, HSF.

63. Letter, Bunker to Claxton, November 20, 1919, HSF.

64. MacCaughey was the president of the Ad Club from 1919 to 1921. Marquis Who's Who, *Who Was Who*, 540; letter, Hawaii Consul General Chōnosuke Yada to Foreign Minister Uchida, October 6, 1920, DRO 3.8.2.288–14.

65. *Pacific Commercial Advertiser*, November 6, 1919. Trent, who was a president of Honolulu's white YMCA and was considered to be a friend of the Japanese community, told a Japanese friend of his that the Japanese language school problem could cause problems for Hawaii's chances of achieving statehood, and he volunteered to present white opinion to the Japanese community. Letter, Acting Consul General Eiichi Furuya to Foreign Minister Uchida, November 7, 1919, DRO 3.8.2.288–14. Also see Nobuhiro Adachi, *Linguistic Americanization of Japanese-Americans in Hawaii* (Ōsaka: Ōsaka Kyōiku Tosho, 1998), 40–43, for Hawaii elites' perspectives on statehood.

66. *Maui News*, November 7, 1919.

67. Palmer's "congregation at the Central Union Church included many of Hawaii's leading capitalists." During the 1920 strike, Palmer also preached a sermon to present a plan for ending the strike. Reinecke, *Feigned*, 110.

68. *Pacific Commercial Advertiser*, November 10, 1919.

69. *Hawaii Educational Review* (February 1920): 22–23.

70. Okihiro, *Cane Fires*, 67. Fred Kinzaburo Makino was born in Yokohama in 1877, and came to Hawaii in 1899 to help his brother's business. During the 1909 sugar plantation strike, Makino was jailed for being a leader of the higher-wage movement. This experience made Makino realize the need for a Japanese newspaper, which he started in 1912 as the *Hawai Hōchi*. Compilation of Committee for the Publication of Kinzaburō Makiko's Biography, *Life of Kinzaburō Makino* (Honolulu: Hawai Hōchi, 1965), 18–19; Masayo Umezawa Duus, *The Japanese Conspiracy: The Oahu Sugar Strike of 1920* (Berkeley: University of California, 1999), 101–103.

71. *Honolulu Star Bulletin*, November 7, 1919.

72. *Pacific Commercial Advertiser*, November 7, 10, 1919.

73. *Pacific Commercial Advertiser*, November 7, 1919. Born in 1873, after graduating from the English Law School in Tokyo, Sōga came to Hawaii in 1896, and began his career at the *Yamato Shinbun* (which changed its name to *Nippū Jiji*) as editor and later president. In the 1909 plantation strike, Sōga was jailed with Makino for supporting laborers, but he later associated more with elites in the Japanese immigrant community. Duus, *Japanese Conspiracy*, 102–103.

74. *Pacific Commercial Advertiser*, November 6, 1919.

75. Letter, Claxton to Bunker, December 6, 1919, HSF.

76. Charles L. Lewis, *Philander Priestley Claxton* (Knoxville: University of Tennessee Press, 1948), 191, 207; Luebke, "Legal Restrictions," 6.

77. Confidential Memorandum, ONI Section B [Intelligence] to State, MID, Interior (Education), Operations, August 20, 1919, HSF.

78. Okihiro, *Cane Fires*, 102–103. This was despite the fact that Japan was allied with the United States during World War I.

79. Ibid., 131, 295.

80. Confidential Memorandum, ONI Section B [Intelligence] to State Department, MID, Interior (Education), Operations, August 20, 1919, HSF. In *Taiheiyō no Rakuen*, Okumura was very critical of the Japanese who resisted the various language-school control bills, and wrote in August 1919 (but not published until later) that:

"The movement of the anti-school control law, conducting throughout the Islands and working at the legislature, ended with success. It was a big celebration, giving letters of thanks to the leaders of the association and parties for the teachers to thank for their efforts. However, it is wondered if this movement actually hindered the Japanese future and our relationship with America. . . . If the Americanization of the Japanese in Hawaii is the key to our success for the future, the movement against the school control bill is considered to have destroyed the foundation of our success." (Translation by the author)

Okumura's solution to the school control bill would have been to place these schools under government supervision and sever ties with religious organizations. Takie Okumura, *Taiheiyō no Rakuen* [Paradise in the Pacific] (n.d., n.p.), 276–277.

81. Office of Naval Intelligence (Washington, D.C.) to State Department, Operations, and Military Intelligence Division, August 14, 1918, RG 165 MID, National Archives File No. 1052–37/1; see also Okihiro, *Cane Fires*, 102–105.

82. This bill was probably the so-called Lyman's bill. C. J. McCarthy to Secretary of Interior, January 31, 1921, File of the Governors, McCarthy, General Files, U.S. Department, Interior Department, Re: Japanese Language Schools. Cited in Okihiro, *Cane Fires*, 108. Although appointed by the President, Hawaii's governor reported to the Secretary of the Interior. Fuchs, *Hawaii Pono*, 184.

83. Letter, Sidney Gulick to Claxton, November 13, 1919, HSF.

84. Letter, Gulick to Claxton, November 13, 1919, HSF. Sidney L. Gulick, *Hawaii's American-Japanese Problem* (Honolulu: Honolulu Star-Bulletin, 1915), 20. Gulick's idea of controlling Japanese language schools in 1918, which was based on his observation of Hawaii's Japanese situation in 1915, was identical to the one that Judd proposed later in 1919. Judd was in a personal contact with Gulick. After Judd's proposal was tabled, he wrote Gulick that he was concerned as to how American "children of Japanese blood" became a "great danger to the nation." Judd continued that they were being "trained by their parents in Hawaii in the idea that they are subjects of the Mikado." Letter, A. F. Judd to Gulick, October 14, 1919, Houghton Library, Harvard University, Gulick Papers.

85. Letter, Bunker to Claxton, December 23, 1919, HSF.

86. Ibid.

87. McCarthy's speech was reprinted in the *Pacific Commercial Advertiser*, December 29, 1919.

88. Letter, Bunker to Claxton, December 23, 1919, HSF.

89. The "Big Five" were C. Brewer & Co. Ltd., Castle & Cook Ltd., American Factors Ltd., Alexander & Baldwin, Ltd., and Theo. H. Davies & Company Ltd. Fuchs, *Hawaii Pono*, 22, 244–245.

90. Ibid., 186–187.

91. This hearing was about a proposal to rescind the Chinese Exclusion Act of 1882, and to recruit Chinese to alleviate Hawaii's labor shortage. McCarthy went to Washington, D.C. and attended the hearing on February 29, 1920. This probably was McCarthy's trip to the national capital that Bunker mentioned to Claxton.

92. U.S. Congress, Senate, Subcommittee of the Committee on Immigration, *Japanese in Hawaii Hearings, 66th Congress, 2nd session, 1920* (Washington, D.C.: GPO, 1920), 31.

93. *Honolulu Advertiser*, August 6, 1918; cited in Hunter, *Buddhism in Hawaii*, 107.

94. Fuchs, *Hawaii Pono*, 187. Phelan proposed disallowing the children of "aliens ineligible to citizenship," that is, the children of Asian immigrants and residents, including the Nisei, to become citizens. Daniels, *Politics*, 88, 104; Okihiro, *Cane Fires*, 159.

95. Ozawa, *Hawai Nihongo Gakkō*, 99.

96. Okihiro, *Cane Fires*, 67.

97. U.S. Congress, Senate, Subcommittee of the Committee on Immigration, *Japanese in Hawaii Hearings*, 30.

98. Hawkins, "Politics, Education, and Language Policy," 46.

99. Gail Y. Miyasaki, "The Schooling of the Nisei in Hawaii," *Educational Perspectives* 20 (winter 1981): 21; Fuchs, *Hawaii Pono*, 266.

100. U.S. Congress, House, Committee on Immigration and Naturalization, *Japanese Immigration Hearings, 66th Congress, 2nd session, 1921* (Washington, D.C.: GPO, 1921; reprint, New York: Arno Press, 1978), 811.

101. Telegram, Bunker to MacCaughey, May 28, 1920, HSF.

102. Halsted, "Sharpened Tongues," 82.

103. Bunker also wrote chapters one and two. The fourth and fifth chapters were written by Kemp, while the sixth and eighth were produced by Twiss, and Kolbe was in charge of chapter seven. Letter, Bunker to Claxton, November 20, 1919, HSF. For fuller analyses of the report, see: Tamura, *Americanization*, 199; Fuchs, *Hawaii Pono*, 270–273; Wist, *A Century of Public Education*.

104. U.S. Department of the Interior, Bureau of Education, *A Survey of Education in Hawaii*, Bulletin 1920, no. 16. (Washington, D.C.: GPO), 109.

105. Okumura, *Seventy Years of Divine Blessings* (Honolulu: n.p., 1940), 41.

106. U.S. Department of the Interior, *A Survey of Education*, 111.

107. Ibid., 114.

108. Okumura, *Taiheiyō no Rakuen*, 259.

109. The report indicated the Hawaii Japanese Education Association was established in 1914, but it was the preparation to organize the association. U.S. Department of the Interior, *A Survey of Education*, 114–115.

110. This was at the first Hawaii Japanese Education Association meeting on February 23, 1915. Hawaii Japanese Education Association, *Hawai Nihongo Kyōikushi*, 22–23.

111. U.S. Department of the Interior, *A Survey of Education*, 115.

112. Ibid., 118–119.

113. Ibid., 116.

114. Ibid., 125–133.

115. Ibid., 134–137.

116. Ibid., 134.

117. Ibid., 139–142.

118. Ibid., 142.

119. Lorrin A. Thurston, *The Foreign Language School Question: An Address to the Honolulu Social Science Association, November 8, 1920* (Honolulu: n.p., 1920), 17.

120. Hunter, *Buddhism in Hawaii*, 127.

121. Halsted, "Sharpened Tongues," 95–97.

122. A companion law, Act 36, specified criteria for non-English language

schoolteachers to obtain certificates from the DPI through exams on English and American ideals. Halsted, "Sharpened Tongues," 98.

3: Closing a Loophole

Epigraph: Cited in U.S. Congress, House, Committee on Immigration and Naturalization, *Japanese Immigration Hearings, 66th Congress, 2nd session, 1921* (Washington, D.C.: GPO, 1921; reprint, New York: Arno Press, 1978), 237. *Epigraph:* U.S. Congress, *Japanese Immigration,* 543.

1. Roger Daniels, *Asian America: Chinese and Japanese in the United States since 1850* (Seattle: University of Washington Press, 1988), 63, 115.

2. Daniels, *The Politics of Prejudice: The Anti-Japanese Movement in California and the Struggle for Japanese Exclusion* (Berkeley: University of California Press, 1962), 82.

3. Daniels, *Politics,* 68.

4. Ibid., 91.

5. This was a part of Reverend Paul B. Waterhouse's testimony at the 1920 Congressional Hearings on Japanese immigration in California. U.S. Congress, *Japanese Immigration,* 983.

6. Nisei were most frequently employed in jobs dealing with their Japanese American communities since the dominant society closed opportunities for their career advancement. On this transition, see Yuji Ichioka, *The Issei: The World of the First Generation Japanese Immigrants, 1885–1924* (New York: Free Press, 1988); and David K. Yoo, *Growing Up Nisei: Race, Generation, and Culture among Japanese Americans of California, 1924–49* (Urbana: University of Illinois Press, 2000).

7. *Rafu Shinpō,* August 19, 1920.

8. Ibid., August 19, 1920.

9. Ibid., August 13, 1920.

10. Ibid., August 19, 1920.

11. Ken Ishikawa, *Beikoku Kashū Nihongo Gakuen ni kansuru Kenkyū* [A study of Japanese language institutes in California] (n.p., 1923), 12.

12. Reginald Bell, *Public School Education of Second-Generation Japanese in California* (Stanford: Stanford University Press, 1935; reprint, New York: Arno Press, 1978), 22.

13. Keizō Sano also was a member of the Japanese Presbyterian Church of San Francisco. Ryō Yoshida, *Amerika Nihonjin Imin to Kirisutokyō Shakai* [Japanese immigrants in America and Christian society] (Tokyo: Nihon Tosho Center, 1995), 201.

14. Shinichi Katō, *Beikoku Nikkeijin Hyakunenshi* [A history of one hundred years of the Japanese and Japanese Americans in the United States] (Tokyo: Shin Nichibei Shinbun Sha, 1961), 115–116. For the locations of the schools, see the Sacramento Japan Town map in Wayne Maeda's *Changing Dreams and Treasured Memories: A Story of Japanese Americans in the Sacramento Region* (Sacramento: Sacramento Japanese American Citizens League, 2000), 270; and a map of San Francisco Japan Town in

Sandra C. Taylor, *Jewel of the Desert: Japanese American Internment at Topaz* (Berkeley: University of California Press, 1993), 33.

15. Daniels, *Politics,* 34, 40. Although most of the Japanese parents refused to send their children to the Oriental School, two Japanese children showed up at the school. Later, one of them stopped attending after meeting with San Francisco Consul General Ueno. Charles Wollenberg, *All Deliberate Speed: Segregation and Exclusion in California Schools, 1855–1975* (Berkeley: University of California Press, 1976), 54, 61; Japanese Foreign Ministry, *Nihon Gaikō Bunsho: Taibei Imin Mondai Keika Gaiyō* [Documents on Japanese foreign policy: A summary of the development of the Japanese immigration question in the United States] (Tokyo: Japanese Foreign Ministry, 1933; reprint, Tokyo: Japanese Foreign Ministry, 1972), 156.

A Canadian report revealed that the Hawaiian Sugar Planters' Association secretly supported the League in order to stop the hemorrhage of Issei plantation workers who were leaving the Islands in droves for better working conditions in California. W. L. MacKenzie King, *Report of the Royal Commission Appointed to Inquire into the Methods by Which Oriental Laborers Have Been Induced to Come to Canada* (Ottawa: Government Printing Bureau, 1908), 54; T. Iyenaga and Kenoske Satō, *Japan and the California Problem* (New York: G. P. Putnam, 1921), 72. Between 1905 and 1916, of the 62,647 Japanese who migrated to Hawaii, 28,068 Japanese (44.8 percent) left for the West Coast, and 30,119 Japanese (48.1 percent) returned home. Gary Y. Okihiro, *Cane Fires: The Anti-Japanese Movement in Hawaii, 1865–1945* (Philadelphia: Temple University Press, 1991), 36.

16. Katō, *Beikoku Nikkeijin,* 116.

17. Ishikawa, *Beikoku Kashū Nihongo Gakuen,* 63.

18. Suzuki was the principal of the Kinmon Gakuen from 1911 to 1930. Hokka Nihongo Gakuen Kyōkai, eds., *Beikoku Kashū Nihongo Gakuen Enkakushi* [A brief history of the Japanese language schools in California] (San Francisco: Hokka Nihongo Gakuen Kyōkai, 1930), 6.

19. Ichioka, *Issei,* 197–200.

20. Ibid., *Issei,* 197–203.

21. The survey appeared in *Sangyō Gō* (San Francisco: Nichibei Shinbunsha, 1918); cited in Ishikawa, *Beikoku Kashū Nihongo Gakuen,* 24.

22. Tomitarō Karasawa, *Kyōkasho no Rekishi* [History of textbooks] (Tokyo: Gyōsei, 1989), 9, 19.

23. Masakazu Iwata, *Planted in Good Soil: A History of the Issei in United States Agriculture* (New York: Peter Lang, 1992), 393–394.

24. According to John Modell, "Los Angeles was almost without agitators," during the 1913 peak of Japanese agricultural development. See his *The Economics and Politics of Racial Accommodation: The Japanese of Los Angeles, 1900–1942* (Urbana: University of Illinois, 1977), 38.

25. This teachers' association later developed into a more centralized organization, the *Nanka Nihongo Gakuen Kyōkai* (Southern California Japanese Language Insti-

tute Association) in 1925. Japanese Chamber of Commerce of Southern California, *Japanese in Southern California: A History of 70 Years* (Los Angeles: Japanese Chamber of Commerce of Southern California, 1960), 286. See Tamiko Tanaka, "The Japanese Language School in Relation to Assimilation" (master's thesis, University of Southern California, 1935) for the Southern California Japanese language schools' development in 1930s.

26. *Rafu Shinpō*, October 3, 1919.

27. Hokka Nihongo Gakuen Kyōkai, *Beikoku Kashū Nihongo*, 86, 91, 98.

28. James M. Inman, *Forum* 65 (January 1921): 1–8; *Rafu Shinpō*, May 22, June 25, 1920.

29. Daniels, *Politics*, 84–85.

30. *Rafu Shinpō*, June 25, 1920; Inman, *Forum;* Daniels, *Asian America*, 146.

31. State Board of Control of California, *California and the Oriental: Japanese, Chinese, and Hindus* (Sacramento: California State Printing Office, 1920).

32. Daniels, *Politics*, 88.

33. State Board of Control of California, *California and the Oriental*, 11.

34. In the 1919 annual meeting of the Japanese Teachers Association of America, it was reported that Japanese students in Isleton were not allowed to attend public schools where Japanese children below the fifth grade were sent to a segregated school. At the public school, nine Japanese students and four Chinese students attended with nine white children. At the segregated school, there were twenty-seven Japanese and seven Chinese students. However, by the time of the annual meeting, all of the Japanese students from the first to eighth grades had been segregated. Hokka Nihongo Gakuen Kyōkai, *Beikoku Kashū Nihongo*, 88.

35. State Board of Control of California, *California and the Oriental*, 11–12.

36. Ibid., 197.

37. *Rafu Shinpō*, June 27, 1920.

38. *Grizzly Bear*, June 1925, 13; Daniels, *Politics*, 91.

39. Daniels, *Politics*, 82.

40. U.S. Congress, *Japanese Immigration*, 281. The Japanese Association of America disseminated a pamphlet explaining the procedures for expatriation in 1922, but its complicated procedures and costs helped dissuade most Issei parents from completing applications for their children. Ichioka, *Issei*, 204–206; Toyotomi Morimoto, *Japanese Americans and Cultural Continuity: Maintaining Language and Heritage* (New York: Garland, 1997), 40. Issei parents may also have ignored the procedure if they never planned to return to Japan.

41. U.S. Congress, *Japanese Immigration*, 338–339. The date of the *Ōfu Nippō* article was February 4, 1920.

42. U.S. Congress, *Japanese Immigration*, 281.

43. Ibid., 281–283. *A Survey of Education in Hawaii* by the U.S. Bureau of Education was published in June 1920. See chapter 2.

44. U.S. Congress, *Japanese Immigration*, 282–283.

45. Ibid., 229.

46. *Rafu Shinpō*, August 18, 1920. *Ōfu Nippō*, July 15, 16, 1920.

47. Letter, Sidney L. Gulick to Albert Johnson, June 29, 1920. Records of the United States House of Representatives, 66th Congress, Committee on Immigration and Naturalization, Folder: H.R. 66A-F18.3, Box 492, National Archives.

48. Japanese Foreign Ministry, *Nihon Gaikō Bunsho: Taibei Imin Mondai Keika Gaiyō*, 623-630.

49. Japanese Foreign Ministry, *Nihon Gaikō Bunsho: Taibei Imin Mondai Keika Gaiyō Fuzokusho* [Documents on Japanese foreign policy: Documents accompanying a summary of the development of the Japanese immigration question in the United States] (Tokyo: Japanese Foreign Ministry, 1973), 613-614.

50. Ibid., 618-619.

51. Daniels, *Politics*, 91.

52. *Grizzly Bear*, October 1920, 24.

53. Daniels, *Politics*, 85.

54. *Grizzly Bear*, October 1920, 2.

55. Ibid., August 1920, 21.

56. Ibid., October 1920, 2.

57. Ibid., June 1920, 4-5.

58. Ibid., November 1920, 1-2.

59. Another similar novel was Peter B. Kyne's *The Pride of Palomar*, which also was serialized nationally in 1920 and published as a book in 1921. Daniels, *Politics*, 92; Carey McWilliams, *Prejudice, Japanese-Americans: Symbol of Racial Intolerance* (Boston: Little, Brown and Co., 1944), 60-61.

60. Letter, Consul General Shichitarō Yada to Foreign Minister Yasuya Uchida, February 1, 1921, DRO, 3.8.2.339-1.

61. Wallace Irwin, *Seed of the Sun* (New York: George H. Doran Co., 1921), 114-117.

62. Ibid., 116.

63. Daniels, *Politics*, 90.

64. *Nichibei*, October 12, 1920.

65. U.S. Congress, *Japanese Immigration*, 979-982.

66. Letter, Paul B. Waterhouse to Albert Johnson, January 28, 1921. Folder: H.R. 66A-F18.3. Committee on Immigration and Naturalization. Records of the United States House of Representatives, 66th Congress, Record Group 233, National Archives Building, Washington, D.C.

67. U.S. Congress, *Japanese Immigration*, 541-543.

68. The number of Nikkei students attending California public schools was taken from Department of Commerce, Bureau of Census, *Fourteenth Census of the United States Taken in the Year 1920*, vol. 2, *Population* (Washington D.C.: Bureau of Census, 1922), 1054. Thus the percentage (42 percent) indicating the ratio of the number of students who went to Japanese language schools compared with the large

number of Nikkei students who attended California's public schools is very approximate, especially as the former statistic came from a 1923 survey and the latter is from the 1920 census. The former statistic also might include some kindergartners.

69. Ichioka, *Issei*, 157; Ichioka, "Japanese Associations and the Japanese Government: A Special Relationship, 1909–1926," *Pacific Historical Review* 46 (1977): 409–438.

70. Ichioka, *Issei*, 205. Abe wrote over a thousand essays for the *Shin Sekai*. See Toyoji Abe, *Toki no Kage* [Shadow of time] (n.p., Yuka Abe, 1968), iv. For Japanese in Oregon, see Eiichirō Azuma, "History of Issei Pioneers in Oregon, 1880–1952," in *In This Great Land of Freedom: The Japanese Pioneers of Oregon*, eds. Lane Ryo Hirabayashi, Akemi Kikumura-Yano, and James A. Hirabayashi (Los Angeles: Japanese American National Museum, 1993), 6–47.

71. Morimoto, *Japanese Americans*, 36.

72. Ichioka, *Issei*, 205.

73. *Nichibei*, October 17, 1920; Ichioka, *Issei*, 206–207.

74. Ishikawa, *Beikoku Kashū Nihongo Gakuen*, 16; Hokka Nihongo Gakuen Kyōkai, *Beikoku Kashū Nihongo*, 102. This was taken from a memorandum circulated with the second newsletter of the Association of Japanese Language Institutes, December 1920.

75. Hokka Nihongo Gakuen Kyōkai, *Beikoku Kashū Nihongo*, 98, 102; Ichioka, *Issei*, 207.

76. Around that time, only one of the eight volumes had been completed. *Rafu Shinpō*, August 12, 1920.

77. Hokka Nihongo Gakuen Kyōkai, *Beikoku Kashū Nihongo*, 162–164, 96–102.

78. *Nichibei*, December 12, 1920; *Ōfu Nippō*, December 11, 1920.

79. *Nichibei*, October 14, 1920; *Ōfu Nippō*, October 25, 1920.

80. *Ōfu Nippō*, July 31, 1920. Also see *Ōfu Nippō*, February 12, 1921. After the 1921 school segregation law, the Florin Grammar School became a segregated school. Nisei were not allowed to go to a new school building constructed for white children. This segregation was maintained for sixteen years. In California, at least five districts actually practiced school segregation: Sacramento County, Florin, Courtland, Isleton, and Walnut Grove. Maeda, *Changing Dreams*, 110.

81. *Ōfu Nippō*, December 6, 1920.

82. *Nichibei*, November 19, 1920. According to the *Nichibei*, Ōta was recalled to Japan by the Japanese Foreign Ministry for his mismanagement of the picture bride issue and the initiative. This is not clear from Ōta's resume in the Japanese Foreign Ministry as he was appointed consul at the Japanese embassy in China only five years later.

83. *Ōfu Nippō*, September 3, 1920.

84. Daniels, *Politics*, 90–91.

85. Ichioka, *Issei*, 226–234.

86. Daniels, *Politics*, 88.

87. *Nichibei*, November 17–24, 1920.

88. Ibid., November 20, 1920.

89. Ibid., November 21, 1920.

90. Ibid., November 25, 1920.

91. Gijō Ozawa, *Hawai Nihongo Gakkō Kyōikushi* [Educational history of Japanese language schools in Hawaii] (Honolulu: Hawai Kyōiku Kai, 1972), 121; Ann L. Halsted, "Sharpened Tongues: The Controversy over the 'Americanization' of Japanese Language Schools in Hawaii, 1919–1927" (Ph.D. diss., Stanford University, 1989), 97.

92. *Nichibei*, November 25, 26, 1920.

93. Katō, *Beikoku Nikkeijin*, 119.

94. *Ōfu Nippō*, January 14, 1921.

95. Sharkey's Senate Bill 223 was introduced to the assembly on January 17. It would have prohibited organizing, conducting, or teaching in any foreign language schools. Lyon's Bill 547 was a copy of Hawaii's Act 30 that was submitted to the senate on January 20. Letter, Consul General Shichitarō Yada to Foreign Minister Yasuya Uchida, January 22, 1921; and letter, Yada to Uchida, January 29, 1921, MT 3.8.2.339-7. "The 1921 State Legislature of California; poll-taxes; laws and regulations relating to school-children," Reel 763, Library of Congress Microfilm Set, *Japanese Ministry of Foreign Affairs, Tokyo, Japan, 1868–1945* (hereafter JMFA/LC).

96. *Ōfu Nippō*, March 14, 1921.

97. Ibid., April 13, 1921.

98. Takimoto visited Wood to discuss what they should expect, if the bill would pass. Telegram, Yada to Uchida, May 19, 1921, DRO 3.8.2.339-1-8.

99. *Grizzly Bear*, November 1922, 15.

100. Yoshihide Matsubayashi, "The Japanese Language Schools in Hawaii and California from 1892 to 1941" (Ph.D. diss., University of San Francisco, 1984), 148.

101. Matsubayashi, "The Japanese Language Schools," 149–151.

102. *Facts and Faces of the Governing Bodies of California* (Sacramento: Moe & Co., 1919), 108.

103. *Sacramento Bee*, March 22, 1921; reprinted in the *Placer Herald*, March 26, 1921.

104. U.S. Congress, *Japanese Immigration*, 322–323.

105. *Ōfu Nippō*, January 7, 1921.

106. Green's bill passed the assembly on April 1 and the senate on April 26, 1921. Telegram, Consul General Yada to Uchida, April 4, 1921; telegram, Yada to Uchida, April 28, 1921. While Green's bill became a law, Mather's bill passed both the senate and assembly, but California's governor did not sign the bill. Morimoto, *Japanese Americans*, 37.

107. Telegram, Yada to Uchida, May 2, 1921, DRO 3.8.2.339-1-8.

108. Telegram, Yada to Uchida, June 6, 1921, MT 3.8.2.339-7. "The 1921 State Legislature of California; poll-taxes; laws and regulations relating to school-children," Reel 762, JMFA/LC; *Ōfu Nippō*, July 27, 1921.

109. Telegram, Yada to Uchida, July 28, 1921, DRO 3.8.2.339-1-8.

110. This is taken from a petition prepared by Tamezō Takimoto, General Secretary of the Japanese Association of America, to appeal to the Senate Education Committee to fight the 1923 Inman private school control bill. Letter, Yada to Uchida, April 12, 1923, DRO 3.8.2.339-1-3.

111. The statistics were taken from a report prepared by Takimoto for Yada. Letter, Yada to Uchida, January 6, 1923, DRO 3.8.2.339-1-8. See the Appendix for a copy of the 1921 examination.

112. From Takimoto's report. Letter, Yada to Uchida, January 6, 1923, DRO 3.8.2.339-1-8. In Los Angeles, the report prepared by Consul General Unojirō Ōyama indicates that, of the 220 examinees for 1921 and 1922 together, 165 passed, 46 failed, and 9 passed conditionally. Letter, Ōyama to Uchida, February 23, 1923, DRO 3.8.2.339-1-8.

113. Letter, Yada to Uchida, January 6, 1923, DRO 3.8.2.339-1-8.

114. Morimoto, *Japanese Americans*, 45.

115. Cited from the Japanese Association of America's petition prepared by Takimoto to the Senate Education Committee to fight for the 1923 Inman private school control bill. Letter, Yada to Uchida, April 12, 1923, DRO 3.8.2.339-1-3.

116. *Sacramento Bee*, November 17, 1922; cited in Matsubayashi, "The Japanese Language Schools," 152.

117. *Sacramento Bee*, November 17, 1922; cited in Matsubayashi, "The Japanese Language Schools," 152-153.

118. *Sacramento Bee*, December 18, 1922; cited in Matsubayashi, "The Japanese Language Schools," 155.

119. Letter, Sam H. Cohn to K. C. Leebrick, December 12, 1922, Hawaii (Territorial) Department of Public Instruction, "Newspaper Clippings Relating to Language School Matters, Book V," 3, uncataloged, Archives of Hawaii; cited in Halsted, "Sharpened Tongues," 130.

120. Letter, K. C. Leebrick to V. S. McClatchy, February 16, 1923, Hawaii (Territorial) Department of Public Instruction, "Newspaper Clippings Relating to Language School Matters, Book V," uncataloged, Archives of Hawaii; cited in Halsted, "Sharpened Tongues," 130-131.

121. Telegram, Yada to Uchida, January 20, 1923, DRO 3.8.2.339-1-3.

122. Matsubayashi, "The Japanese Language Schools," 155.

123. *Ōfu Nippō*, January 11, 1923.

124. *Nichibei*, January 5, 1923.

125. Ibid., January 6, 1923.

126. Ibid., January 9, 1923.

127. *Grizzly Bear*, February 1923, 3.

128. Ibid., March 1923, 18.

129. *Nichibei*, January 9, 1923. After completion, the textbooks were supposed to be sent to the Japanese Ministry of Education to receive a "grammar check." This,

however, became a controversy within the Nikkei community. The *Ōfu Nippō* criticized the Japanese Association's decision on this matter. *Ōfu Nippō*, January 11, 1923.

130. Presumably, these were Reverend Harue Shibata of the First Japanese Baptist Church and Reverend K. Muraoka of the Mahew Community Baptist Church of Sacramento. See Sumio Koga, ed., *A Centennial Legacy: History of the Japanese Christian Missions in North America, 1877–1977*, vol. 1 (Chicago: Norbart Inc., 1977), 140, 157.

131. *Ōfu Nippō*, February 2, 1923.

132. Ibid., February 7, 1923.

133. Elsewhere Ichihashi expressed his opinion of Japanese language schools that "these schools have been unsuccessful in their primary function," teaching Japanese language to Nisei, but "done remarkably well . . . in teaching proper conduct and behavior." Yamato Ichihashi, *Japanese in the United States: A Critical Study of the Problems of the Japanese Immigrants and Their Children* (Stanford: Stanford University Press, 1932), 331. For Ichihashi's view on his son's Japanese language education, see Gordon H. Chang, *Morning Glory, Evening Shadow: Yamato Ichihashi and His Internment Writings, 1942–1945* (Stanford: Stanford University Press, 1997), 74.

134. *Nichibei*, February 18, 1923.

135. *Ōfu Nippō*, March 8, 1923.

136. Telegram, Yada to Uchida, March 9, 1923, DRO 3.8.2.339–1–3.

137. Daniels, *Politics*, 50.

138. Telegram, Uchida to Yada, March 11, 1923, DRO 3.8.2.339–1–3.

139. Ibid., April 2, 1923, DRO 3.8.2.339–1–3.

140. Telegram, Yada to Uchida, March 22, 1923, DRO 3.8.2.339–1–3.

141. Ibid., March 28, 1923, DRO 3.8.2.339–1–3. The note included a cryptic suggestion to recruit the supervisors of congressmen Johnson and Phelan.

142. Telegram, Yada to Uchida, March 22, 1923, DRO 3.8.2.339–1–3.

143. Ibid., March 30, 1923, DRO 3.8.2.339–1–3.

144. One of the committee members withdrew his vote because he was involved with a religious school. *Ōfu Nippō*, March 30, 1923.

145. Telegram, Yada to Uchida, March 31, 1923, DRO 3.8.2.339–1–3.

146. Telegram, Yada to Uchida, April 12, 1923, DRO 3.8.2.339–1–3; and Telegram, Yada to Uchida, May 21, 1923, DRO 3.8.2.339–1–3.

147. *Ōfu Nippō*, June 21, 1923.

148. David George Herman, "Neighbors on the Golden Mountain: The Americanization of Immigrants in California Public Instruction as an Agency of Ethnic Assimilation" (Ph.D. diss., University of California, 1971), 616; Morimoto, *Japanese Americans*, 39.

149. The California textbook series, however, suffered from a poor reputation as being "full of misprints," "too difficult," and "worse than Monbushō textbooks." Despite this, it went through several revisions and printings before 1941. Morimoto, *Japanese Americans*, 46–47.

150. Katō, *Beikoku Nikkeijin*, 120.

151. Reginald Bell, *Public School Education of Second-Generation Japanese in California* (Stanford: Stanford University Press, 1935; reprint, New York: Arno Press, 1978), 20.

152. These were the suggestions Vice Foreign Minister Hanihara presented. *Ōfu Nippō*, November 4, 1920.

153. *Ōfu Nippō*, November 4, 1920.

154. Telegram, Vice Foreign Minister Masanao Hanihara to Vice Minister of Education Takaichirō Akaji, July 17, 1922, DRO 3.10.2.54.

155. Letter, Akaji to Hanihara, August 24, 1922, DRO 3.10.2.54.

4: A Transplanted Attack

An earlier version of this chapter appeared in the *Pacific Northwest Quarterly* 94 (2003): 140–150.

Epigraph: U.S. Congress, House, Committee on Immigration and Naturalization, *Japanese Immigration Hearings, 66th Congress, 2nd session, 1921* (reprint, New York: Arno Press, 1978), 1199.

1. S. Frank Miyamoto, *Social Solidarity among the Japanese in Seattle* (Seattle: University of Washington Press, 1939), 64.

2. Kazuo Itō, *Issei: A History of Japanese Immigrants in North America*, trans. Shinichirō Nakamura and Jean S. Gerard (Seattle: Japanese Community Service, 1973), 136.

3. Itō, *Issei*, 592.

4. Myron E. Powers, "Telic Attempts of Two Racial Groups to Retain their Social Inheritance" (master's thesis, University of Washington, 1932), 24.

5. Miyamoto, *Social Solidarity*, 65.

6. Mitsuhiro Sakaguchi, *Nihonjin Amerika Iminshi* [A history of Japanese immigration to America] (Tokyo: Fuji Shuppan, 2001), 172; Powers, "Telic Attempts," 24.

7. When the construction fee was solicited, these prominent Japanese happened to pass through Seattle and made contributions. Yoriaki Nakagawa, *Akiko* (Seattle: Yoriaki Nakagawa, 1934), 235–236; Itō, *Issei*, 592.

8. Powers, "Telic Attempts," 25.

9. U.S. Congress, House, Committee on Immigration and Naturalization, *Japanese Immigration*, 1177. Sakamoto eight years later founded the *Japanese American Courier*.

10. U.S. Congress, House, Committee on Immigration and Naturalization, *Japanese Immigration*, 1177–1178; U.S. Bureau of the Census, *Fourteenth Census of the United States Taken in the Year 1920*, vol. 2, *Population* (Washington, D.C.: Bureau of Census, 1922), 1054.

For an interesting study of Nisei students at Seattle public schools two decades later, see Yoon K. Pak, *Wherever I Go, I Will Always be a Loyal American: Schooling Seattle's Japanese Americans during World War II* (New York: RoutledgeFalmer, 2002).

11. Ronald E. Magden, *Furusato: Tacoma-Pierce County Japanese 1888–1988* (Tacoma, WA: Nikkeijinkai, 1998), 23.

12. The hearings were held from June 12 to 20, and again on September 25, 1919.

13. Issei were not allowed to become citizens. See Frank F. Chuman, *Bamboo People: The Law and Japanese-Americans* (Del Mar, CA: Publisher's Inc., 1976).

14. U.S. Congress, House, Committee on Immigration and Naturalization, *Percentage Plans for Restriction of Immigration, 66th Congress, 1st session, 1919* (Washington, D.C.: G.P.O., 1919), 32, 258.

15. U.S. Congress, House, Committee on Immigration and Naturalization, *Percentage Plans*, 191.

16. Yūji Ichioka, *The Issei: The World of the First Generation Japanese Immigrants, 1885–1924* (New York: Free Press, 1988), 204–205. Roger Daniels, *The Politics of Prejudice: The Anti-Japanese Movement in California and the Struggle for Japanese Exclusion* (Berkeley: University of California Press, 1962), 63. For the impact of the law in Washington, see John Adrian Rademaker, "The Ecological Position of the Japanese Farmers in the State of Washington" (Ph.D. diss., University of Washington, 1939), and John Isao Nishinori, "Japanese Farms in Washington" (master's thesis, University of Washington, 1926).

17. U.S. Congress, House, Committee on Immigration and Naturalization, *Percentage Plans*, 50. Gulick expressed his idea of establishing a school control law back in 1915 when he visited Japanese schools in Hawaii. See chapter 1.

18. Ibid., 51.

19. Miller Freeman, *The Memoirs of Miller Freeman, 1875–1955* (n.p., William B. Freeman Family, 1956); U.S. Congress, House, Committee on Immigration and Naturalization, *Percentage Plans*, 235.

20. U.S. Congress, House, Committee on Immigration and Naturalization, *Percentage Plans*, 220. The postwar recession and the influx of the Industrial Workers of the World to Seattle also made it harder for veterans to resettle. White veterans not only blamed Japanese but also condemned others of color for their troubles. Dana Frank, *Purchasing Power: Consumer Organizing, Gender, and the Seattle Labor Movement, 1919–1929* (Cambridge, MA: Cambridge University Press, 1994), 20.

21. Douglas R. Pullen, "The Administration of Washington State Governor Louis F. Hart, 1919–1925" (Ph.D. diss., University of Washington, 1974), 234.

22. U.S. Congress, House, Committee on Immigration and Naturalization, *Percentage Plans*, 225.

23. Ibid., 234.

24. Ibid., 75. Contrary to Murphy's statement, S. Frank Miyamoto states that Murphy knew Seattle Issei were not illiterate, since "he was working with us . . . he must have seen that all the Issei read and wrote Japanese. The Issei's Bible and hymn books were all printed in Japanese." Miyamoto's statement was obtained from personal communications with Miyamoto, February 25, 2003.

The 1920 census also indicates that only 8.4 percent of Nikkei over age ten were illiterate. U.S. Bureau of the Census, *Abstract of the Fourteenth Census of the United States, 1920* (Washington, D.C.: 1923), 104; U.S. Bureau of the Census, Fourteenth Census, 1153.

25. U.S. Congress, House, Committee on Immigration and Naturalization, *Percentage Plans*, 73.

26. U.S. Bureau of the Census, *Abstract of the Fourteenth Census*, 104.

27. U.S. Bureau of the Census, *Fourteenth Census*, 76.

28. Rademaker, "Ecological Position," 37–38.

29. *Congressional Record*, 66th Cong., 1st sess., 1919, 58, pt. 4:3292. Also, see *Seattle Star* August 1, 1919. Before the actual mass meeting was held, the August 7, 1919 *Seattle Star* announced that the Immigration Committee cancelled their visit to Seattle because the House did not recess.

30. *Seattle Star*, August 7, 1919.

31. Ibid., August 12, 1919.

32. Ibid., August 13, 1919.

33. Ibid., August 1, 1919. The August 22, 1919 *Seattle Star* spelling was "Kannair."

34. Ibid., August 11, 12, 1919.

35. *Tacoma Times*, July 30, 31, 1919; cited in Magden, *Furusato*, 57.

36. In the early twentieth century, some of the Japanese exclusion incidents included a boycott of Japanese restaurants in 1900, suspension of barbers' licenses in 1902, and recurring Japanese-worker exclusion at lumber mills in the 1910s. The existing prohibition law on foreigners' fishing was reactivated, and an attempt to exclude Japanese grocers also occurred in 1914. Kōjirō Takeuchi, *Beikoku Seihokubu Nippon Iminshi* [History of Japanese immigration in northwest America] (Seattle: North American Daily News, 1928; reprint, Tokyo: Yūshōdō, 1994), 156–198. Furthermore, there were several legislative attempts to abolish Japanese entrepreneurs through a permit or license system on hotels, pawnshops, employment agencies, and dancehalls between 1919 and 1920; Magden, *Furusato*, 25–26.

37. Shortly after the League was formed, Sullivan resigned on September 9, 1919, after being appointed as the primary investigator on the Japanese situation by the American Legion. U.S. Congress, House, Committee on Immigration and Naturalization, *Japanese Immigration*, 1405. Also in Thomas H. Heuterman, *The Burning Horse: Japanese-American Experience in the Yakima Valley, 1920–1942* (Cheney, WA: Eastern Washington University Press, 1995), 20. By the time the immigration hearings came to Seattle, Miller Freeman was the president of the Anti-Japanese League.

38. See Daniels, *Politics*, 68.

39. *Seattle Star*, August 22, 1919. Pullen, "Administration of Washington," 234.

40. Letter, Consul General Naokichi Matsunaga to Foreign Minister Yasuya Uchida, January 25, 1920. The Diplomatic Record Office, Tokyo (hereafter DRO), 3.8.2.339–3.

41. Letter, Minnie Bean to Attorney General Thompson, August 30, 1919. Attor-

ney General, Alphabetical Correspondence, 1909–1940, Washington State Archives, Olympia.

42. "The New President," *Washington Education Journal* 3 (November 1921): 68.

43. Most of the Japanese farms were located in the Puyallup, Stuck, Green, and White River valleys. Pullen, "Administration of Washington," 224.

44. Letter, Thompson to Bean, September 4, 1919. Attorney General, Alphabetical Correspondence, 1909–1940, Washington State Archives, Olympia.

45. Bean was appointed as superintendent of public schools in Pierce County on September 1, 1919. *Tacoma News Tribune*, August 28, 1919.

46. U.S. Congress, House, Committee on Immigration and Naturalization, *Japanese Immigration*, 1177. Geographically, the Tacoma Japanese Language School was also in Pierce County, but the City of Tacoma was not in Bean's jurisdiction. The Fife Japanese Language School was established in 1909 and the Firwood Japanese Language School began in 1915. Tacoma Shūhōsha, *Tacoma Oyobi Chihō Nihonjinshi* [A history of Japanese Tacoma and vicinity] (Tacoma: Tacoma Shūhōsha, 1941), 76.

47. *Hokubei Jiji*, September 3, 1919.

48. Josephine Corliss Preston, "Department of Public Instruction," *Northwest Journal of Education* 31 (December 1919), 106.

49. Magden, *Furusato*, 58.

50. In order to investigate the necessity of a Japanese school, the Japanese Association conducted a survey of the number of Nikkei children in Tacoma. According to the October 1911 survey, there were thirty-three children, ranging in age from one to fourteen years old. James Watanabe, *History of the Japanese of Tacoma* (Tacoma: Pacific Northwest District Council, Japanese American Citizens League, 1986), 54.

51. Magden, *Furusato*, 70.

52. Watanabe, *History of the Japanese*, 55.

53. Parents paid a monthly tuition of 50 cents per kindergartner and $2 per elementary school student. Magden, *Furusato*, 70.

54. Watanabe, *History of the Japanese*, 68.

55. Magden, *Furusato*, 72.

56. Yamasaki became an Issei community leader and served as the executive secretary for the Tacoma Japanese Association in 1915. Watanabe, *History of the Japanese*, 67; Magden, *Furusato*, 49.

57. Itō, *Issei*, 601; Magden, *Furusato*, 72. Pacific swimming excursions became problematic, because of hostility from locals; by 1933 they found no appropriate places available. Tacoma Shūhōsha, *Tacoma Oyobi*, 43–48.

58. Magden, *Furusato*, 71–72.

59. Tacoma Shūhōsha, *Tacoma Oyobi*, 39.

60. Magden, *Furusato*, 70.

61. Tacoma Shūhōsha, *Tacoma Oyobi*, 41; Magden, *Furusato*, 74; Itō, *Issei*, 601.

62. Magden, *Furusato*, 81.

63. Tacoma Shūhōsha, *Tacoma Oyobi*, 41–42; Magden, *Furusato*, 74. The Sunday School lasted until 1939, when Yamasaki returned to Japan as a representative of the

Northwest American Japanese Association to pay respect to the Japanese Imperial Army in Japan, Korea, and China. Tacoma Shūhōsha, *Tacoma Oyobi*, 72.

64. Previously, the Tacoma Japanese Language School had rented a house at 411 S. 15th Ave. for $18 per month since its opening in 1911.

65. Magden, *Furusato*, 74; Tacoma Shūhōsha, *Tacoma Oyobi*, 40.

66. Tacoma Shūhōsha, *Tacoma Oyobi*, 40. The number of picture brides who came to Washington, Montana, parts of Idaho, and the Territory of Alaska (the jurisdiction of Beikoku Seihoku Renraku Nihonjinkai) were: 150 (1915), 144 (1916), 206 (1917), 281 (1918), 267 (1919), and 99 (1920). U.S. Congress, House, Committee on Immigration and Naturalization, *Japanese Immigration*, 1207.

67. *Hokubei Jiji*, December 21, 1918.

68. Ibid., February 10, 1919.

69. Ibid., February 4, 1919.

70. Ibid., April 22, 24, 1919.

71. Takeuchi, *Beikoku Seihokubu*, 180–181.

72. *Hokubei Jiji*, August 27, 31, September 2, 3, 1918.

73. Itō, *Issei*, 85, 703.

74. Ibid., 136.

75. *Hokubei Jiji*, August 27, 31, September 2, 3, 1918.

76. Itō, *Issei*, 597. The Japanese Foreign Ministry usually chose the path of avoiding conflict with discriminatory measures against Japanese immigrants so as not to endanger Japanese–U.S. relations.

77. Tacoma Shūhōsha, *Tacoma Oyobi*, 38.

78. Masato Yamasaki, "Yamaoka Ototaka-shi no Kokugo Gakkō Kaizenron o Hyōsu" [Critiquing Mr. Ototaka Yamaoka's suggestion for the evolution of Japanese language schools], *Hankyō* 1, no. 2 (September 1918): 2–3.

79. Tacoma Shūhōsha, *Tacoma Oyobi*, 161.

80. *Hokubei Jiji*, August 16, 17, 1918. The United North American Japanese Association conducted a survey on the advantages and disadvantages of Japanese language schools in 1922. The survey results showed that Japanese language education did not negatively affect children's public school grades. It also indicated that Japanese language education would help Nikkei children if they went to Japan and tried to find work. It concluded that many of the Issei parents perceived the necessity of Japanese language schools, which were not harmful to Nisei living conditions. Sakaguchi, 184–186.

81. Takeuchi, *Beikoku Seihokubu*, 428.

82. Ibid., 415.

83. Ichioka, *Issei*, 203.

84. U.S. Congress, House, Committee on Immigration and Naturalization, *Japanese Immigration*, 383.

85. Takeuchi, *Beikoku Seihokubu*, 428.

86. According to Ichioka, an educational committee of the Pacific Coast Japanese

Association Deliberative Council launched a textbook compilation project, but "only five textbooks had been compiled by 1918 to replace the Japanese Ministry of Education series." Ichioka, *Issei*, 205. Ichioka does not mention the details of these early textbooks if they were published.

87. Each volume was developed for one grade; volumes 1 through 8 cover grades one through eight. Although there is only one text per grade, they included lessons from history, geography, biology, novels, folk stories, and biographies, but basically were designed to develop students' reading ability in Japanese. They are written in three writing systems—*katakana* and *hiragana* for the lower levels, and *kanji* (Chinese characters) for the upper levels. For an analysis of the Washington textbook series, see Noriko Asato, "The Issei Challenge to Preserve Japanese Heritage during the Period of Americanization," in *Nikkei in the Pacific Northwest: Japanese Americans and Japanese Canadians in the Twentieth Century*, eds. Louis Fiset and Gail M. Nomura (Seattle: University of Washington Press, 2005). For a comparison of Washington's and California's textbooks, see Teruko I. Kumei, "Making 'A Bridge over the Pacific': Japanese Language Schools in the United States, 1900–1941," *American Studies in Scandinavia* 32 (2000): 65–86.

88. Beikoku Seihokubu Renraku Nihonjinkai, *Kaimu Oyobi Kaikei Hōkoku* [Minutes and financial report] (Seattle: Beikoku Seihokubu Renraku Nihonjinkai, 1922), 23.

89. Takeuchi, *Beikoku Seihokubu*, 430–431; Katherine J. Lentz, "Japanese-American Relations in Seattle" (master's thesis, University of Washington, 1924), 11. The reason that twice as many first through fourth grade textbooks were published was that there were fewer older Nisei, and the student's attrition rate was high in the upper levels.

90. U.S. Congress, House, Committee on Immigration and Naturalization, *Japanese Immigration*, 1177–1178. The data was submitted to the committee hearings, and the figures cited in the study are based on the 1920 statistics. Also see Beikoku Seihokubu Renraku Nihonjinkai, *Beikoku Seihokubu Zairyū Nihonjin Hatten Ryakushi* [An overview of the historical development of Japanese in northwest America] (Seattle: Beikoku Seihokubu Renraku Nihonjinkai, 1923), 41–44.

91. *Tacoma Daily Ledger*, July 2, 1920.

92. U.S. Congress, House, Committee on Immigration and Naturalization, *Japanese Immigration*, 1192.

93. *Seattle Star*, August 5, 1920.

94. Takeuchi, *Beikoku Seihokubu*, 432. Takeuchi and the *Seattle Star* differ on the date that Johnson and Raker visited the Japanese language school.

95. This bill also would have prohibited an alien who had declared his/her intention of becoming an American citizen to teach without a permit from the Superintendent of Public Instruction. "Senate Bill 140," State of Washington, *Printed Bills of the Legislature, 17th Session, Senate* (Olympia: State of Washington Printing Office, 1921).

96. California's law passed its legislature in June 1921. *Ōfu Nippō*, June 7, 1921. Ann Halsted, "Sharpened Tongues: The Controversy Over the 'Americanization' of

Japanese Language Schools in Hawaii, 1919–1927" (Ph.D. diss., Stanford University, 1989), 97.

97. This resolution was passed at a legislative committee meeting of the Washington Education Association in Tacoma. "Proceedings of Saturday Morning Session, October 16, 1920," *Northwest Journal of Education* 32 (November 1920), 78. Takeuchi also wrote that a proposal for foreign language control was resolved at the Washington Education Association's annual meeting at Yakima. Takeuchi, *Beikoku Seihokubu*, 429. However, the *Northwest Journal of Education*, the official association journal before it was taken over by the *Washington Education Journal*, does not mention the resolution at the Yakima conference.

98. U.S. Congress, House, Committee on Immigration and Naturalization, *Japanese Immigration*, 1177. In 1920, there were 806 Nisei elementary school pupils and 87 high school students in Seattle, which represented 0.0189 percent and 0.00992 percent of the total number of public students, respectively. U.S. Congress, House, Committee on Immigration and Naturalization, *Japanese Immigration*, 1178.

99. Magden credits lobbyists for "engineering" the victory. Magden, *Furusato*, 61.

100. "Senate Bill 120." State of Washington, *Printed Bills of the Legislature, 18th Session, Senate* (Olympia: State of Washington Printing Office, 1923).

101. Pullen, "Administration of Washington," 245; Rademaker, "Ecological Position," 91 ff.

102. The 1923 Washington Alien Land Law was passed by the House on February 16, and by the Senate on February 28. It was signed by the governor on March 10, 1923. Nishinori, "Japanese Farms," 64.

103. For example, the legislator who introduced Nebraska's alien land law confessed that a friend from California had asked him to do so. See Hiram Hisanori Kanō, *A History of the Japanese in Nebraska* (Scottsbluff, NE: Scottsbluff Public Library, 1984), 11, 13.

104. Rademaker, "Ecological Position," 35.

105. Katsutoshi Kurokawa, *Amerika Rōdō Undō to Nihonjin Imin: Shiatoru ni okeru Haiseki to Rentai* [The American labor movement and Japanese immigrants: Exclusion and solidarity] (Okayama, Japan: Daigaku Kyōiku Shuppan, 1998), 63, 71.

106. *Seattle Union Record*, Dec. 16, 1920; cited in Kurokawa, *Amerika Rōdō Undō*, 82–83. For more on Japanese relations with the council, see Frank, *Purchasing Power*, 38.

107. *Seattle Star*, August 29, 1919.

108. Letter, Seattle Consul General Naokichi Matsunaga to Foreign Minister Yasuya Uchida, January 25, 1920, DRO 3.8.2.339–3.

109. For more about these local battles, see Takeuchi, *Beikoku Seihokubu*, 171.

110. Pak, *Wherever I Go*, 44, 48–49, 64.

111. Ibid., 50, 71.

112. Roderick D. McKenzie, *Oriental Exclusion: The Effect of American Immigra-*

tion Laws, Regulations and Judicial Decisions upon the Chinese and Japanese on the American Pacific Coast (New York: Institute of Pacific Relations, 1927), 172.

113. Toyotomi Morimoto, *Japanese Americans and Cultural Continuity: Maintaining Language and Heritage* (New York: Garland Publishing, 1997), 54.

114. Miyamoto, *Social Solidarity*, 111.

115. Ichioka, *Issei*, 202.

116. Yakima Nihonjinkai, *Yakimaheigen Nihonjinshi* [The history of the Japanese in the Yakima Valley] (Yakima, WA: Yakima Nihonjinkai, 1935), 145–147. Japanese anthropologist Masako Notoji, however, asserts that Yakima Nikkei were still uncertain of the goal for Nisei education, and highlighted their strong desire to maintain ethnic identity. According to her, although they tried to raise Nisei as American citizens with the Yamato spirit, any kind of Nisei achievement was interpreted with "the sense of ethnic identity and pride." Masako Notoji, "From Graveyard to Baseball: The Quest for Ethnic Identity in the Prewar Japanese Immigrant Community in the Yakima Valley," *Japanese Journal of American Studies* 3 (1989): 48.

117. Itō, *Issei*, 603.

5: Conclusion

1. Yoshihide Matsubayashi, "The Japanese Language Schools in Hawaii and California from 1892 to 1941" (Ph.D. diss., University of San Francisco, 1984), 140.

2. Matsubayashi, "Japanese Language Schools," 141–143.

3. Ann L. Halsted, "Sharpened Tongues: The Controversy Over the 'Americanization' of Japanese Language Schools in Hawaii, 1919–1927" (Ph.D. diss., Stanford University, 1989), 98.

4. "$6,000 for Americanization," *Japan Review* 3 (1921): 209.

5. Halsted, "Sharpened Tongues," 114.

6. Dennis M. Ogawa, *Kodomo no tame ni—For the Sake of the Children: The Japanese American Experience in Hawaii* (Honolulu: University of Hawai'i Press, 1978), 146.

7. Gijō Ozawa, *Hawai Nihongo Gakkō Kyōikushi* [Educational history of Japanese language schools in Hawaii] (Honolulu: Hawaii Kyōiku Kai, 1972), 128.

8. Yukuji Okita, *Hawai Nikkei Imin no Kyōikushi: Nichibei Bunka, Sono Deai to Sōkoku* [History of Japanese immigrant education in Hawaii: Encounter and conflict of Japanese and American culture] (Tokyo: Minerva Shobō, 1997), 244.

9. Okita, *Hawai Nikkei Imin*, 244; Halsted, "Sharpened Tongues," 173, 176.

10. *Nippū Jiji*, December 4, 1922; cited in Okita, *Hawai Nikkei Imin*, 244.

11. Halsted, "Sharpened Tongues," 189.

12. Ibid., 115.

13. Kōichi G. Harada, "A Survey of the Japanese Language Schools in Hawaii" (master's thesis, University of Hawai'i, 1934), 68–69.

14. Halsted, "Sharpened Tongues," 176.

15. Ibid., 190.

16. Matsubayashi, "Japanese Language Schools," 171.

17. Clark Spurlock, *Education and the Supreme Court* (Urbana: University of Illinois Press, 1955), 172. Although Chinese and Korean language schools were not the target, some of these schools joined Japanese colleagues in fighting Hawaii's language school laws.

18. Halsted, "Sharpened Tongues," 191.

19. Ibid., 192.

20. The test case was moved to the Ninth Circuit Court of Appeals in San Francisco on August 8, 1925. Halsted, "Sharpened Tongues," 192.

21. U.S. Department of the Interior. Bureau of Education, *A Survey of Education in Hawaii, Bulletin 1920, no. 16* (Washington, D.C.: GPO, 1920), 134.

22. *Farrington v. Tokushige*, 273 U.S. 284; cited in Halsted, "Sharpened Tongues," 180.

23. Halsted, "Sharpened Tongues," 193.

24. Thornton Sherburne Hardy, *Wallace Rider Farrington* (Honolulu: Honolulu Star-Bulletin, 1935), 122; cited in Halsted, 193.

25. *Farrington v. Tokushige*, 272 U.S. 284, Brief for Appellees, 55, 77; cited in Halsted, "Sharpened Tongues," 185–186.

26. Halsted, "Sharpened Tongues," 193.

27. *Farrington v. Tokushige*, 273 U.S. 284; cited in Halsted, "Sharpened Tongues," 195.

28. Japanese language schools prospered in the 1930s. However, they were closed during World War II. After World War II, see Noriko Shimada, "Wartime Dissolution and Revival of the Japanese Language Schools in Hawai'i: Persistence of Ethnic Culture," *Journal of Asian American Studies* 1 (June 1998): 121–151.

29. *Nebraska Session Laws, 1919*, chap. 249, 1019; cited in Frederick C. Luebke, "Legal Restrictions on Foreign Languages in the Great Plains States, 1917–1923," in *Language in Conflict: Linguistic Acculturation on the Great Plains*, ed. Paul Schach (Lincoln: University of Nebraska Press, 1980), 13.

30. Luebke, "Legal Restrictions," 14–15.

31. Ibid., 15.

32. *Pierce v. Society of Sisters*, 268 U.S. 510 (1925), 532–533; cited in Kenneth B. O'Brien, Jr., "Education, Americanization and the Supreme Court: The 1920's," *American Quarterly* 13 (1961): 167–168.

33. O'Brien, "Education, Americanization and the Supreme Court," 171.

34. William G. Ross, *Forging New Freedoms: Nativism, Education, and the Constitution, 1917–1927* (Lincoln: University of Nebraska Press, 1994), 185.

35. Personal communications with S. Frank Miyamoto, February 25, 2003.

36. Ibid.

37. Ibid.

38. Milton M. Gordon, *Assimilation in American Life: The Role of Race, Religion, and National Origins* (New York: Oxford University Press, 1964), 98–99.

39. Personal communications with S. Frank Miyamoto, February 25, 2003.

40. For Miyamoto, voluntary associations were placed in contrast with "communal organizations," which are based on "blood ties or long-standing traditional ties." Typical examples of a communal organization are kinship organizations or the Catholic Church, which, according to Miyamoto, "prevented their youths from broadening their social contacts."

41. Personal communications with S. Frank Miyamoto, February 25, 2003. Also see Eileen H. Tamura, *Americanization, Acculturation, and Ethnic Identity: The Nisei Generation in Hawaii* (Urbana: University of Illinois Press, 1994), 151.

42. Bill Hosokawa, *Nisei: The Quiet Americans* (New York: William Morrow and Co., 1969), 159.

43. Edith Yonenaka's and Timmy Hirata's recollections, cited in Tamura, *Americanization*, 154.

44. Harada, "A Survey of the Japanese Language Schools in Hawaii," 102.

45. Hokka Nihongo Gakuen Kyōkai, eds., *Beikoku Kashū Nihongo Gakuen Enkakushi* [A brief history of the Japanese language schools in California] (San Francisco: Hokka Nihongo Gakuen Kyōkai, 1930), 235–264; and Ken Ishikawa, *Beikoku Kashū Nihongo Gakuen ni Kansuru Kenkyū* [A study of Japanese language institutes in California] (n.p., 1923), 30–32. The number of Nikkei students attending California public schools was taken from Department of Commerce, Bureau of Census, *Fourteenth Census of the United States Taken in the Year 1920, vol. 2, Population* (Washington, D.C.: Bureau of Census, 1922), 1054.

46. U.S. Congress, House, Committee on Immigration and Naturalization, *Japanese Immigration Hearings, 66th Congress, 2nd session, 1921* (reprint, New York: Arno Press, 1978), 1177–1178; Department of Commerce, Bureau of Census, *Fourteenth Census of the United States Taken in the Year 1920, vol. 2, Population* (Washington, D.C.: Bureau of Census, 1922), 1054.

47. Franklin Odo, *No Sword to Bury: Japanese Americans in Hawai'i during World War II* (Philadelphia: Temple University Press, 2004), 59; Mariko Takagi, "Moral Education in Pre-War Japanese Language Schools in Hawaii" (master's thesis, University of Hawai'i, 1987), 19.

48. Takagi, "Moral Education," 114–115.

49. Daniel Inouye, *Journey to Washington* (Englewood Cliffs, NJ: Prentice-Hall, 1967), 36.

50. Odo, *No Sword to Bury*, 268.

51. Ibid., 59.

52. Ibid., 43.

53. Ibid., 267.

54. Ibid., 47–48.

55. Personal communications with S. Frank Miyamoto, February 25, 2003.

56. Los Angeles Consul General Unojirō Ōyama to Foreign Minister Yasuya Uchida, July 5, 1919, DRO 3.10.2.1.

57. Roger Daniels, *Asian America: Chinese and Japanese in the United States since 1850* (Seattle: University of Washington Press, 1988), 73, 115.

58. Joyce Kuo, "Excluded, Segregated, and Forgotten: A History View of the Discrimination against Chinese Americans in Public Schools," *Chinese America, History and Perspectives*, 2000, 33.

59. The 1860 school law segregated children of black, Chinese, and Indian descent from public schools. Kuo, "Excluded, Segregated, and Forgotten," 4–5.

60. Another alternative was Christian missionary schools, which offered English-language instruction to school-aged children and adults, using the Bible as a medium. Kuo, "Excluded, Segregated, and Forgotten," 5.

61. Charles Wollenberg, *All Deliberate Speed: Segregation and Exclusion in California Schools, 1855–1975* (Berkeley: University of California Press, 1976), 36.

62. Kuo, "Excluded, Segregated, and Forgotten," 8.

63. Shien-woo Kung, *Chinese in American Life: Some Aspects of Their History, Status, Problems, and Contributions* (Seattle: University of Washington Press, 1962), 220–221.

64. U.S. Department of the Interior, Bureau of Education, *A Survey of Education*, 12.

65. Wayne Patterson, *The Ilse: First Generation Korean Immigrants in Hawai'i 1903–1973* (Honolulu: University of Hawai'i Press and Center for Korean Studies, University of Hawai'i, 2000), 117–118.

66. Ibid., 118.

67. Ibid., 118–119.

68. Patterson, *Ilse*, 119–120.

69. In his study of nineteenth-century educational reform, revisionist education historian Michael B. Katz demonstrated that public schools reflected perspectives of the social and economic elite who tried to gain social control by teaching specific values to children. See his book, *The Irony of Early School Reform: Educational Innovation in Mid-Nineteenth Century Massachusetts* (Cambridge, MA: Harvard University Press, 1968).

70. Congressman Albert Johnson actually submitted a bill to revoke Nisei American citizenship in 1920. Teruko Kumei, "'The Twain Shall Meet' in the Nisei?: Japanese Language Education and U.S.-Japan Relations, 1900–1940," in *New Worlds, New Lives: Globalization and People of Japanese Descent in the Americas and from Latin America in Japan*, eds. Lane Ryo Hirabayashi, Akemi Kikumura-Yano, and James A. Hirabayashi (Stanford: Stanford University Press, 2002), 113. McClatchy and the California Immigration Committee also conducted a campaign to amend the Constitution to deprive Nisei of their American citizenship. Kent Edward Haldan, "'Our Japanese Citizens': A Study of Race, Class, and Ethnicity in Three Japanese American Communities in Santa Barbara County, 1900–1960" (Ph.D. diss., University of California at Berkeley, 2000), 45.

Bibliography

Abe, Toyoji. *Toki no Kage* [Shadow of time]. n.p.: Yuka Abe, 1968.

Adachi, Nobuhiro. *Linguistic Americanization of Japanese-Americans in Hawaii.* Ōsaka: Ōsaka Kyōiku Tosho, 1998.

Allen, Riley. "Education and Race Problems in Hawaii." *American Review of Reviews* (December 1921): 613–624.

Asato, Noriko. "The Issei Challenge to Preserve Japanese Heritage during the Period of Americanization." In *Nikkei in the Pacific Northwest: Japanese Americans and Japanese Canadians in the Twentieth Century,* eds. Louis Fiset and Gail M. Nomura. Seattle: University of Washington Press, 2005.

———. "Mandating Americanization: Japanese Language Schools and the Federal Survey of Education in Hawaii, 1916–1920." *History of Education Quarterly* 43 (2003): 10–38.

———. "Ousting Japanese Language Schools: Americanization and Cultural Maintenance in Washington State, 1919–27." *Pacific Northwest Quarterly* 94 (2003): 140–150.

Attorney General. Alphabetical Correspondence, 1909–1940. Washington State Archives.

Azuma, Eiichirō. "History of Issei Pioneers in Oregon, 1880–1952." In *In This Great Land of Freedom: The Japanese Pioneers of Oregon,* ed. Lane Ryo Hirabayashi, Akemi Kikumura-Yano, and James A. Hirabayashi, 6–47. Los Angeles: Japanese American National Museum, 1993.

Beikoku Seihokubu Renraku Nihonjinkai. *Kaimu Oyobi Kaikei Hōkoku* [Minutes and financial report]. Seattle: Beikoku Seihokubu Renraku Nihonjinkai, 1922.

———. *Beikoku Seihokubu Zairyū Nihonjin Hatten Ryakushi* [An overview of the historical development of Japanese in northwest America]. Seattle: Beikoku Seihokubu Renraku Nihonjinkai, 1923.

Bell, Reginald. *Public School Education of Second-Generation Japanese in California.* Stanford: Stanford University Press, 1935. Reprint. New York: Arno Press, 1978.

Chang, Gordon H. *Morning Glory, Evening Shadow: Yamato Ichihashi and His Internment Writings, 1942–1945.* Stanford: Stanford University Press, 1997.

Chuman, Frank F. *Bamboo People: The Law and Japanese-Americans.* Del Mar, CA: Publisher's Inc., 1976.

Compilation of Committee for the Publication of Kinzaburō Makiko's Biography. *Life of Kinzaburō Makino.* Honolulu: Hawai Hōchi, 1965.

Conroy, Hilary. *The Japanese Frontier in Hawaii, 1868–1898.* Berkeley: University of California Press, 1953.

Daniels, Roger. *Asian America: Chinese and Japanese in the United States since 1850.* Seattle: University of Washington Press, 1988.

———. *The Politics of Prejudice: The Anti-Japanese Movement in California and the Struggle for Japanese Exclusion.* Berkeley: University of California Press, 1962.

Dore, Ronald P. *Education in Tokugawa Japan.* Berkeley: University of California Press, 1965.

Duus, Masayo Umezawa. *The Japanese Conspiracy: The Oahu Sugar Strike of 1920.* Berkeley: University of California, 1999.

Facts and Faces of the Governing Bodies of California. Sacramento: Moe & Co., 1919.

Frank, Dana. *Purchasing Power: Consumer Organizing, Gender, and the Seattle Labor Movement, 1919–1929.* Cambridge: Cambridge University Press, 1994.

Freeman, Miller. *The Memoirs of Miller Freeman, 1875–1955.* n.p.: William B. Freeman Family, 1956.

Fuchs, Lawrence H. *Hawaii Pono: A Social History.* New York: Harcourt, Brace & World, 1961.

Godo, Yoshihisa, and Yūjiro Hayami. *Accommodation of Education in Modern Economic Growth: A Comparison of Japan with the United States.* Asian Development Bank. Available from http://www.adbi.org/PDF/wp/wp4/wp4.pdf. Accessed June 14 2002.

Gordon, Milton M. *Assimilation in American Life: The Role of Race, Religion, and National Origins.* New York: Oxford University Press, 1964.

Gulick Family Papers. Houghton Library, Harvard University.

Gulick, Sidney L. *American Democracy and Asiatic Citizenship.* New York: Charles Scribner's Sons, 1918.

———. *The American Japanese Problem.* New York: Charles Scribner's Sons, 1914.

———. *Hawaii's American-Japanese Problem.* Honolulu: Honolulu Star-Bulletin, 1915.

Haldan, Kent Edward. "'Our Japanese Citizens': A Study of Race, Class, and Ethnicity in Three Japanese American Communities in Santa Barbara County, 1900–1960." Ph.D. diss., University of California at Berkeley, 2000.

Halsted, Ann L. "Sharpened Tongues: The Controversy over the 'Americanization' of Japanese Language Schools in Hawaii, 1919–1927." Ph.D. diss., Stanford University, 1989.

Harada, Koichi G. "A Survey of the Japanese Language Schools in Hawaii." Master's thesis, University of Hawai'i, 1934.

Hardy, Thornton Sherburne. *Wallace Rider Farrington.* Honolulu: Honolulu Star-Bulletin, 1935.

Hartmann, Edward G. *The Movement to Americanize the Immigrant.* New York: Columbia University Press, 1948.

Hawaii Education Association. *Hawai Nihongo Kyōikushi* [History of Japanese education in Hawaii]. Honolulu: Hawaii Education Association, 1937.

Hawkins, John N. "Politics, Education, and Language Policy: The Case of Japanese Language Schools in Hawaii." *Amerasia* 5 (1978): 39–56.

Hayashi, Brian Masaru. *"For the Sake of Our Japanese Brethren": Assimilation, Nationalism, and Protestantism among the Japanese of Los Angeles, 1895–1942*. Stanford: Stanford University Press, 1995.

Herman, David George. "Neighbors on the Golden Mountain: The Americanization of Immigrants in California Public Instruction as an Agency of Ethnic Assimilation." Ph.D. diss., University of California, 1971.

Heuterman, Thomas H. *The Burning Horse: Japanese-American Experience in the Yakima Valley, 1920–1942*. Cheney, WA: Eastern Washington University Press, 1995.

Hokka Nihongo Gakuen Kyōkai. *Beikoku Kashū Nihongo Gakuen Enkakushi* [A brief history of the Japanese language schools in California]. San Francisco: Hokka Nihongo Gakuen Kyōkai, 1930.

Honda, Chie. "Dai Niji Sekai Taisen-mae no Hawai ni Okeru Jōdoshinshū Honpa Hongwanji no Nihongo Gakkō" [Jodoshinshu Honpa Hongwanji's Japanese language schools in Hawaii before World War II]. In *America no Nikkeijin— Toshi, Shakai, Seikatsu* [Nikkei in America—cities, society, life], ed. Toshio Yanagida, 173–197. Tokyo: Dobunkan, 1995.

Honpa Hongwanji. *Honpa Hongwanji Hawai Kaikyō 35-nen Kiyō* [35th bulletin of the Honpa Hongwanji Mission in Hawaii]. Honolulu: Honpa Hongwanji, 1931.

Hosokawa, Bill. *Nisei: The Quiet Americans*. New York: William Morrow and Co., 1969.

Hunter, Louise H. *Buddhism in Hawaii: Its Impact on a Yankee Community*. Honolulu: University of Hawai'i Press, 1971.

Ichihashi, Yamato. *Japanese in the United States: A Critical Study of the Problems of the Japanese Immigrants and Their Children*. Stanford: Stanford University Press, 1932.

Ichioka, Yuji. "A Historian by Happenstance." *Amerasia Journal* 26 (2000): 31–54.

———. *The Issei: The World of the First Generation Japanese Immigrants, 1885–1924*. New York: Free Press, 1988.

———. "Japanese Associations and the Japanese Government: A Special Relationship, 1909–1926." *Pacific Historical Review* 46 (1977): 409–438.

Imamura, Yemyō. *Hawai Kaikyōshi* [History of missionary work in Hawaii]. Honolulu: Honpa Hongwanji, 1918.

Inouye, Daniel. *Journey to Washington*. Englewood Cliffs, NJ: Prentice-Hall, 1967.

Iriye, Akira. *Pacific Estrangement: Japanese and American Expansion, 1897–1911*. Cambridge, MA: Harvard University Press, 1972.

Irons, Peter. *Justice at War: The Story of the Japanese American Internment Cases*. Berkeley: University of California Press, 1983.

———. *Justice Delayed: The Record of the Japanese American Internment Cases*. Middletown, CT: Wesleyan University Press, 1989.

Irwin, Wallace. *Seed of the Sun*. New York: George H. Doran Co., 1921.

Ishikawa, Ken. *Beikoku Kashū Nihongo Gakuen ni Kansuru Kenkyū* [A study of Japanese language institutes in California]. n.p., 1923.

Itō, Kazuo. *Issei: A History of Japanese Immigrants in North America.* Trans. by Shinichirō Nakamura and Jean S. Gerard. Seattle: Japanese Community Service, 1973.

Iwata, Masakazu. *Planted in Good Soil: A History of the Issei in United States Agriculture.* New York: Peter Lang, 1992.

Iyenaga, T., and Kenoske Satō. *Japan and the California Problem.* New York: G. P. Putnam, 1921.

James, Thomas. *Exile within the Schooling of Japanese Americans, 1942–1945.* Cambridge, MA: Harvard University Press, 1987.

Japan. Foreign Ministry. Japanese Diplomatic Record Office, Tokyo.

Japanese Chamber of Commerce of Southern California. *Japanese in Southern California: A History of 70 Years.* Los Angeles: Japanese Chamber of Commerce of Southern California, 1960.

Japanese Foreign Ministry. *Ryōjikan Shitsumu Sankōsho* [Consular guidebook]. Tokyo: Japanese Foreign Ministry, 1916.

———. *Nihon Gaikō Bunsho: Taibei Imin Mondai Keika Gaiyō* [Documents on Japanese foreign policy: A summary of the development of the Japanese immigration question in the United States]. Tokyo: Japanese Foreign Ministry, 1933. Reprint. Tokyo: Japanese Foreign Ministry, 1972.

———. *Nihon Gaikō Bunsho: Taibei Imin Mondai Keika Gaiyō Fuzokusho* [Documents on Japanese foreign policy: Documents accompanying a summary of the development of the Japanese immigration question in the United States]. Tokyo: Japanese Foreign Ministry, 1973.

Japanese Ministry of Foreign Affairs, 1868–1945. Library of Congress Microfilm Set.

Kano, Hiram Hisanori. *A History of the Japanese in Nebraska.* Scottsbluff, NE: Scottsbluff Public Library, 1984.

Karasawa, Tomitarō. *Kyōkasho no Rekishi* [History of textbooks]. Tokyo: Gyōsei, 1989.

Katō, Shinichi. *Beikoku Nikkeijin Hyakunenshi* [A history of one hundred years of the Japanese and Japanese Americans in the United States]. Tokyo: Shin Nichibei Shinbun Sha, 1961.

Katz, Michael B. *The Irony of Early School Reform: Educational Innovation in Mid-Nineteenth Century Massachusetts.* Cambridge, MA: Harvard University Press, 1968.

King, W. L. MacKenzie. *Report of the Royal Commission Appointed to Inquire into the Methods by Which Oriental Laborers Have Been Induced to Come to Canada.* Ottawa: Government Printing Bureau, 1908.

Koga, Sumio. *A Centennial Legacy: History of the Japanese Christian Missions in North America, 1877–1977.* Vol. 1. Chicago: Norbart Inc., 1977.

Kumei, Teruko. "Making 'a Bridge over the Pacific': Japanese Language Schools in the United States, 1900–1941." *American Studies in Scandinavia* 32 (2000): 65–86.

———. "Nichibei 'Shinkō no Rensa': America no Nisei Kyōiku to Gaimushō" [America and Japan's "chain of relationship": Nisei education in America and the Japanese foreign ministry]. In *"Zaigai Shitei" Kyōiku no Kitei Yōin to Ibunkakan Kyōiku ni Kansuru Kenkyū* [A study of stipulation factors for the education of "Japanese children overseas" and crosscultural education], ed. Masaru Kojima, 39–54. n.p., 2000.

———. "'The Twain Shall Meet' in the Nisei?: Japanese Language Education and U.S.-Japan Relations, 1900–1940." In *New Worlds, New Lives: Globalization and People of Japanese Descent in the Americas and from Latin America in Japan*, ed. Lane Ryo Hirabayashi, Akemi Kikumura-Yano, and James A. Hirabayashi, 108–125. Stanford: Stanford University Press, 2002.

Kung, Shien-Woo. *Chinese in American Life: Some Aspects of Their History, Status, Problems, and Contributions.* Seattle: University of Washington Press, 1962.

Kuo, Joyce. "Excluded, Segregated, and Forgotten: A History View of the Discrimination against Chinese Americans in Public Schools." *Chinese America, History and Perspectives* (2000): 32–48.

Kurokawa, Katsutoshi. *Amerika Rōdō Undō to Nihonjin Imin: Shiatoru ni Okeru Haiseki to Rentai* [The American labor movement and Japanese immigrants: Exclusion and solidarity]. Okayama, Japan: Daigaku Kyōiku Shuppan, 1998.

Lentz, Katherine J. "Japanese-American Relations in Seattle." Master's thesis, University of Washington, 1924.

Lewis, Charles L. *Philander Priestley Claxton.* Knoxville: University of Tennessee Press, 1948.

Luebke, Frederick C. "Legal Restrictions on Foreign Languages in the Great Plains States, 1917–1923." In *Language in Conflict: Linguistic Acculturation on the Great Plains*, ed. Paul Schach, 1–19. Lincoln: University of Nebraska Press, 1980.

MacCaughey, Vaughan. "Some Outstanding Educational Problems of Hawaii." *School and Society* 9 (January 1919): 99–105.

Maeda, Wayne. *Changing Dreams and Treasured Memories: A Story of Japanese Americans in the Sacramento Region.* Sacramento, CA: Sacramento Japanese American Citizens League, 2000.

Magden, Ronald E. *Furusato: Tacoma-Pierce County Japanese 1888–1988.* Tacoma, WA: Nikkeijinkai, 1998.

Marquis Who's Who. *Who Was Who in America.* Vol. 3. Chicago: Marquis Who's Who, 1963.

Matsubayashi, Yoshihide. "The Japanese Language Schools in Hawaii and California from 1892 to 1941." Ph.D. diss., University of San Francisco, 1984.

McKenzie, Roderick D. *Oriental Exclusion: The Effect of American Immigration Laws, Regulations and Judicial Decisions upon the Chinese and Japanese on the American Pacific Coast.* New York: Institute of Pacific Relations, 1927.

McWilliams, Carey. *Prejudice, Japanese-Americans: Symbol of Racial Intolerance.* Boston: Little, Brown and Co., 1944.

Miyamoto, S. Frank. *Social Solidarity among the Japanese in Seattle.* Seattle: University of Washington Press, 1939.

Miyasaki, Gail Y. "The Schooling of the Nisei in Hawaii." *Educational Perspectives* 20 (winter 1981): 20–25.

Modell, John. *The Economics and Politics of Racial Accommodation: The Japanese of Los Angeles, 1900–1942.* Urbana: University of Illinois, 1977.

Morimoto, Toyotomi. *Japanese Americans and Cultural Continuity: Maintaining Language and Heritage.* New York: Garland Publishing, 1997.

Nakagawa, Fusa. *Tosa kara Hawai e* [From Tosa to Hawaii]. Kochi, Japan: Committee of Okumuma Takie to Hawai Nikkei Iminten, 2000.

Nakagawa, Yoriaki. *Akiko.* Seattle: Yoriaki Nakagawa, 1934.

"New President, The." *Washington Education Journal* 3 (November 1921): 68.

Nishinori, John Isao. "Japanese Farms in Washington." Master's thesis, University of Washington, 1926.

Notoji, Masako. "From Graveyard to Baseball: The Quest for Ethnic Identity in the Prewar Japanese Immigrant Community in the Yakima Valley." *Japanese Journal of American Studies* 3 (1989): 29–63.

O'Brien, Kenneth B. "Education, Americanization and the Supreme Court: The 1920's." *American Quarterly* 13 (1961): 161–171.

Odo, Franklin. *No Sword to Bury: Japanese Americans in Hawai'i during World War II.* Philadelphia: Temple University Press, 2004.

Ogawa, Dennis M. *Kodomo no Tame ni—For the Sake of the Children: The Japanese American Experience in Hawaii.* Honolulu: University of Hawai'i Press, 1978.

Okihiro, Gary Y. *Cane Fires: The Anti-Japanese Movement in Hawaii, 1865–1945.* Philadelphia: Temple University Press, 1991.

Okita, Yukuji. *Hawai Nikkei Imin no Kyōikushi: Nichibei Bunka, Sono Deai to Sōkoku* [History of Japanese immigrant education in Hawaii: Encounter and conflict of Japanese and American culture]. Tokyo: Minerva, 1997.

Okumura, Takie. *Seventy Years of Divine Blessings.* Honolulu: n.p., 1940.

———. *Taiheiyō no Rakuen* [Paradise in the Pacific]: n.p., n.d.

Ozawa, Gijo. *Hawai Nihongo Gakkō Kyōikushi* [Educational history of Japanese language schools in Hawaii]. Honolulu: Hawai Kyōiku Kai, 1972.

Pacific Japanese Mission of the Methodist Episcopal Church (North). *26th Annual Session*, 1925.

Pak, Yoon K. *Wherever I Go, I Will Always Be a Loyal American: Schooling Seattle's Japanese Americans during World War II.* New York: RoutledgeFalmer, 2002.

Papers of the Survey of Race Relations in the Pacific West, Hoover Institution Archives.

Passin, Herbert. *Society and Education in Japan.* New York: Teachers College Press, 1965.

Patterson, Wayne. *The Ilse: First Generation Korean Immigrants in Hawai'i 1903–1973.* Honolulu: University of Hawai'i Press and Center for Korean Studies, University of Hawai'i Press, 2000.

Powers, Myron E. "Telic Attempts of Two Racial Groups to Retain Their Social Inheritance." Master's thesis, University of Washington, 1932.

Preston, Josephine Corliss. "Department of Public Instruction." *Northwest Journal of Education* 31 (December 1919): 106.

"Proceedings of Saturday Morning Session, October 16, 1920." *Northwest Journal of Education* 32 (November 1920): 78.

Publication Committee. "A History of Japanese Immigrants in Hawaii." *Hawaii Nihonjin Iminshi* [A History of Japanese immigration in Hawaii]. Honolulu: United Japanese Society of Hawaii, 1964.

Pullen, Douglas R. "The Administration of Washington State Governor Louis F. Hart, 1919–1925." Ph.D. diss., University of Washington, 1974.

Rademaker, John Adrian. "The Ecological Position of the Japanese Farmers in the State of Washington." Ph.D. diss., University of Washington, 1939.

Ravitch, Diane. *Left Back: A Century of Failed School Reforms.* New York: Simon & Schuster, 2000.

Records of the Office of Education. RG 12. National Archives, College Park, MD.

Reinecke, John E. *Language and Dialect in Hawaii: A Sociolinguistic History to 1935,* ed. Stanley M. Tsuzaki. Honolulu: University of Hawai'i Press, 1969.

———. *Feigned Necessity: Hawaii's Attempt to Obtain Chinese Contract Labor, 1921–1923.* San Francisco: Chinese Materials Center, 1979.

Ross, William G. *Forging New Freedoms: Nativism, Education, and the Constitution, 1917–1927.* Lincoln: University of Nebraska Press, 1994.

Rubinger, Richard. *Private Academies of Tokugawa Japan.* Princeton, NJ: Princeton University Press, 1982.

Sakaguchi, Mitsuhiro. *Nihonjin Amerika Iminshi* [A history of Japanese immigration to America]. Tokyo: Fuji Shuppan, 2001.

Satō, Shintarō. "Kaigai Hōjin Gakkō no Genjō ni Tsuite" [Conditions of Japanese schools overseas]. *Teikoku Kyōiku* (August 1938): 23–38.

Shimada, Noriko. "Okumura Takie to Shibusawa Eiichi: Nichibei kara Mita Hawai ni Okeru Hainichi Yobō Keihatsu Undō" [Takie Okumura and Eiichi Shibusawa: A movement to Americanize Japanese to prevent anti-Japanese sentiment in Hawaii from the perspective of Japan-US relations]. *Nihon Joshi Daigaku Kiyō* 43 (1994): 39–56.

———. "Wartime Dissolution and Revival of the Japanese Language Schools in Hawai'i: Persistence of Ethnic Culture." *Journal of Asian American Studies* 1 (1998): 121–151.

Siddall, John William. *Men of Hawaii.* Honolulu: Honolulu Star-Bulletin, 1917.

"$6,000 for Americanization." *Japan Review* 3 (1921): 209.

Smith, William Carlson. *Americans in Process: A Study of Our Citizens of Oriental Ancestry.* Ann Arbor, MI: Edwards Brothers, 1937. Reprint. New York: Arno Press, 1970.

Spurlock, Clark. *Education and the Supreme Court.* Urbana: University of Illinois Press, 1955.

State Board of Control of California. *California and the Oriental: Japanese, Chinese, and Hindus*. Sacramento: California State Printing Office, 1920.

State of Washington. *Printed Bills of the Legislature, 17th Session, Senate*. Olympia, WA: State of Washington Printing Office, 1921.

———. *Printed Bills of the Legislature, 18th Session, Senate*. Olympia, WA: State of Washington Printing Office, 1923.

Tacoma Shūhōsha. *Tacoma Oyobi Chihō Nihonjinshi* [A history of Japanese in Tacoma and vicinity]. Tacoma, WA: Tacoma Shūhōsha, 1941.

Takagi, Mariko. "Moral Education in Pre-War Japanese Language Schools in Hawaii." Master's thesis, University of Hawai'i, 1987.

Takaki, Ronald. *Pau Hana: Plantation Life and Labor in Hawaii, 1835–1920*. Honolulu: University of Hawai'i Press, 1983.

———. *Strangers from a Different Shore: A History of Asian Americans*. Boston: Little, Brown, 1989.

Takeuchi, Kōjirō. *Beikoku Seihokubu Nippon Iminshi* [History of Japanese immigration in northwest America]. Seattle: North American Daily News, 1928. Reprint. Tokyo: Yūshōdō, 1994.

Tamura, Eileen H. *Americanization, Acculturation, and Ethnic Identity: The Nisei Generation in Hawaii*. Urbana: University of Illinois Press, 1994.

Tamura, Linda. *The Hood River Issei: An Oral History of Japanese Settlers in Oregon's Hood River Valley*. Urbana: University of Illinois Press, 1993.

Tanaka, Tamiko. "The Japanese Language School in Relation to Assimilation." Master's thesis, University of Southern California, 1935.

Taylor, Sandra C. *Advocate of Understanding: Sidney Gulick and the Search for Peace with Japan*. Kent, OH: Kent State University Press, 1984.

———. *Jewel of the Desert: Japanese American Internment at Topaz*. Berkeley: University of California Press, 1993.

Thompson, Frank V. *Schooling of the Immigrant*. New York: Harper & Brothers, 1920.

Thurston, Lorrin A. *The Foreign Language School Question: An Address to the Honolulu Social Science Association, November 8, 1920*. Honolulu: n.p., 1920.

United States Bureau of the Census. *Abstract of the Fourteenth Census of the United States, 1920*. Washington, D.C: GPO, 1923.

———. *Fourteenth Census of the United States Taken in the Year 1920*. Vol. 2, *Population*. Washington, D.C: GPO, 1922.

United States Congress. House. Committee on Immigration and Naturalization. *Percentage Plans for Restriction of Immigration. 66th Congress, 1st Session*. Washington, D.C.: GPO, 1919.

———. *Japanese Immigration Hearings. 66th Congress, 2nd Session*. Washington, D.C.: GPO, 1921. Reprint. New York: Arno Press, 1978.

United States Congress. House. Committee on the Territories. *Proposed Amendments of the Organic Act of the Territory of Hawaii. 66th Congress, 2nd Session*. Washington, D.C.: GPO, 1920.

United States Congress. Senate. Subcommittee of the Committee on Immigration. *Japanese in Hawaii Hearings. 66th Congress, 2nd Session.* Washington, D.C.: GPO, 1920.

United States Department of the Interior. Bureau of Education. *A Survey of Education in Hawaii, Bulletin No. 16.* Washington, D.C.: GPO, 1920.

Van Sant, John E. *Pacific Pioneers: Japanese Journeys to America and Hawaii, 1850–80.* Urbana: University of Illinois Press, 2000.

Washimi, Sadanobu. "Hawai Jōdoshū to Nihongo Gakkō" [Hawaii Jōdoshū and Japanese language schools]. In *Bukkyō Kyōka Kenkyū* [A study of Buddhist teachings], ed. Committee of Celebrating Mizutani Kōshō's Seventieth Birthday, 481–496. Kyoto: Shimonkaku, 1998.

Watanabe, James. *History of the Japanese of Tacoma.* Tacoma, WA: Pacific Northwest District Council, Japanese American Citizens League, 1986.

Wist, Benjamin O. *A Century of Public Education in Hawaii.* Honolulu: Hawaii Educational Review, 1940.

Wollenberg, Charles. *All Deliberate Speed: Segregation and Exclusion in California Schools, 1855–1975.* Berkeley: University of California Press, 1976.

Yakima Nihonjinkai. *Yakimaheigen Nihonjinshi* [The history of the Japanese in the Yakima Valley]. Yakima, WA: Yakima Nihonjinkai, 1935.

Yamasaki, Masato. "Yamaoka Ototaka-shi no Kokugo Gakkō Kaizenron o Hyōsu" [Critiquing Mr. Ototaka Yamaoka's suggestion for the evolution of Japanese language schools]. *Hankyō* 1, no. 2 (September 1918): 2–3.

Yoo, David K. *Growing Up Nisei: Race, Generation, and Culture among Japanese Americans of California, 1924–49.* Urbana: University of Illinois Press, 2000.

Yoshida, Ryō. *Amerika Nihonjin Imin to Kirisutokyō Shakai* [Japanese immigrants in America and Christian society]. Tokyo: Nihon Tosho Center, 1995.

Newspapers and Periodicals

Grizzly Bear
Hawai Hōchi
Hawai Shokumin Shinbun
Hawaii Educational Review
Hokubei Jiji
Honolulu Star-Bulletin
Maui News
Nichibei
Nippū Jiji
Ōfu Nippō
Pacific Commercial Advertiser
Placer Herald
Rafu Shinpō

Seattle Star
Seattle Union Record
Shin Sekai
Tacoma Daily Ledger
Tacoma News Tribune
Tacoma Times
Washington Education Journal
Yamato Shinbun

Index

About the Author

Noriko Asato is associate professor in the Library and Information Science Program, University of Hawaiʻi at Mānoa. She has published several journal articles on Japanese language schools. Her essay on the first Japanese language textbook series in the contiguous United States, "The Issei Challenge to Preserve Japanese Heritage during the Period of Americanization: An Analysis of Seattle's *Nihongo Tokuhon*, 1920," appeared in Gail Nomura and Louis Fiset's, *Nikkei in the Pacific Northwest: Japanese Americans and Japanese Canadians in the Twentieth Century* (Seattle: University of Washington Press, 2005). Asato previously coordinated the Japanese language program at the University of Nebraska. A native of Yokohama, Asato has an MA from the University of Wisconsin and a PhD from Purdue University.

Printed in the United States
By Bookmasters